GIVING USA™ 2006

Some sections of *Giving USA 2006* are online at www.givingusa.org/downloads2006.

User id: givingusa

Password: givingusa2006

GIVING USA™
2006

The Annual Report on Philanthropy for the Year 2005

51st Annual Issue

Researched and Written at

The Center on Philanthropy
AT INDIANA UNIVERSITY
INDIANA UNIVERSITY—PURDUE UNIVERSITY INDIANAPOLIS

Publisher

GIVINGUSA
F O U N D A T I O N

Photo credits and information

We asked photographers from around the world to submit their best work for use in the 2006 edition of *Giving USA*, and almost 100 photos were sent in to be judged by a blue-ribbon panel. The best of the best are found on the cover and inside pages.

Cover photo: First place award.
6-year-old Safitriani sits on a can of cooking oil distributed by Save the Children in the Cure IDP camp, Laweung village, Indonesia
Organization: Save the Children, Wilton, Conn. Photographer: S. Michael Bisceglie, Readsboro, Vt.

Back cover: Second place award.
Habitat for Humanity volunteers build houses on the Mall in Washington after Hurricane Katrina. The houses were moved to the Gulf when they were completed.
Organization: Habitat for Humanity, Americus, Ga. Photographer: Holly Eaton, Habitat for Humanity, Americus, Ga.

Runners-up
Facing Page:
A volunteer holds a child at a Red Cross shelter.
Organization: Cincinnati chapter of the American Red Cross. Photographer: Dave Bushle.

Page iv:
The hands speak volumes about giving, but it is interesting to note that the coins being held date to ancient times and are indicative of the ones given to Jesus by the widow.
Organization: City Union Mission, Kansas City, Mo. Photographer: Dennis Chapman, Kansas City, Mo.

Page 56:
Some of the first beneficiaries of a new school feeding program in Benguela province, Angola, enjoy a hot lunch.
Organization: World Food Programme of the United Nations. Photographer: Marcelo Spina Hering, Italy

Page 227:
A mother and her children wait hopefully at the City Union Mission in Kansas City.
Organization: City Union Mission, Kansas City, Mo. Photographer: Dennis Chapman, Kansas City, Mo.

Giving USA Foundation™ welcomes the use and citation of information from *Giving USA*. The preferred citation for *Giving USA* is: *Giving USA*, a publication of the Giving USA Foundation™, researched and written by the Center on Philanthropy at Indiana University. For scholarly citations, the preferred form is the American Psychological Association style for a periodical published annually, as follows: Title of chapter, *Giving USA 2006*, page number. Speakers are encouraged to cite *Giving USA* and should credit the publication or Giving USA Foundation when using data or charts from this work.

Giving USA is a public outreach initiative of the Giving USA Foundation. The Foundation, established by the Giving Institute: Leading Consultants to Non-Profits, endeavors to advance research and education in philanthropy.

ISSN: 0436-0257
ISBN: 0-9786199-0-0

Contributors

Philanthropy Circle
$15,000
Center on Philanthropy at Indiana University
Marts & Lundy, Inc.

Patron
$5,000–$7,999
IDC
Viscern/Ketchum/RSI

Partner
$2,500–$4,999
Alexander Haas Martin & Partners, Inc.
Alexander Macnab & Company
The Alford Group Inc.
Campbell & Company
CCS Fund Raising
The Clements Group, LC
Greater St. Louis Community Foundation
Claude Grizzard, Sr.
Hodge, Cramer & Associates, Inc.
Raising More Money
Raybin Associates, Inc.
Ruotolo Associates Inc.

Developer
$2,000–$2499
David & Linda Shaheen Foundation
The Oram Group, Inc.

Builder
$1,000–$1,999
A.L. Brourman Associates, Inc.
Jimmie Alford, CFRE and Maree Bullock
Arnoult & Associates, Inc.
L. Gregg Carlson
The Collins Group
Durkin Associates
Jaques & Company, Inc.

Contributors

Builder (continued)
$1,000–$1,999

Joyaux Associates
The Kellogg Organization, Inc.
Stephanie and David R. Luckes
Thomas W. Mesaros, CFRE
Miller Group Worldwide, LLC
National Community Development Services, Inc.
Payne Forrester & Associates
Remington Group
Robert B. Sharp Company of Colorado, Inc.
Semple Bixel Associates, Inc.
Smith Beers Yunker & Company, Inc.
StaleyRobeson®

Sponsorship
$500–$900

American Association of Museums
Blackburn Associates, Inc.
Cardaronella Stirling Associates
Carlton & Company
Carol O'Brien Associates, Inc.
Covenant Group
Edith H. Falk, CFRE
Fund Inc®
Jeanne Sigler & Associates, Inc.
JF Smith Group, Inc.
Orange County Chapter of AFP
Whitney Jones, Inc.
Woodburn, Kyle & Company

Friends
$1–$499

Rita Fuerst Adams
Melissa S. Brown
Randee Dalzell
Finger Lakes Chapter of the AFP
Clark & Marilyn Gafke
Jeffrey Byrne & Associates, Inc.
Thomas Kovach
Michelle Verrone
Bruce J. Wenger

GIVING USA 2006

Contents

Foreword ii
Acknowledgments v

Overview of factors influencing giving in 2005 1

Overview of Giving in 2005
Key findings 11
Giving USA: The Numbers 18

Special Section: Giving for Disasters 57

Sources of Contributions
Giving by individuals 66
Giving by bequest 78
Giving by foundations 87
Giving by corporations 94

Uses of Contributions
Giving to religion 107
Giving to education 121
Giving to foundations 131
Giving to health 135
Giving to human services 144
Giving to arts, culture, and humanities 154
Giving to public-society benefit 163
Giving to environment and animals 173
Giving to international affairs 180

Legal and Legislative Issues 187

Giving Data
Gifts of $5 million or more in 2005 196
Data tables for charts in *Giving USA*: The Numbers 204

Methodology
Brief summary of methods used 214
Glossary 223
Summary of the National Taxonomy of Exempt Entities 228

Giving Institute and the Giving USA Foundation™ 231

Committees, Advisory Council, and Staff 234

Index 237

Order Forms 239

Foreword

The year 2005 dramatized the roles philanthropy plays in our lives, whether in the United States or worldwide. The year saw extraordinary philanthropic response to an unusual sequence of three major natural disasters. Yet, the stock market, which is an important determinant of giving for individuals and foundations, ended the year at nearly the same level as in December 2004. There were dramatically high corporate profits and growth in gross domestic product, which boosted corporate contributions. Charitable bequests are estimated to have fallen. The combined result is that charitable giving rose to $260.28 billion, showing growth of 6.1 percent (2.7 percent adjusted for inflation).

Driving the change in giving upward were corporate donations, which grew by an unprecedented 22.5 percent (18.5 percent adjusted for inflation), following two years of very strong growth in gross domestic product and in corporate profits before taxes. Individual giving, always the largest single source of donations, rose by 6.4 percent (2.9 percent adjusted for inflation). Foundation grantmaking rose, partly because of an increase in the number of foundations and partly because the stock market rose in 2004 and held steady in 2005. Charitable bequests are estimated to have fallen in 2005, largely due to a decline in the number of deaths.

Gifts for disaster relief began in late 2004 after a tsunami struck nations around the Indian Ocean. Contributions from U.S. donors for relief and recovery work reached nearly $2 billion, with most of that amount contributed in 2005.

In August 2005, Hurricane Katrina struck the southern United States, followed within six weeks by two more Category 5 hurricanes. Contributions for relief rose to $1 billion within three weeks of Katrina and had reached more than $3 billion by year-end. Recovery aid continued to flow well into 2006.

Less than six weeks after Hurricane Katrina, an earthquake devastated communities in the Kashmiri mountains along the border of Pakistan and India. American donors contributed an estimated $100 million to relief efforts, including major corporate donations. In some other previous international natural disasters, donations to the American Red Cross, often the largest single recipient of aid, have been between $14 million and $50 million.[1]

All together, disaster contributions made in 2005 came to an estimated $7.37 billion, or 2.8 percent of the estimated total charitable giving. Individuals contributed the bulk of the total, accounting for an estimated $5.83 billion, or 79 percent of the total. Corporations gave an estimated $1.38 billion, or 19 percent of the total. The balance,

---

[1]   The American Red Cross received: $50 million for relief work after Hurricane Mitch (1998); $39 million for aid during the Balkan crises (1999); and $14 million after an earthquake in India (2001).

an estimated $160 million ($0.16 billion), was paid by foundations in 2005, for 2 percent of the total.

Even with overall growth in charitable giving, some subsectors grew more than others. The arts, culture, and humanities subsector and the health subsector saw inflation-adjusted giving decline in 2005. There is no definitive research that can show whether giving to organizations in these subsectors dropped because of contributions made for disaster relief or for other reasons. Both are subsectors that experience variations in giving with economic changes, with capital campaigns, and with other causes, so many options may need to be investigated before drawing firm conclusions.

Subsectors that saw double-digit increases include human services, environment and animals, and international affairs. For organizations in the human services and environment/animals subsectors, growth was strong even before disaster giving is included. In the international affairs subsector, there appears to have been some "crowding out," so that organizations not directly engaged in disaster relief work saw their contributions fall. The net effect without disaster giving was a drop of 1.9 percent (-5.1 percent adjusted for inflation). Thus, 2005 results parallel what economists Mark Wilhelm and David Ribar reported in an April 2002 article in the *Journal of Political Economy*: relief giving is associated with a drop of 5 percent in giving to international affairs organizations not providing disaster relief.

In its annual survey, *Giving USA* found an unusually high percentage of organizations—more than 59 percent—reporting that charitable gifts increased from 2004 to 2005. About 13 percent said that contributions in 2005 were within 1 percent of the amount raised for 2004, and 28 percent reported a decline in charitable dollars received. In prior years, back to 2000, no more than 56 percent of organizations reported an increase and no fewer than 36 percent saw a decrease. The responses for 2005 suggest an upturn in giving, with a higher percentage reporting growth and a lower share reporting a decline.

Giving USA combines data from a number of sources to present a series of simultaneous estimates about charitable giving for a year. It is an invaluable resource for understanding current and past charitable giving, which helps organizations anticipate their options in the future. The results for 2005 show us that Americans are always generous and especially so when the vagaries of Mother Nature strike. We are pleased to present these data to the American public and the philanthropic community so that they can use the numbers to guide their charitable activities.

Richard T. Jolly
Chair
Giving USA Foundation™

George C. Ruotolo, Jr., CFRE
Acting Chair
Giving Institute: Leading
Consultants to Non-Profits

Eugene R. Tempel, Ed.D., CFRE
Executive Director
The Center on Philanthropy
at Indiana University

Acknowledgments

Giving USA is possible only through the support of generous donors, whose gifts help fund the work needed to conduct the only annual national survey of a random sample of thousands of nonprofit organizations. Thank you to each individual and organization who has contributed to *Giving USA*. Your funding assures the high quality of the results presented and the comprehensive nature of the "yearbook of philanthropy."

In addition to gifts of money, many members of Giving Institute: Leading Consultants to Non-Profits also contribute significant time to *Giving USA*. This year's edition has benefited immeasurably from the wise counsel of Richard T. Jolly, chair of the Giving USA Foundation, and James D. Yunker, chair of the *Giving USA* Editorial Review Board. The names of members of the Giving USA Foundation board and the Editorial Review Board appear in the section that begins on page 234. My thanks go to all.

A volunteer advisory board assists the research team in developing and reviewing the *Giving USA* estimates. Members of the Advisory Council on Methodology give their time and generously share their own research and solutions to methodological puzzles. Thank you to each. They are recognized by name and affiliation on page 235.

Images on this year's cover were selected from many entries submitted in a contest arranged by Del Martin of Alexander Haas Martin & Partners, Inc. of Atlanta. Judges are named in the section that begins on page 234. The copyright page contains more information about the photographs featured. We thank the entrants for sharing their images and helping to commemorate the most unusual year of 2005.

A special feature of *Giving USA 2006* is the first-ever publication in "hard copy" of findings from the Center on Philanthropy Panel Study from 2003. This is made possible thanks to the Campbell & Company Research Fellowship awarded to Takayuki Yoshioka, a doctoral student at the Center on Philanthropy. *Giving USA* acknowledges with gratitude the Campbell & Company gift and Mr. Yoshioka's work.

Working at a major research institution devoted to increasing the understanding of philanthropy means there are numerous colleagues who share an interest in and have skills for researching this subject. This year, students and staff of the Center's research department made significant contributions, including writing chapters; cross-checking figures; and proofreading text, tables, and graphics. A list of chapter authors and other project staff appears on page 236.

This book and its related products—PowerPoint slides, quarterly newsletters, and more—benefit from the skills of Nancy Sixsmith of ConText Editorial Services (Bloomington, IN), J. Heidi Newman of Mark My Word! (Indianapolis), and Rich Metter of Rich Metter Graphics (New York City) with special thanks to Ainsley, Daniel, and Keir. Printing is undertaken by IPC Print Services in St. Joseph, Michigan.

My deepest appreciation goes to my family. Thanks, guys!

Melissa S. Brown
Managing Editor, *Giving USA 2006*

Overview of factors influencing giving in 2005

This section reviews some of the factors affecting giving for each major source of donations and summarizes findings about gifts made to some subsectors, including key results from a survey of households. Online, at at the site referenced at the front of this book, you will find other information about how to use *Giving USA* for benchmarking, about size definitions used in the *Giving USA* survey, and other answers to frequently asked questions.

Through direct giving, living individuals typically account for three-quarters (or so) of the total, and bequests account for about 7 percent, so individuals (living and deceased) account for more than 80 percent of total giving each year. Economic and social factors that affect individual giving are key determinants of the overall changes in giving in each year.

When disaster contributions are included, giving in 2005 rose to an estimated $260.28 billion, a growth of 6.1 percent (2.7 percent adjusted for inflation). Before disaster giving is included, giving rose to $252.99 billion, which is a change of 3.2 percent (and a decline of 0.2 percent after adjustment for inflation). Estimates are rounded to the nearest $10 million ($0.01 billion) before they are summed and before percentages are calculated.

The estimates of giving for 2005, with disaster giving excluded, did not rise faster because the estimates rest on information about the U.S. economy. There were conflicting economic trends in the year, with strong growth in gross domestic product (GDP) and corporate profits,[1] which lifted corporate giving estimates, but a nearly flat stock market when looking at the beginning and end of the year,[2] which added little to household or foundation giving estimates. Government reports showed that personal income rose, but studies by the U.S. Census Bureau and the U.S. Bureau of Labor Statistics found that many households saw comparatively slow rates of income growth in recent years, and some saw income decline after adjustment for inflation.[3]

Although not reflected in the estimating procedures, it is also possible that uncertainties resulting from rising fuel prices, which contributed to a consumer confidence index drop in October,[4] media coverage of a feared "housing bubble" that was predicted to burst,[5] and other concerns about future economic security also influenced some households' decisions about whether to give at all—and if they give, how much to give and to which causes.

Wealthiest households realizing gains; most families' income not rising as fast as inflation

Households typically contribute three-quarters or more of the total donated in the United States in a year. Household giving is associated with assets (or wealth) growth, personal income growth, tax rate changes, and prior levels of giving.

Overview of factors influencing giving in 2005

In 2005, business writers and economic analysts noted reports from the U.S. Census Bureau and the U.S. Department of Labor that showed two separate trends for economic prosperity underway in the United States: wealth and income were growing for households at the highest ends of the economic spectrum, but had fallen or stayed flat over several years for the vast majority of households.[6] Both trends have implications for philanthropic giving.

The wealthiest households often consider a complex matrix of their wealth and their income when making giving decisions, yet many families can consider only income in their giving decisions. As their income rises, giving also rises; when income stays flat or falls, giving follows.[7]

Major gifts linked to stock market

Just under 9 percent of households with income of $100,000 or more accounted for 43 percent of contributions claimed on 2003 tax returns (including the estimated giving by households that do not itemize deductions for gifts).[8] When the nation's wealthiest families see income and wealth increase, major gifts rise noticeably. This is tracked in several places, including the Center on Philanthropy's Million Dollar List, the *Chronicle of Philanthropy*'s annual summary of the top 60 donors, the announcement of campaigns, and in other ways. In 2005, the number of million dollar gifts rose in comparison to 2004 (although total dollars fell, in part because no charitable bequests or pledges of $1 billion or more were announced in 2005 as happened in 2004).

The *Chronicle of Philanthropy* reported that "a flat stock market and skepticism about how much additional money charities with large endowments need for their work were among the key reasons that 2005 was not as strong a year for megagifts."[9] The same article reported that an increasing number of older, wealthy donors made large gifts as part of their long-term plans to distribute assets before death. This was one reason given for the number of "new names" on the annual list of the 60 individual donors (including couples) who made the largest gifts in the year.

Average households are important contributors

Based on information from 2003 tax returns (the most recent year available) combined with an estimate of giving by nonitemizing households that uses data from the Center on Philanthropy Panel Study, tax filers with income below $100,000 (91 percent of tax filers) accounted for an estimated 57 percent of all individual charitable giving. When the "average" household sees wages and other income grow very slowly, there will be an impact on charitable giving, especially among causes and at gift amounts most likely to be supported by "average" families.

From the Center on Philanthropy Panel Study, we know that the highest percentages of "average" households contributed to five types of causes in both 2000 and 2002 (the most recent data available). The percentage of households supporting various types of causes is shown in Table 1.

Table 1
Percentage of households contributing to charity, by type of cause, 2002
For income below $100,000 and income of $100,000 and above

	All	Income < $100,00	Income $100,000+
Donors to anything	67	62	92
Religion	45	42	61
Charities that help people meet their basic needs	29	23	49
Combined funds (United Way and similar organizations)	27	26	47
Health-related charities	21	18	36
Educational organizations	15	11	34
Charities serving youth and families	11	10	21
Arts, culture, and humanities charities	8	6	18
Environmental/animal-related organizations	8	5	11
Neighborhood or community development groups	6	7	17
International aid, relief, or peace/security charities	4	4	7

Data: Center on Philanthropy Panel Study, from the Center on Philanthropy at Indiana University.
Data collected in 2003 about giving in 2002 (most recent available in spring 2006).

On average, households with income of $100,000 or more give a higher amount than do lower-income households, even when both support the same type of charity. Thus, a small percentage of households in the highest-income group can account for a sizeable share of all giving to any one type of charity.

Table 2 shows estimated percentages of charitable dollars by type of cause and income level of household donors. This table does not include donations from the mega-donors listed on the *Chronicle of Philanthropy* list. It differs slightly from the tax data, in which 43 percent of charitable contributions come from households with income above $100,000. In the Center on Philanthropy Panel Study, there are many high-income households, but not enough to fully represent the level of giving from those families in the total picture of charitable contributions. The subsector most likely to be skewed is education (which regularly receives 50 percent or more of the dollar amount of largest gifts). The second largest recipient of large gifts from mega-donors is often private or independent foundations, which are not included in the Center on Philanthropy Panel Study.

Table 2
By type of cause, the percentage of dollars donated by households in two income groups

	Income < $100,000	Income $100,000+*
To anything	61	39
Religion	66	34
Combined funds	50	50
Charities that help people meet their basic needs	59	41
Health-related charities	42	58
Educational institutions	37	63
Arts, culture, and humanities charities	48	52
Charities serving youth and families	65	35
Neighborhood/community development groups	67	33
Environmental organizations	54	46
International aid, relief, or peace/security charities	66	34

*Weighted estimates using family weights in the study, which are calculated to represent the population overall. However, the nation's top 1 percent of families by wealth disproportionately account for charitable giving to many types of causes and are not disproportionately accounted for in this survey.
Data: Center on Philanthropy Panel Study, from the Center on Philanthropy at Indiana University.
Data collected in 2003 about giving in 2002 (most recent available as of spring 2006).

Religion and human services charities are among the most frequently supported charities that appear to depend more on donations from "average" families than do some other types of charities:

- 66 percent of all reported dollars given to religion in the study were from households with income below $100,000;

- 65 percent of the dollar amount of gifts to charities that serve youths and families came from families with income below $100,000; and

- 59 percent of the reported donations to charities that help people meet their basic needs come from families with income below $100,000.

Other types of charities also rely on donations from "average" households:

- 67 percent of reported contributions to neighborhood or community development groups came from households with income below $100,000; as did

- 66 percent of donations for international aid, relief, or peace and security issues.

Changing sense of financial security might affect giving

Factors beyond income and assets can affect households' sense of financial security. In 2005, one such source of anxiety was energy prices. Gasoline prices rose to $3.03 per gallon,[10] and the cost of natural gas for heating and cooking increased, on average, 38 percent from the previous year.[11] As households grappled with higher expenses, they might have reduced some charitable giving.

Research by INDEPENDENT SECTOR in 2001 found that 71 percent of households that did not make charitable gifts answered "yes" when asked if they were worried about having enough money in the future. Among noncontributing households, 65 percent said they could not afford to contribute to charity, which was much more frequently mentioned than the next-highest reason: not being asked (12 percent).[12]

During four months of 2005, donors get extra tax benefits from giving

Some individual donors are highly motivated by the tax benefits of giving, especially when deciding how much to give in a particular year. For 2005, some nonprofit organizations reported benefiting from the provisions of the Katrina Emergency Tax Relief Act (KETRA), which provided an exceptional, one-time incentive by effectively increasing the tax deductibility of some types of gifts (cash to a charity—not stock to a foundation) for some types of donors (those able to contribute 100 percent of their adjusted gross income) or those with incomes above certain thresholds, who are typically required to reduce deductions by 3 percent. The provisions of KETRA are discussed more fully in the legal-legislative chapter. KETRA also lifted the typical 10 percent limit for corporations claiming charitable deductions to a one-time 15 percent limit for some types of donations. Few corporations reach the 10 percent cap in a year. It is unknown how many took advantage of the KETRA provision; when they did contribute, it is unknown how much corporate contributions may have increased.

Foundation grantmaking linked to stock market performance

Foundation grantmaking, at about 11 percent a year since 2000, is the next largest source of philanthropy after individual giving. Even though an increasing percentage of foundations are "pass through"—making gifts to charitable recipients the same year in which the foundation receives a gift from its donor(s)—the bulk of foundation grantmaking is still from endowed foundations that draw up their grantmaking budgets based on assets and interest earned.

The stock market rose 3 percent (0.2 percent adjusted for inflation) from the beginning of the year to the end, based on the Standard & Poor's 500 Index, whereas other markets such as the NASDAQ and Russell 1000 also showed increases of 1.4 and 4.4 percent, respectively (before inflation adjustments).[13] The S&P 500 is closely correlated with foundation grantmaking levels.

Corporate giving follows economic growth of corporations

GDP is one factor that is strongly associated with corporate giving. When GDP grows, corporate giving also increases. For 2005, GDP rose 3.5 percent (after adjustment for inflation), following a 4.3 percent increase in 2004. Combined, these two years of strong overall economic growth are predicted to lift corporate giving by more than $1 billion.

Corporate profits before tax increased 35.8 percent (32 percent adjusted for inflation using the Consumer Price Index, consistent with other inflation adjustment in *Giving USA*). Corporate pretax profits were an estimated $1.44 trillion, according to March 2006 estimates from the Bureau of Economic Analysis.[14] Although corporate profits are strong, they had a lesser impact on the corporate giving estimate for 2005 than did GDP growth.

This exceptionally high profit growth was attributed to increases in profits in all sectors, with the largest growth in utilities and manufacturing. About half the increase in manufacturing profits was attributed by the Bureau of Economic Analysis to growth in profits in the petroleum industry. Another factor in the high growth was a tax law change in the Job Creation and Worker Assistance Act and the Job Growth and Tax Relief Reconciliation Act, which allowed firms to accelerate depreciation for capital expenses (which raises profits before tax).[15]

Bequest giving falls as death rate falls

Estimates of bequest giving depend on two variables: the number of people who died who had wills with charitable bequests and the value of the estates of the people who died. In 2004, the death rate for adults fell to a record low.[16] It is estimated to be similarly low in 2005. A lower rate of death among adults aged 55 and above affects bequests received at charities in two ways. First, more donors who created charitable bequests are living past their previously estimated lifespan; second, those who do live longer may need more of their assets for their own support, resulting (possibly) in smaller estates after death.

Giving is in response to needs or to maximize opportunities

Three major natural disasters in 2005 generated at least $7.37 billion in contributions (3 percent of total estimated giving): the late December 2004 tsunami in the Indian Ocean; Hurricane Katrina (followed by Hurricanes Rita and Wilma) along the Gulf Coast of the United States; and an earthquake in the mountains of Pakistan, in which at least 73,000 lives were lost immediately and more died after the event because of food shortages and exposure.

In addition to the charitable contributions made, the recovery and rebuilding efforts engaged people very directly in ways that are not counted as charitable giving for tax purposes. Churches collected truckloads of goods and organized and sent teams of volunteers.[17] Schools organized drives to collect supplies, books, and equipment to restore classrooms in schools in Louisiana, Mississippi, and Alabama.[18] Clubs of co-workers and other groups of people organized temporary or even semipermanent homes for survivors of the disasters who relocated.[19]

Lower incomes = rising needs for human services

Data about incomes and poverty levels for 2005 were not available in early 2006. The nation's official poverty rate rose slightly from 12.5 percent in 2003 to 12.7 percent in 2004, according to a report released in August 2005 by the U.S. Census Bureau. The percentage of the nation's population without health insurance coverage remained stable, at 15.7 percent in 2004.[20] Even for those not living in poverty, real (inflation-adjusted) median earnings of men age 15 and older who worked full-time, year-round declined 2.3 percent between 2003 and 2004, to $40,798. Women with similar work situations saw their earnings decline by 1 percent, to $31,223.

The U.S. Department of Agriculture released a study in October 2005, based on data collected from 48,000 households in December 2004. In that survey, 11.9 percent of households reported not having enough food at some point in 2004 because they had insufficient money or other resources for food. This is the highest percentage since 1998. The 2004 data are the most recent available.[21] The National Low Income Housing Coalition stated that for the first time, a full-time minimum wage earner could not afford rent for a one-bedroom apartment in any area of the country.[22]

Changes in charitable receipts at organizations

Giving USA found that 59 percent of organizations responding to its survey reported an increase in charitable receipts in 2005. This was true even before adding contributions made specifically for the disaster relief campaigns. About 13 percent of organizations reported that there was no change in 2005 compared with 2004, and about 28 percent said their contributions went down in 2005 when compared with 2004. These figures include the lowest share of declines in the *Giving USA* survey since 2000 and the highest percentage of growth. They are also close to the results found by the Association of Fundraising Professionals (AFP) in a poll of members. AFP reported that 63 percent reported growth in giving, 13 percent said no change, and 24 percent reported a decline.[23] A poll conducted by Guidestar found that 22 percent reported decreased contributions from 2004 to 2005, 26 percent stayed the same, 49 percent reported increased contributions, and 3 percent did not know.[24]

Disaster giving

Disaster giving was tracked more closely in 2005 than it had been during prior disasters. The Conference Board and the Panel Study of Income Dynamics at the University of Michigan surveyed households. The U.S. Chamber of Commerce and the Committee to Encourage Corporate Philanthropy tracked corporation contributions. The Foundation Center monitored foundation grantmaking. The Center on Philanthropy at Indiana University kept lists with hundreds of organizations and the amounts they reported receiving in gifts for tsunami relief, hurricane relief, and earthquake relief. Even with a great deal of information, estimates are still estimates. No single effort made an attempt to count the same type of gift, nor did the various sources involved collaborate ahead of time on what was counted (gifts, pledges, in-kind gifts, cash gifts only, transfers from other charities as a gift, etc.).

The best estimate available in early 2006 is that contributions for the tsunami relief totaled $1.92 billion, of which $1.76 billion can be confirmed as received by 85 charities that provided information about their charitable receipts for tsunami relief. A total of $5.30 billion was contributed for Katrina relief according to the information available about donors, and from recipient organizations we can track receipts of cash and in-kind contributions totaling $3.51 billion, which does not include much of the giving to congregations and other religious organizations.

At least 15 percent of giving is for long-term investment

It is not possible to collect exact information about every gift made to determine whether it is for current operations (salaries, rent, and other expenses) or is a contribution for an endowment (to help generate income for future costs), for a building, or for a planned activity to occur in the future. Nonetheless, it is possible to use available data sources to find an amount that is reported to be for "noncurrent" purposes.

For 2004, *Giving USA* finds more than $36 billion contributed to endowments, capital campaigns, deferred gifts, such as a trust (in which the control of the assets passes to the recipient in the future), and other types of future expenditures:

$20.32 billion to foundations (much of which is for endowments that generate interest for future giving);[25]

$1.24 billion given to the four largest commercially sponsored donor-advised funds (Fidelity, Schwab, Vanguard, and National Philanthropic Trust).[26] About 20 to 25 percent of assets in these donor-advised funds are directed to charitable recipients in a year, yet the total amount contributed to the top four funds is shown here as "for long-term investment";[27]

$2.60 billion granted by foundations for capital purposes (some of which appears in the amount given to higher education institutions and cannot easily be removed from either figure);[28]

$11.40 billion for capital purposes at higher education institutions, which admittedly includes some double-counting of foundation grants;[29]

$0.25 billion in deferred gifts recorded at health organizations;[30]

$0.15 billion to hospitals and health systems for an endowment or a capital campaign, including multiyear commitments and bequests announced but not necessarily received by the intended beneficiary in 2004;[31]

$0.87 billion for art museums for an endowment or a capital campaign, or an in-kind gift of art. The amount here includes multiyear commitments for campaigns and bequests announced but not necessarily received by the intended beneficiary in 2004.[32]

$36.83 billion total

Overview of factors influencing giving in 2005

$36.83 billion is 15 percent of the revised estimate of $244.94 billion for 2004 giving and represents a fairly conservative estimate of the amount of giving that is for an endowment or is to be used to build a structure that will last for many years. Some of the gifts counted here are in-kind contributions of items for a permanent collection (e.g., at an art museum).

1   Bureau of Economic Analysis, March 30, 2006, press release about corporate profits, www.bea.gov.
2   Standard & Poor's 500 Index, measured 1,211.92 at close on December 31, 2004 and 1,248.29 at close on December 30 (last trading day) 2005. Adjusted for inflation, this is a change of 0.2 percent.
3   Bureau of Labor Statistics, December 6, 2005.
4   V. Bajaj, Home sale prices decline; Consumer confidence drops, *New York Times*, October 26, 2005.
5   Fannie [Mae] sees higher odds of regional housing busts, *Wall Street Journal Abstracts*, June 20, 2005.
6   Some examples: Michael Mandel, economics editor at *Business Week*, wrote, "Since the end of 2003, average real wages have fallen by 3.2%, while productivity is up by 5.1%. Even managers... have seen a 4% decline in real wages since the end of 2003..." *Business Week*, December 7, 2005. Dr. Mandel drew his conclusions from data released December 6 by the U.S. Bureau of Labor Statistics. Steven Rattner, an investment banker, wrote, "...the bottom 80% endures economic stagnation, including real [inflation-adjusted] wages that haven't risen in 14 months, according to the Bureau of Labor Statistics. Economists Thomas Piketty and Emmanuel Saez calculated (using data from the Internal Revenue Service, hardly a hotbed of partisanship) that the share of income going to the top 1% of households nearly doubled, to 14.7% in 2002, up from a low of 7.7% in the early 1970s." *Business Week*, August 8, 2005. Paul Krugman, professor of economics and international affairs at Princeton and op-ed columnist for the *New York Times*, wrote, "...in August [2005], the Census Bureau released family income data for 2004....most families actually lost economic ground. Real median household income—the income of households in the middle of the income distribution, adjusted for inflation—fell for the fifth year in a row." *New York Times*, December 5, 2005.
7   P. Schervish and J. Havens, Wealth and commonwealth: New findings on wherewithal and philanthropy, *Nonprofit and Voluntary Sector Quarterly*, March 2001.
8   *Giving USA* calculations using data from the IRS for contributions itemized by tax filers in various income categories; plus an amount estimated for gifts made by households that do not itemize any charitable contributions, whose income is not known but who are most likely to be in the group with income below $100,000, as in higher income groups, 87 percent of returns included itemized charitable gifts. In 2003, *Giving USA* estimates a total of $180.19 billion in total household/individual giving. Using IRS data about itemized gifts, $77.75 billion came from the 8.8 percent of households with income of $100,000 or more, and $67.95 billion came from households with income below $100,000. *Giving USA* estimates that $34.49 billion came from households that did not itemize contributions. (Thus approximately 43 percent of individual giving in 2003 was from high-income households, and 57 percent was from households with income below $100,000.)
9   M. DiMento and N. Lewis, How the wealthy give, *Chronicle of Philanthropy*, February 23, 2006, www.philanthropy.com.
10 Energy Information Association, Retail Gasoline Historical Prices, www.eia.doe.gov
11 M. Lavelle, The Big Chill, *US News & World Report*, December 19, 2005; pp. 59-62, 64-65, http://web.lexis-nexis.com/universe.
12 C. Toppe, A. Kirsch, and J. Michel, *Giving & Volunteering in the United States, 2001*, INDEPENDENT SECTOR, www.independentsector.org.
13 NASDAQ measured 2175.44 at close on December 31, 2004 and 2205.32 at close on December 30 (last trading day) 2005. Russell 1000 measured 650.99 at close on December 31, 2004 and 679.42 at close on December 30, 2005.

14   Bureau of Economic Analysis, News release: Gross Domestic Product and Corporate Profits, March 30, 2006, www.bea.gov.

15   Bureau of Economic Analysis, March 30, 2006, news release as in note 11.

16   Miniño A.M., Heron M., Smith B.L., Deaths: Preliminary data for 2004. Health E-Stats. Released April 19, 2006, National Health and Vital Statistics, www.cdc.gov/nchs.

17   J. Howard Price, Keep the Faith, and They Will Come; Religious folk step forward to clean up after Katrina, *The Washington Times*, October 27, 2005.

18   L. Hague, Kaneland Students Paying it Forward Penny, School Supplies Drive Doing Better Than Expected, *Chicago Daily Herald*, December 14, 2005.

19   Hurricane Briefs, *The Advocate*, December 16, 2005.

20   *Income, Poverty and Health Insurance in the United States, 2004*, U.S. Census Bureau, released August 2005, www.census.gov.

21   M. Nord, M. Andrews, and S. Carlson, *Household food security in the United States, 2004*, Economic Research Report Number ERR11, October, 2005, www.ers.usda.gov.

22   NLIHC Releases 2005 Housing Affordability Report, December 13, 2005, press release, www.nlihc.org.

23   Nearly two-thirds of U.S. and Canadian charities raise more funds in 2005, April 3, 2006, press release, www.afpnet.org.

24   Charities Predict Stagnant or Declining End-of-Year Fundraising, November 17, 2005, news release, www.guidestar.org.

25   The Foundation Center, Growth in Giving, April 2006.

26   *Giving USA 2005*, Table 6, page 160, using information from IRS Forms 990 and reported by the *Chronicle of Philanthropy*.

27   See the public-society benefit chapter in this edition and in prior editions of *Giving USA*.

28   The Foundation Center, Foundation Giving Priorities, February 2006, p. 46.

29   Data from the Council for Aid to Education. Used with permission.

30   Association for Healthcare Philanthropy, 2004 giving report.

31   Compiled by *Giving USA* from the Million Dollar List for 2004 as released by the Center on Philanthropy at Indiana University. Excludes foundation grants announced for endowment or capital purposes because they are included in the previous information from the Foundation Center.

32   Compiled by *Giving USA* from the Million Dollar List for 2004 as released by the Center on Philanthropy at Indiana University. Excludes foundation grants announced for endowment or capital purposes because they are included in the previous information from the Foundation Center.

Key findings

Total charitable giving for 2005 is estimated to be $260.28 billion. This is an increase of 6.1 percent compared with the revised estimate of $245.22 billion for 2004. Adjusted for inflation, the increase is 2.7 percent.

An estimated $7.37 billion in disaster relief giving is included in the total for 2005. Without this additional amount—and assuming that the disaster relief amount is all new money that would not have been donated if there had been no disasters—the change from 2004 to 2005 is from $245.22 billion to $252.99 billion, or an increase of 3.2 percent (and a decrease of 0.2 percent adjusted for inflation).

Individual contributions reached an estimated $199.07 billion in 2005, an increase of 6.4 percent (2.9 percent adjusted for inflation). Individuals gave an estimated $5.83 billion in disaster relief contributions in 2005. With that amount not included in the estimate, individual giving would be $193.24 billion, an increase of 3.3 percent over the revised estimate of $187.11 billion for 2004 (and a decline of 0.1 percent compared with 2004 after adjustment for inflation). This assumes that none of the disaster relief contributions would have been made to other charities had there been no disasters. Individual giving, including the estimate for disaster relief contributions, was 76.5 percent of the total estimated giving for 2005.

Charitable bequests are estimated to be $17.44 billion for 2005, a drop of 5.5 percent compared with the revised estimate of $18.46 billion for 2004. This is a decline of 8.6 percent when adjusted for inflation. No charitable bequests are known to be for disaster relief in 2005. Charitable bequests are estimated to be 6.7 percent of total giving for 2005.

Foundation grantmaking rose to an estimated $30.0 billion for 2005, for independent, community, and operating foundations, based on the Foundation Center's survey conducted in January and February 2006. This is an increase of 5.6 percent (2.1 percent adjusted for inflation) compared with the revised amount of $28.41 billion for 2004, which reflects grantmaking reported on IRS forms 990-PF and 990 (for community foundations) filed for 2004 and tabulated by the Foundation Center. An estimated $160 million in grants paid in 2005 was for disaster relief, with additional commitments announced for future grantmaking. Without the paid disaster relief grants included, the estimate of foundation grantmaking for 2005 is $29.84 billion, an increase of 5.0 percent (1.5 percent adjusted for inflation). Foundation grantmaking is estimated to be 11.5 percent of total giving in 2005.

Corporate giving in 2005 reached an estimated $13.77 billion, counting $3.6 billion in corporate foundation grantmaking as estimated by the Foundation Center, which includes some corporate foundation relief giving. Corporate giving increased an

Key findings

estimated 22.5 percent over the revised total of $11.24 billion for 2004 (18.5 percent adjusted for inflation). Of the amount for 2005, an estimated $1.38 billion is for disaster relief giving, including both cash and in-kind donations. Without that amount, the estimate for corporate giving is $12.47 billion, an increase of 10.9 percent (7.3 percent adjusted for inflation). Corporate contributions are an estimated 5.3 percent of total contributions for 2005.

Gifts to religious organizations rose to an estimated $93.18 billion, an increase of 5.9 percent (2.5 percent adjusted for inflation) over the revised estimate of $87.95 billion for 2004. Gifts to religious organizations in 2005 include an estimated $431 million donated for disaster relief. Without this amount included, the estimate is $92.75 billion in 2005, a change of 5.5 percent (2.0 percent adjusted for inflation). Uncounted are in-kind donations and thousands of volunteer hours contributed through congregations directly to regions affected and survivors of the natural disasters. Giving to religious organizations included in the *Giving USA* study is estimated to be 35.8 percent of total giving in 2005.

Giving to educational organizations is estimated at $38.56 billion for 2005, an increase of 13.1 percent (9.4 percent adjusted for inflation). This estimate is based on a combination of sources, including findings from the Council for Aid to Education through June 2005 and a *Giving USA* survey for all of 2005. Very little of the education estimate reflects donations for disaster relief or recovery. Giving to educational organizations is estimated to be 14.8 percent of total giving in 2005.

Giving to foundations is estimated by the Foundation Center to be $21.70 billion, a change of 6.8 percent (3.3 percent adjusted for inflation) compared with the $20.32 billion reported by the Foundation Center in gifts to foundations in 2004. About $50 million ($0.05 billion) in 2005 was reported in gifts to community foundations for disaster relief activities. For 2005, gifts to foundations are approximately 8.3 percent of all giving.

Gifts to health organizations are estimated to be $22.54 billion in 2005, an increase of 2.7 percent (and a decline of 0.7 percent adjusted for inflation) compared with 2004. Very little of the giving to health-related organizations reported for 2005 was for disaster relief, although health care organizations were directly engaged in providing rescue and relief services, and often the personnel of these organizations were on the "front lines" of disaster relief efforts. Gifts to health organizations are an estimated 8.7 percent of total charitable giving for 2005.

Giving to human services organizations rose to $25.36 billion in 2005. The estimate is 32.3 percent more than the estimate of $19.17 billion for 2004 (28.0 percent adjusted for inflation). It includes $3.31 billion in disaster aid contributions. The *Giving USA* survey found an increase of 15.0 percent (11.3 percent adjusted for inflation) even before the addition of disaster gifts. This growth, before disaster giving is included, reverses a prior three-year decline in inflation-adjusted giving to human services organizations. Giving for human services organizations was 9.7 percent of total estimated giving.

Giving for public-society benefit organizations reached an estimated $14.03 billion, an increase of 8.3 percent (4.7 adjusted for inflation). This includes an estimated $263 million in contributions for disaster relief. With those contributions excluded, giving to organizations in this subsector was $13.77 billion, or an increase of 6.2 percent (2.8 percent adjusted for inflation) compared with 2004. Giving for organizations in this subsector, which includes United Ways, Jewish Federations, commercially sponsored donor-advised funds, civil rights organizations, and a number of other types of charities, was 5.4 percent of total estimated giving for 2005.

Contributions for organizations in the arts, culture, and humanities subsector dropped by 3.4 percent in 2005, to $13.51 billion. This is a decline of 6.6 percent adjusted for inflation. Approximately $40 million was contributed to organizations in this subsector for disaster relief. Gifts to arts, culture, or humanities organizations were 5.2 percent of total estimated giving for 2005.

Gifts for organizations in the environment and animals subsector reached an estimated $8.86 billion, an increase of 16.4 percent (12.6 percent adjusted for inflation). This year's estimate includes about $30 million of contributions received by animal welfare organizations that organized disaster relief efforts for pets. Without this, giving to organizations in this subsector was $8.83 billion, an increase of 16.0 percent (12.2 percent adjusted for inflation). Giving for organizations in the environment and animals subsector was 3.4 percent of total estimated giving.

Gifts to organizations engaged in international affairs, including international relief and aid, reached an estimated $6.39 billion in 2005, reflecting an estimated $1.14 billion in relief contributions after the tsunami of December 2004 and the earthquake of October 2005. The total in 2005 is a change of 19.4 percent (15.6 percent adjusted for inflation). Without the amount for disaster relief, giving to organizations in this subsector fell to $5.25 billion, a drop of 1.9 percent (-5.1 percent adjusted for inflation). Giving for organizations in the international affairs subsector was 2.5 percent of total estimated giving.

Unallocated contributions are estimated to be $16.15 billion, or 6.2 percent of the total. Unallocated giving includes gifts to newly formed organizations; individual and corporate deductions expected to be claimed in 2005 for gifts made in prior years (carried over); amounts that donors deduct at a value different from what the nonprofit reports as revenue; gifts and grants to government entities claimed by donors but not reported as received at a 501(c)(3) charity; and foundation grants to organizations located in another country.

Giving USA: The Numbers

2005 contributions: $260.28 billion by source of contributions

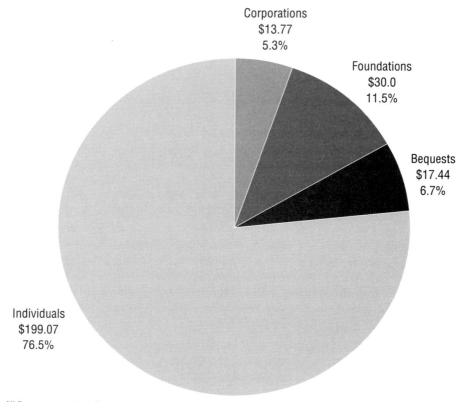

All figures are rounded. Total may not be 100%.

- Total estimated charitable giving in 2005 reached $260.28 billion. This is an increase of 6.1 percent (2.7 percent adjusted for inflation).
- The total includes _Giving USA_'s estimates of contributions made in 2005 for disaster relief, based on data available in April 2006:
  - Individuals (79 percent of disaster giving) — $5.83 billion
  - Independent, community, and operating foundations (2 percent of disaster giving, estimated by the Foundation Center) — $0.16 billion
  - Corporations (19 percent of disaster giving) — $1.38 billion
  - Total — $7.37 billion

Giving USA: The Numbers

- The estimates here assume that most disaster relief giving was in addition to all other contributions that the donor would normally make. This assumption is supported by survey results for household donors for disaster giving in 2005 (the Conference Board and the Center on Philanthropy), the receipts reported to *Giving USA* in its survey for this edition, experience after the attacks of September 11, 2001, and the reports of charities themselves in 2005 in polls taken by the Association of Fundraising Professionals and Guidestar.

- Individual or household donors contributed an estimated $199.07 billion, or 76.5 percent of total estimated giving. The estimate of giving by individuals or households includes: 1) estimated charitable deductions claimed on tax returns; 2) an estimate for giving by households that do not itemize deductions; and 3) an estimate based on household surveys for relief giving after the tsunami and after the hurricanes.

- No data are available as of early 2006 for the potential impact on individual or corporate giving of the Katrina Emergency Tax Relief Act (KETRA). Anecdotal reports suggest that some donors increased their contributions in late 2005 to benefit from that act's provisions. The estimate here does not include gifts that might have been prompted by the KETRA provisions.

- Charitable bequests were estimated to be $17.44 billion, or 6.7 percent of total estimated giving. The estimate of charitable bequests includes an estimate for the amount contributed by estates that will file an estate tax return for 2005 and an amount for estates that are not required to file a federal estate tax return.

- The sum of gifts by living individuals and through charitable bequests is $216.51 billion, which represents 83.2 percent of estimated total giving for 2005. This is the lowest percentage ever for personal gifts (from living individuals and bequests). It is lower because corporate giving grew to exceptionally high levels in 2005 with contributions for disaster relief. Also, foundation grantmaking is estimated to be near its all-time high of 11.8 percent (reached in 2001).

- Grantmaking by independent (private), community, and operating foundations was estimated by the Foundation Center to be $30.0 billion. This is 11.5 percent of total estimated giving.

- Corporate giving, including approximately $3.6 billion in grants from corporate foundations, according to the Foundation Center, is estimated to be $13.77 billion or 5.3 percent of total contributions in 2005. This includes estimated relief giving in cash and in-kind, based on counts prepared by the U.S. Chamber of Commerce.

Giving USA: The Numbers

2005 contributions: $260.28 billion by type of recipient organization

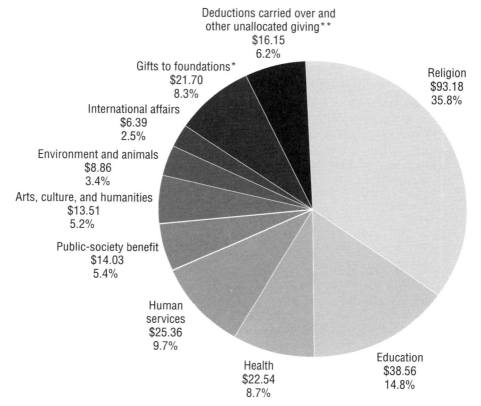

Deductions carried over and
other unallocated giving**
$16.15
6.2%

Gifts to foundations*
$21.70
8.3%

International affairs
$6.39
2.5%

Environment and animals
$8.86
3.4%

Arts, culture, and humanities
$13.51
5.2%

Public-society benefit
$14.03
5.4%

Human
services
$25.36
9.7%

Health
$22.54
8.7%

Religion
$93.18
35.8%

Education
$38.56
14.8%

All figures are rounded. Total may not be 100%.
* Foundation Center estimate.
** See last bullet point on facing page for definition.

Giving USA: The Numbers

- Religious organizations received an estimated $93.18 billion in charitable gifts in 2005, or 35.8 percent of the total. This includes $431 million in disaster relief gifts tracked at denominational relief organizations, ministries, and missions.

- Educational institutions received an estimated $38.56 billion, which is 14.8 percent of the total. About $10 million of disaster giving was reportedly made directly to organizations in the education subsector. Some disaster relief giving went to educational institutions through other charities, such as the Bush-Clinton Katrina Fund, and is recorded in the subsector of the original recipient.

- Health organizations received an estimated $22.54 billion, or 8.7 percent of the total. About $9 million in disaster giving was reportedly made initially to health organizations. Many health organizations received support from charities that were the initial recipients of a donation, including congregations, United Ways, or the Bush-Clinton relief fund.

- Human services organizations received $25.36 billion, or 9.7 percent of the total. This includes an estimated $3.31 billion in disaster relief gifts reported as received at organizations in this subsector. The largest single recipient was the American Red Cross, which received $2.4 billion in 2005 for the three disasters.

- Public-society benefit organizations received an estimated $14.03 billion, or 5.4 percent of the total. This includes an estimated $263 million ($0.26 billion) in disaster relief gifts tracked as received at organizations in this subsector.

- Arts, culture, and humanities organizations received an estimated $13.51 billion, or 5.2 percent of the total. This includes $38 million ($0.04 billion) in disaster relief for museums and support for Architecture for Humanity and other rebuilding efforts focused in the arts.

- Environment/animals organizations received an estimated $8.86 billion, or 3.4 percent of the total. This includes approximately $29 million ($0.03 billion) in disaster relief for animals or the environment.

- International affairs organizations received an estimated $6.39 billion, or 2.5 percent of the total. This includes $1.14 billion in estimated disaster relief.

- The Foundation Center estimates giving of $21.70 billion to foundations in 2005, or 8.3 percent of the total. Announced disaster relief gifts of $51 million ($0.05 billion) to community foundations are included in this estimate.

- Deductions carried over and unallocated giving are estimated at $16.15 billion or 6.2 percent of the total. This amount represents individual and corporate deductions expected to be claimed in 2005 for gifts made in prior years (carried over), amounts that donors deduct at a value different from what the nonprofit reports as revenue, gifts and grants to government entities, foundation grants to organizations located in another country, and contributions to new organizations not yet allocated to a subsector.

Giving USA: The Numbers

**Estimated giving for disasters compared with known receipts
at charitable organizations, 2005
($ in billions)**

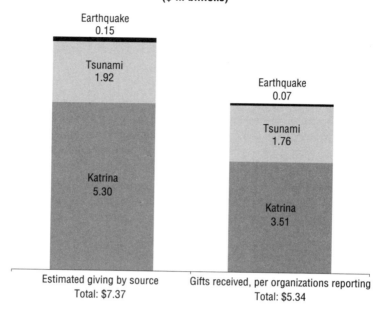

- The total estimate for giving to disasters in 2005 is $7.37 billion. This estimate is based on the best available data in early 2006, and it includes cash and in-kind giving from individuals, corporations, and foundations. This is an estimate of the sources of relief giving.

- To estimate the distribution of relief contributions by type of recipient (see page 20), *Giving USA* asked all survey recipients about disaster relief receipts and supplemented survey responses with data from the Center on Philanthropy at Indiana University for organizations that did not return the survey. The amount that could be tracked by those two methods reached $5.34 billion. This amount does not include many congregations or public agencies, such as schools or public hospitals.

- Both of these estimates (sources and types of recipients) include some value for in-kind donations, especially from corporations, which contributed supplies, equipment, medicines, and much more. Not all corporations reported a value for their in-kind gifts. Where a dollar value was available, it was included.

- Some of the giving estimated here is likely to have replaced gifts that otherwise would have been made in 2005, yet no data are available about the dollar value of gifts that would have been made if there had been no disasters (what economists call "crowding-out"). The entire amount here is added to estimates of charitable giving generated following *Giving USA*'s usual estimating procedures for contributions.

Giving USA: The Numbers

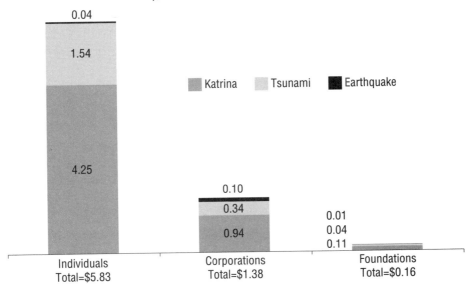

Estimates of disaster contributions by donor type, 2005
($ in billions: total=$7.37 billion)

Legend: Katrina — Tsunami — Earthquake

Individuals
Total=$5.83

Corporations
Total=$1.38

Foundations
Total=$0.16

Data sources: The Center on Philanthropy at Indiana University, Conference Board, Foundation Center, Panel Study of Income Dynamics, and U.S. Chamber of Commerce

- Individuals contributed an estimated $5.83 billion for disaster relief, with most of that going for hurricane relief ($4.25 billion), followed by $1.54 billion contributed for tsunami relief in 2005, and a more typical disaster contribution of about $40 million ($0.04 billion) for relief after the Pakistan earthquake of October 2005.

- Corporate donors gave an estimated $940 million ($0.94 billion) for hurricane relief. Corporate donors gave an estimated $340 million ($0.34 billion) for tsunami relief in 2005 and an estimated $100 million ($0.1 billion) in relief after the Pakistan earthquake. The U.S. Chamber of Commerce shows an estimated $84 million in disaster relief giving by corporate foundations. To avoid double counting, the overall corporate giving estimate only uses the Foundation Center's reported corporate foundation grantmaking and does not include the corporate foundation grants tracked by the U.S. Chamber of Commerce.

- Independent, community, and operating foundation grant payments for disasters is estimated to have been $160 million ($0.16 billion). Approximately $110 million ($0.11 billion) is thought to be grants paid in 2005 for relief work after the hurricanes and approximately $50 million ($0.05 billion) is thought to be grants paid in 2005 for relief in the Indian Ocean ($0.04 billion) and in Pakistan ($0.01 billion). These are preliminary estimates based on data collected by the Foundation Center through spring 2006. The Foundation Center will release more information in 2006 and 2007.

Giving USA: The Numbers

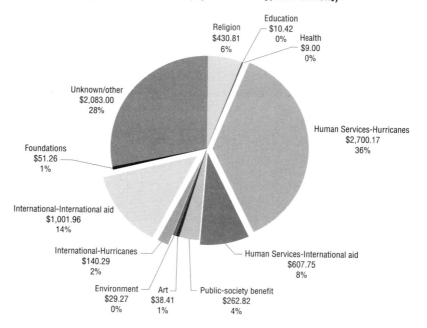

Recipients of disaster relief giving: partial tabulation based on information from early 2006 ($ in millions: total=$7,365 million [$7.37 billion])

- In the wake of the Gulf Coast hurricanes, organizations in the human services subsector reported the highest share of the total received by organizations providing information. Hurricane relief gifts to human services organizations reached at least $2,700.17 million ($2.70 billion).

- Gifts estimated at $140.29 million ($0.14 billion) were given to organizations in the international affairs subsector that provided relief services in the United States after Hurricane Katrina.

- Gifts made for tsunami relief went to organizations in the international subsector, the human services subsector, and the religion subsector. The largest share went to organizations in the international aid subsector, which received at least $1,001.96 million ($1.0 billion).

- Human services organizations in the United States also received funds for tsunami relief, reporting an estimated $607.75 million ($0.61 billion).

- Religious organizations, including the relief programs affiliated with denominations, ministries and missions, received an estimated $430.81 million ($0.43 billion) in relief funding for the two crises: the tsunami and the hurricanes. It is probable that far more was donated through congregations and distributed to recipients not tracked by any source, including *Giving USA* or the Center on Philanthropy.

Giving USA: The Numbers

Changes in giving by source, without and with disaster contributions, 2004–2005 (Not adjusted for inflation)

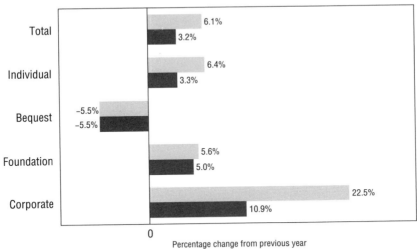

Percentage change from previous year

☐ With disaster giving included   ■ Before disaster giving added

- The *Giving USA* estimates for 2005 include $7.37 billion (rounded to the nearest $10 million) in estimated contributions made for relief. The estimates are preliminary, based on data available in April 2006.

- Before adding disaster relief giving, the sum of estimated giving by all sources is $252.99 billion. Each source estimate includes rounding to the nearest $10 million. The change before adding disaster giving is 3.2 percent more than the revised estimate of $245.22 billion for 2004, not adjusted for inflation.

- If no disaster giving were added, *Giving USA* estimates that individual giving would be $193.24 billion, an increase of 3.3 percent over the revised estimate for 2004 of $187.11 billion.

- The estimate for bequest giving would not change, as no bequests were found directed to disaster relief work, but charitable bequests are down 5.5 percent in 2005 compared with 2004.

- The estimate for foundation giving would be approximately $29.84 billion, a change of 5.0 percent compared with the $28.41 billion in foundation grantmaking in 2004, as reported by the Foundation Center.

- Corporate giving would be an estimated $12.47 billion, or 10.9 percent above the revised estimate of $11.24 billion for 2004.

Giving USA: **The Numbers**

Changes in giving by source, without and with disaster contributions, 2004–2005
(Adjusted for inflation)

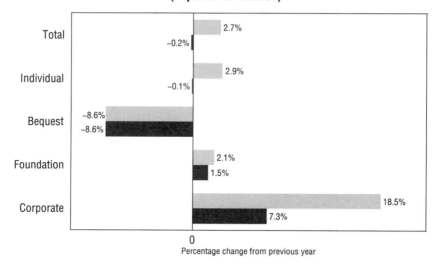

With disaster giving included ■ Before disaster giving added

- Adjusted for inflation, total giving is estimated to have declined by 0.2 percent before disaster giving is added. The estimated decline is attributable to declining bequest amounts and a small decline estimated in giving by individuals before including disaster giving.

- Individual giving with disaster gifts included rose an estimated 2.9 percent (adjusted for inflation). Before adding the disaster amount, individual giving is estimated to have declined by 0.1 percent. This decline reflects a very low inflation-adjusted increase (0.2 percent) in the Standard & Poor's 500 Index, which is used as an indicator of wealth, one of the key factors that is associated with changes in giving.

- No charitable bequests could be found that were directed to disaster relief, although bequest giving did fall for other reasons in 2005.

- Adjusted for inflation, foundation grantmaking rose an estimated 1.5 percent before adding disaster relief gifts. This also reflects a lower rate of increase in the stock market than was seen in 2004, when the Standard & Poor's 500 Index grew by 6.2 percent adjusted for inflation from the end of 2003 through the end of 2004.

- Before adding disaster giving, corporate giving is estimated to have grown by 7.3 percent, adjusted for inflation. This rate of growth reflects very strong growth in gross domestic product and growth in profits before tax in 2004 and 2005.

Giving USA: The Numbers

**Estimated changes in giving by type of recipient,
without and with estimates for disaster relief gifts included, 2004–2005
(Not adjusted for inflation)**

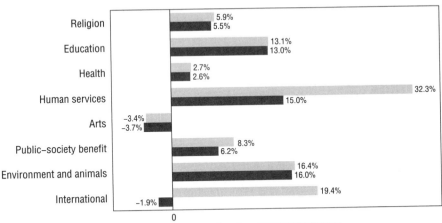

Percentage change from previous year

☐ With disaster giving included   ■ Before disaster giving added

- The Center on Philanthropy tracked relief gifts throughout 2005. Relief gifts predominantly affected three subsectors: Human services; international affairs; and to a lesser extent, public-society benefit.

- Religious organizations include groups such as the Mennonite Central Committee, United Methodist World Relief, Lutheran Services America and many others. With disaster giving added, giving to religion rose by 5.9 percent. Without the gifts to these denominational mission and relief agencies, giving to religious organizations rose 5.5 percent.

- Charitable education organizations received an estimated $10 million in relief gifts. This had just a small impact on the percentage change in giving to this subsector.

- Health organizations received an estimated $9 million in donations for relief work. The impact on the overall percentage change was very small.

- With disaster giving included, giving to the human services subsector grew by 32.3 percent. Even before relief giving, organizations in this subsector reported an unusually strong year, with growth of 15.0 percent in charitable gifts.

- Arts organizations saw charitable gifts decline in 2005 by 3.4 percent with disaster giving included. Relief gifts to arts organizations included donations to Architecture for Humanity and other organizations providing immediate relief and taking part in the rebuilding efforts. Giving to this subsector dropped 3.7 percent before relief gifts were added.

Giving USA: **The Numbers**

- Public-society benefit organizations saw giving rise by 8.3 percent with disaster relief giving included. Before disaster relief contributions of an estimated $263 million to these organizations are added to the total, contributions to organizations in the public-society benefit subsector increased by 6.2 percent.

- Organizations in the environment-animals subsector raised relief funds for animal rescue after the hurricanes, which helped boost giving to this subsector by 16.4 percent. Before the relief amounts, contributions to organizations in this subsector rose by an estimated 16.0 percent.

- With relief gifts included, the international affairs subsector saw giving increase 19.4 percent. Without including relief gifts, contributions to organizations in the international affairs subsector fell by 1.9 percent. This decline, the first since 1997 in this subsector, suggests that at least some gifts that would normally have been made for international affairs went instead for relief work.

Giving USA: The Numbers

**Estimated changes in giving by type of recipient,
without and with estimates for disaster relief gifts included, 2004–2005
(Adjusted for inflation)**

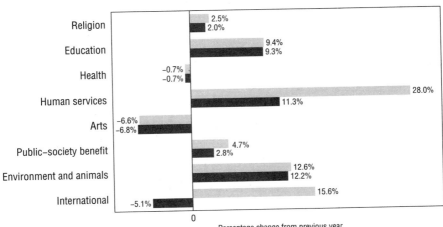

Percentage change from previous year

With disaster giving included ■ Before disaster giving added

- Adjusted for inflation, giving to religious organizations rose 2.5 percent with disaster gifts included and 2.0 percent before adding them.

- Contributions to education organizations rose by 9.4 percent with disaster relief gifts added and 9.3 percent before adding them.

- Giving to health fell by 0.7 percent with disaster relief gifts included. The gifts directly to health organizations that were reported were so low that the change is the same whether they are included or not.

- Giving to human services organizations rose by 28.0 percent with disaster giving included and by 11.3 percent before disaster giving was added.

- Giving for the arts, culture, and humanities subsector fell by 6.6 percent adjusted for inflation with disaster relief gifts included and dropped 6.8 percent before they were added in.

- Giving to organizations in the public-society benefit subsector rose by 4.7 percent adjusted for inflation with disaster gifts included and by 2.8 percent before disaster giving was included.

- Giving to the environment/animals subsector rose 12.6 percent with disaster relief giving included and by 12.2 percent before it was added.

- Giving for the international affairs subsector rose 15.6 percent with disaster relief giving included and fell by 5.1 percent before it was added.

Giving USA: The Numbers

Changes in giving by source, 2004–2005 and 2003–2004

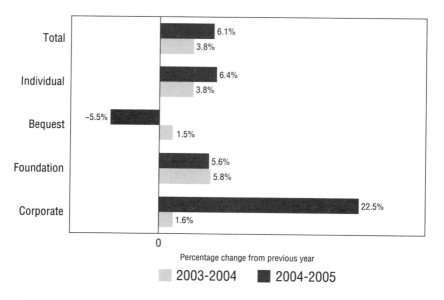

Percentage change from previous year

2003-2004   2004-2005

- This page compares changes between 2004 and 2005 with disaster giving included and changes between 2003 and 2004, all before adjustment for inflation. The next page considers the same years with adjustment for inflation.

- Total giving in 2005 rose by an estimated 6.1 percent, an increase over the change of 3.8 percent in the prior year.

- Individual giving increased in 2005 by an estimated 6.4 percent, a faster rate of growth than between 2003 and 2004, which was 3.8 percent.

- Charitable bequests in 2005 are estimated to have declined 5.5 percent, largely because of fewer deaths. This rate of change is a shift from the 1.5 percent rate of growth seen in 2004.

- Foundation grantmaking is estimated to have increased 5.6 percent in 2005, according to the Foundation Center, a slightly slower rate of growth than was found for 2004. This estimate is for grantmaking by independent, community, and operating foundations. Corporate foundation grantmaking is in the estimate of corporate giving.

- Corporate giving shows an exceptionally high rate of growth in 2005, at 22.5 percent, a big change from the 1.6 percent rate of growth estimated for 2004. The 2005 value reflects increased gross domestic product, increased corporate profits, and about $1.38 billion in disaster relief giving.

Giving USA: The Numbers

Changes in giving by source, 2004–2005 and 2003–2004
(Adjusted for inflation)

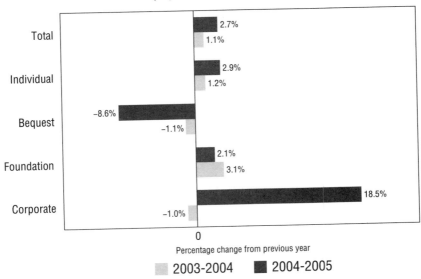

- After adjustment for inflation using the Consumer Price Index, total giving is estimated to have increased by 2.7 percent in 2005, which is greater than the inflation-adjusted increase of 1.1 percent estimated for 2004. The Consumer Price Index measured inflation at 3.5 percent in 2005 and 2.6 percent in 2004. Note that sometimes when adjusting *Giving USA* estimates, the rounding process yields an inflation-adjusted change that differs from the current change minus the inflation rate.

- Individual giving adjusted for inflation is estimated to have increased 2.9 percent in 2005, a faster rate of growth than the 1.2 percent estimated for 2004.

- Contributions by bequest fell in 2005 by an estimated 8.6 percent, following an inflation-adjusted decline of 1.1 percent in 2004.

- Foundation grantmaking adjusted for inflation rose by an estimated 2.1 percent in 2005, a slower rate of growth than the 3.1 percent found in 2004.

- Corporate giving adjusted for inflation increased an estimated 18.5 percent, dramatically above the decline of 1.0 percent found for 2004.

Giving USA: The Numbers

Changes in giving by type of recipient organization, 2004–2005 and 2003–2004

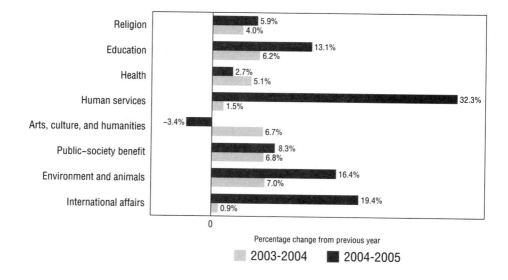

- With disaster giving included, giving to religious organizations rose by 5.9 percent in 2005, a faster rate of change than the 4.0 percent for 2004.

- Giving to the education subsector rose by 13.1 percent in 2005, which is the fastest rate of growth since 2000 for this subsector.

- Giving to health organizations rose by 2.7 percent in 2005, trailing the 5.1 percent increase seen in 2004.

- Giving to human services organizations, which included more than $3.3 billion in disaster relief giving, rose by 32.3 percent in 2005.

- Gifts to the arts, culture, and humanities subsector fell by 3.4 percent in 2005, the first decline since 1998.

- Giving for organizations in the public-society benefit subsector rose by 8.3 percent in 2005, exceeding the 2004 change of 6.8 percent due to the disaster relief giving included for 2005.

- Giving for the environment and animals subsector increased by 16.4 percent in 2005, an unusually high rate of change that follows growth of 7.0 percent in 2004.

- Giving for international affairs organizations, which includes relief giving, grew by 19.4 percent in 2005, compared with the very low rate of growth of 0.9 percent in 2004.

Giving USA: The Numbers

Changes in giving by type of recipient organization, 2004–2005 and 2003–2004 (Adjusted for inflation)

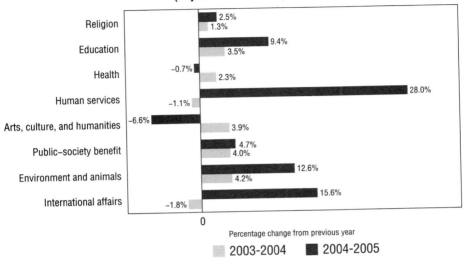

- Adjusted for inflation, gifts to religious organizations grew by 2.5 percent in 2005, compared with a change of 1.3 percent in 2004.

- Gifts to educational organizations in 2005 rose by an inflation-adjusted 9.4 percent, much more than the 3.5 percent rate of growth in 2004.

- Adjusted for inflation, gifts to health organizations dropped by 0.7 percent in 2005, which follows an increase of 2.3 percent in 2004.

- Gifts to human services organizations ended a three-year inflation-adjusted decline in 2005, growing by 28.0 percent. A portion of that is from disaster relief giving, but a nearly equal portion of the change is from other giving to human services.

- Giving to arts, culture, and humanities organizations fell by 6.6 percent after adjustment for inflation. This drop follows healthy growth of 3.9 percent in 2004.

- Giving to organizations in the public-society benefit subsector rose by 4.7 percent in 2005, just slightly more than the 4.0 percent rate of growth found for 2004.

- Gifts to the environment and animals subsector grew by 12.6 percent in 2005, three times more than the 4.2 percent rate of growth found for 2004.

- Giving to the international affairs subsector increased by 15.6 percent after adjustment for inflation. This reflects disaster relief giving and other giving.

Giving USA: The Numbers

Total giving, 1965–2005
($ in billions)

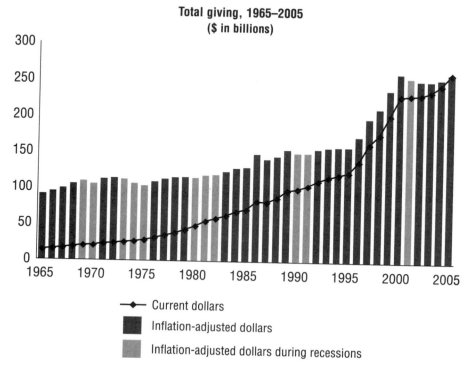

- Current dollars
- Inflation-adjusted dollars
- Inflation-adjusted dollars during recessions

- In current dollars, before adjustment for inflation, estimated giving has increased by $245.57 billion since 1965. Nearly half of that growth (49 percent) has been since 1996, when giving was an estimated $139.10 billion.

- Adjusted for inflation, estimated giving has risen from $91.20 billion in 1965 to $260.28 billion in 2005. This is an increase of more than $169 billion, or 185 percent. Most of that growth has been since 1996, when inflation-adjusted giving was $173.14 billion.

- In 2005, giving of $260.28 billion has not quite surpassed the inflation-adjusted high of $260.53 billion achieved in 2000, which coincided with the end of the so-called "tech bubble" in the stock market.

Giving USA: The Numbers

Total giving by source by five-year spans in inflation-adjusted dollars, 1966–2005
($ in billions)

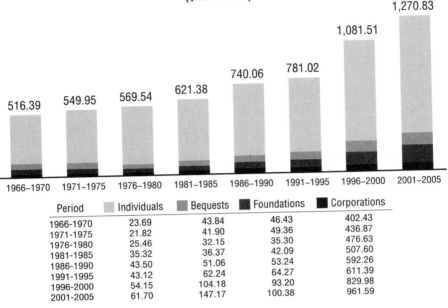

Period	Individuals	Bequests	Foundations	Corporations
1966-1970	23.69	43.84	46.43	402.43
1971-1975	21.82	41.90	49.36	436.87
1976-1980	25.46	32.15	35.30	476.63
1981-1985	35.32	36.37	42.09	507.60
1986-1990	43.50	51.06	53.24	592.26
1991-1995	43.12	62.24	64.27	611.39
1996-2000	54.15	104.18	93.20	829.98
2001-2005	61.70	147.17	100.38	961.59

Giving USA uses the CPI to adjust for inflation.

Adjusted for inflation, giving in the 2001-2005 period was 17.5 percent more than in the prior five-year period of 1996-2000.

The increase seen in all donations for the 2001-2005 period reflects:
- 15.9 percent growth in individual giving;
- 7.7 percent growth in bequest gifts;
- 41.3 percent growth in grants from independent, community, and operating foundations, which is attributed by the Foundation Center to grantmaking at prior levels even as assets fell in the early 2000s, the creation of new foundations, and new gifts made to existing foundations; and
- 13.9 percent increase in corporate giving, including grants from corporate foundations.

Since the 1966-1970 period, there has been a 146.1 percent increase in total giving. This reflects:
- 138.9 percent growth in individual giving;
- 116.2 percent growth in bequest gifts;
- 235.7 percent increase in grantmaking by independent, community, and operating foundations, as tracked by the Foundation Center; and
- 160.4 percent increase in corporate giving, including grants from corporate foundations reported by the Foundation Center.

Giving USA: The Numbers

Giving by individuals, 1965–2005
($ in billions)

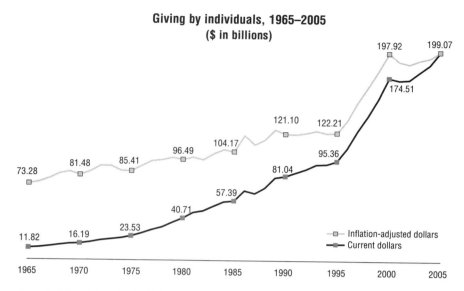

- Charitable giving by individuals and households reached an estimated $199.07 billion in 2005, compared with a revised estimate of $187.11 billion for 2004. This is a growth of 6.4 percent (2.9 percent adjusted for inflation).

- This estimate includes a projection that households itemizing charitable deductions on their tax returns will claim gifts totaling $156.32 billion for 2005. For 2003, households itemized charitable gifts of $145.702 billion. This is the most recent IRS data available in spring 2006.

- The estimate of giving by households that do not itemize charitable deductions is $36.92 billion, or an average of $551 in contributions from each of the 70 or so percent of households that do not itemize charitable deductions.

- The estimate of individual giving is 76.5 percent of total giving for 2005.

- Before adding disaster giving, individual giving is estimated to be $193.24 billion.

- Individual giving includes $5.83 billion in estimated contributions for disaster relief made in 2005. Most studies conducted suggest that almost all disaster relief giving by households was in addition to any other giving those families did. The disaster estimate has been added to the estimate of itemized charitable contributions and donations by households that do not itemize.

- The Katrina Emergency Tax Relief Act (KETRA) may have stimulated some new giving and it may have shifted some giving into 2005 that would have occurred in later years. With no data available in April 2006 about the extent of the impact of the KETRA provision, no adjustment has been made to the *Giving USA* estimate for individual giving in 2005. Please see the Legal/Legislative chapter for a discussion of the Act's provisions.

Giving USA: The Numbers

Giving by bequest, 1965–2005
($ in billions)

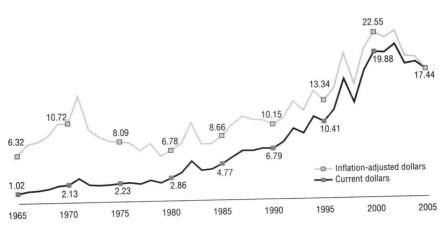

- Charitable bequests in 2005 reached an estimated $17.44 billion. This is a decrease of 5.5 percent compared with the revised estimate of $18.47 billion for 2004. Adjusted for inflation, the decline is 8.6 percent.
- Estimated charitable bequests are 6.7 percent of total giving for 2005.
- Charitable bequests are dropping at least in part because of a slow-down in the number of people dying. The National Center for Health Statistics office reported a decline of 50,000 in the number of deaths in 2004, the sharpest decline in 70 years.
- Another contributing factor to the decline in charitable bequests in recent years is the very slow growth in household assets from 1999 through 2004. John Havens of the Boston College Center on Wealth and Philanthropy reports that, adjusted for inflation, in those years, total household wealth held by all families grew by just 0.2 percent cumulatively.
- Researchers at the Federal Reserve Board released an analysis of the 2004 Survey of Consumer Finances, which shows that for people age 65 and above, on average, net worth fell between 2001 and 2004. Lower net worth means lower charitable bequests, even when all household wealth is averaged across all households. It can also mean lower giving by living individuals.
- About one-fifth ($3.63 billion, or 18 percent) of the dollar amount in the charitable bequest estimate is from estates below the federal estate tax filing threshold. Based on IRS data from estate tax returns for 2004, about 40 percent of the bequest estimate is from 300 or so estates that have a gross estate value of $20 million or more, and the remaining 20 percent of the bequest estimate is from more than 11,000 estates with gross estate value between $1.5 million and $19.99 million.
- Other planned giving instruments such as annuities and trusts are not included in the *Giving USA* estimate of charitable bequests.

Giving USA: The Numbers

Giving by foundations, 1965–2005
($ in billions)

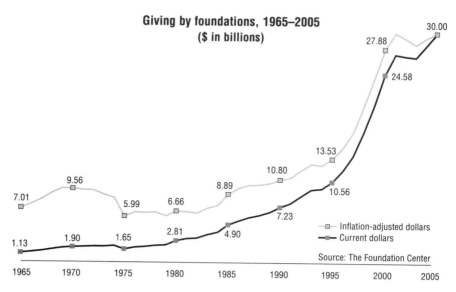

Source: The Foundation Center

- The Foundation Center estimated $30.0 billion in giving in 2005 by independent, community, and operating foundations. This is a 5.6 percent increase in grantmaking by these types of foundations (2.1 percent adjusted for inflation) compared with the final amount of $28.41 billion for 2004.

- The Foundation Center summarized these trends as important to foundation grantmaking in 2005:
  – Growth in foundation assets in 2004
  – New gifts to existing foundations
  – Creation of new foundations in 2004 and 2005.

- The Foundation Center notes that growth in grantmaking in 2005 was lower than the percentage increase in assets in 2004. For independent, community, and operating foundations, grantmaking rose by 5.6 percent and asset values (including new gifts to existing foundations, investment yields, and new foundation creation) rose by 7.1 percent. Grantmaking budgets in 2005 may reflect grantmaker caution in light of a two-year decline in assets from 2000 to 2002 and the practice at many large foundations of basing grantmaking on an average of asset values calculated over several years. Added to these factors was the relatively lackluster performance of the stock market in 2005.

- Foundation grantmaking represented 11.5 percent of all estimated contributions in 2005, which is near the all-time high of 11.8 percent in 2001.

Giving USA: The Numbers

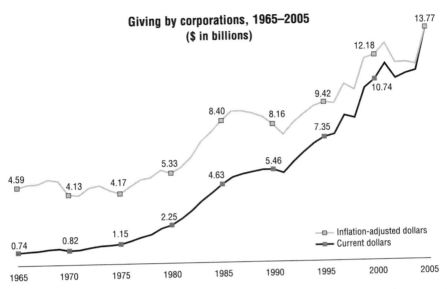

Giving by corporations, 1965–2005
($ in billions)

Inflation-adjusted dollars
Current dollars

- Corporate contributions rose to an estimated $13.77 billion in 2005, an increase of 22.5 percent (18.5 percent adjusted for inflation) compared with the revised estimate of $11.24 billion for 2004.

- Corporate charitable contributions are 5.3 percent of total estimated giving in 2005.

- The growth in corporate giving in 2005 reflects:
  - An estimated $1.38 billion in donations for disaster relief with $84 million removed from that total as potentially double-counted corporate foundation grants.
  - An estimated increase of more than $1 billion associated with increases in gross domestic product and increases in corporate profits.
  - Corporate foundation grantmaking of an estimated $3.6 billion, using data collected by the Foundation Center.
  - Subtraction of corporate gifts of an estimated $3.4 billion made to corporate foundations, based on the past three years of corporate giving to fund corporate foundations and including the creation of the Google Foundation with a gift of $90 million.

- Corporate giving is associated with changes in corporate profits. One profit measure, the Bureau of Economic Analysis's report of corporate profits before tax, showed a very high rate of growth in 2005, which at least partially reflected tax law changes for 2002 through 2005 that affect depreciation. *Giving USA* developed an estimate with an adjusted level of profits to try to take into account the portion of the profit increase attributable to depreciation. The resulting estimate of corporate giving for 2005 was $13.76 billion instead of $13.77.

Giving USA: The Numbers

Giving by source: percentage of the total by five-year spans, 1966–2005

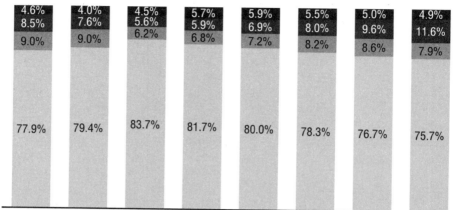

Individuals   Bequests   Foundations   Corporations

- Giving by individuals has maintained a fifty-year trend of being by far the single most important source of donations in the United States.

- Charitable bequests, which increased as a share of the total in 1991-1995 and again from 1996-2000, have declined to just less than 8 percent of all giving for the period 2001-2005.

- Grantmaking by foundations has been a fairly stable 11.5 to 11.8 percent of the total since 2001. For the 2001-2005 period, foundation grantmaking is the largest share after individual giving.

- Donations made by corporations, including corporate foundations, rose slightly as a share of the total in 2005, to 5.3 percent. The share of 4.9 percent for the 2001-2005 period is lower than the five-year spans since 1981, but more than the values for 1966-1980.

Giving USA: The Numbers

Total giving as a percentage of gross domestic product, 1965–2005

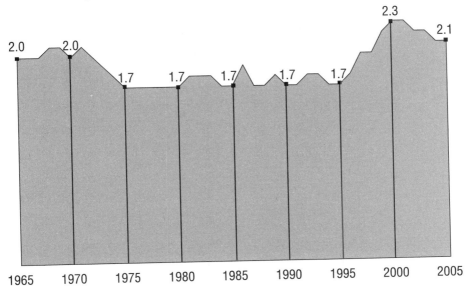

- Total estimated giving of $260.28 billion is 2.1 percent of gross domestic product for 2005. It has remained above 2.0 percent since 1997 after more than 20 years below that amount.

- The high of 2.3 percent was in 2000, when contributions grew by 8 percent for religious organizations and 15.3 percent at educational institutions. In addition, in that year, foundations received $24.71 billion, the third-highest year on record for foundation giving. Those three organizational types combined account for nearly 60 percent of total contributions. Significant gifts to all three in 2000 lifted giving to an exceptional level.

Giving USA: The Numbers

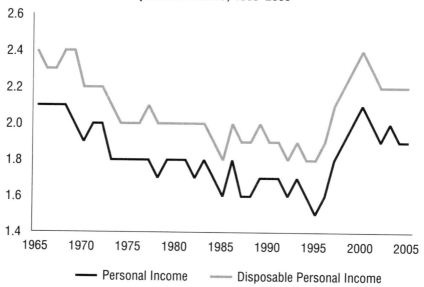

Individual giving as a share of personal income and disposable personal income, 1965–2005

Legend: —— Personal Income —— Disposable Personal Income

- After reaching a peak in 2000, giving as a percentage of personal income and as a percentage of disposable income has leveled off.

- Disposable income reflects personal income less taxes to federal, state and local governments (i.e., it is "after-tax income"). For 2005, the Federal Bureau of Economic Analysis's estimate of personal income was 2.0 percent more than the 2004 estimate, after adjustment for inflation using the Consumer Price Index. Disposable personal income, also reported by the Bureau of Economic Analysis, rose by 0.9 percent in 2005, using the same data source. Growth in giving of 2.9 percent (adjusted for inflation) exceeded the rate of growth in disposable personal income.

Giving USA: The Numbers

Individual giving as a percentage of personal consumption expenditures excluding food and energy, 1965–2005

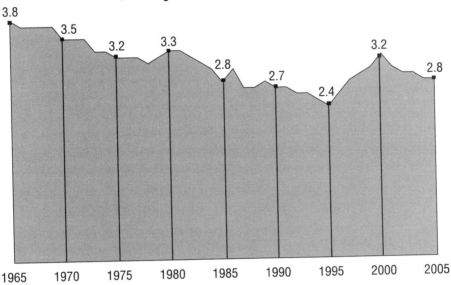

- Giving can be viewed as a form of "consumption," or an expenditure that a household chooses to make among many other possible choices of how to spend its income. One common way to measure expenditures by households is to remove the food and energy costs because they are the most subject to short-term changes. Reflecting this, the U.S. Bureau of Economic Analysis provides a personal consumption expenditures measure excluding food and energy.

- In 1965, household contributions began falling as a share of personal expenditures when food and energy are excluded. The lowest percentage was in 1995, when giving was 2.4 percent of personal expenditures excluding food and energy.

- From 1995 through 2000, charitable giving increased as a percentage of consumption.

- Since 2001, giving has been fairly stable, around 2.8 percent of personal consumption expenditures when food and energy are excluded.

- The values in this graph are generally higher than giving as a percentage of income or as a percentage of disposable income because giving is divided by a smaller amount – expenditures with two big categories (food and energy) excluded.

Giving USA: The Numbers

Corporate giving as a percentage of corporate pretax profits, 1965–2005

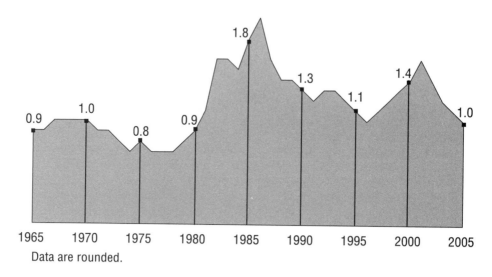

Data are rounded.

- Corporate giving as a percentage of corporate profits is estimated to be 1.0 percent in 2005, one of the lowest levels found since 1980, but close to the 40-year average of 1.2 percent.

- This lower level of giving as a share of profits does not reflect less corporate giving. Instead, the estimated $13.77 billion in corporate giving is calculated as a percentage of dramatically increased profits, and at least a part of the increased profits is attributed to changing rules about depreciation, and not to corporate income.

- The Katrina Emergency Tax Relief Act (KETRA) permitted corporations in 2005 to increase the amount claimed in deductions to 15 percent of income (up from the 10 percent usually in force). It is not clear whether that might affect corporate giving for the year. No adjustment has been made to the 2005 estimate to incorporate any potential impact of KETRA.

- Tax law changes in 2002 and 2003 also shifted how corporations claim depreciation (which affects how profits are calculated) and how corporations value in-kind gifts.

- With the numerous changes in corporate accounting rules in effect since 2001, the measure of corporate giving as a percentage of pretax profits is difficult to interpret and should be cited sparingly.

Giving USA: The Numbers

Giving to religion, 1965–2005
($ in billions)

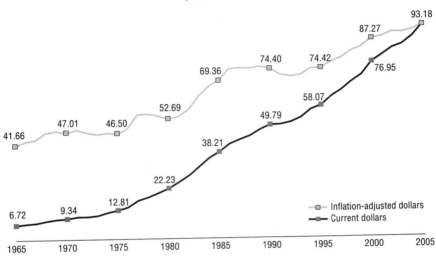

- Giving to religious organizations increased by 5.9 percent (2.5 percent adjusted for inflation), reaching an estimated $93.18 billion in 2005.

- Giving to religious organizations represented 35.8 percent of total estimated charitable contributions in the United States in 2005.

- Religious organizations received contributions of more than $431 million for disaster relief. *Giving USA* does not count the thousands of volunteer hours contributed by members of congregations or the household items collected by congregations to give directly to survivors of natural disasters.

Giving USA: The Numbers

Giving to education, 1965–2005
($ in billions)

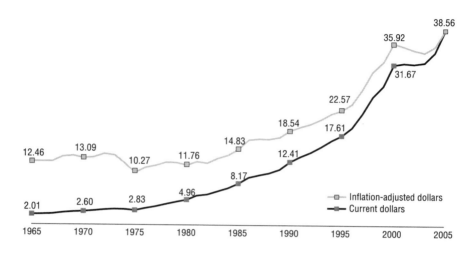

- Charitable gifts to educational organizations reached an estimated $38.56 billion in 2005, an increase of 13.1 percent compared with 2004 (9.4 percent adjusted for inflation).

- Educational organizations received 14.8 percent of estimated total giving.

- The increase was driven by large organizations, most of which are colleges and universities. Among the large institutions that responded to the *Giving USA* survey, nearly two-thirds (64 percent) reported an increase averaging $11 million. All sizes of educational organizations in the *Giving USA* survey reported growth in charitable receipts in 2005.

- Anecdotal reports suggest that at least part of the increase seen in giving to educational institutions in 2005 is attributable to the fact that donors prepaid pledges to benefit from the tax advantages available in the Katrina Emergency Tax Relief Act. This parallels the 14.9 percent increase in giving to education in 1986, when donors made gifts before tax rate changes for 1987 reduced the tax benefit for contributions itemized as tax deductions.

- Donations to educational institutions after Hurricane Katrina included funding for institutions in New Orleans to defray the costs of rebuilding, contributions toward tuition for students relocating to other schools, and a major gift of $50 million for rebuilding public schools in Mississippi. In allocating gifts to recipients, *Giving USA* does not include contributions to public agencies. Those gifts are in "unallocated."

Giving USA: The Numbers

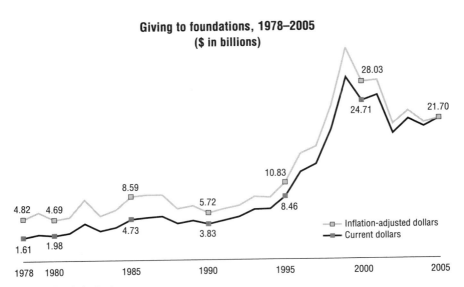

Giving to foundations, 1978–2005
($ in billions)

28.03

24.71

21.70

10.83

8.59

5.72

8.46

4.82   4.69

4.73

3.83

1.61   1.98

— □ — Inflation-adjusted dollars
— ■ — Current dollars

1978 1980   1985   1990   1995   2000   2005

Data: The Foundation Center.
Excludes gifts to corporate foundations.

- The Foundation Center estimates approximately $21.70 billion in gifts to foundations in 2005. This represents approximately 8.3 percent of all giving in 2005.

- The Foundation Center tracks active, grantmaking foundations and reports a total of 65,140 foundations in 2004. The figure for 2005 from the Foundation Center will be released in early 2007.

- In prior years, the Foundation Center has found that for every $1 billion given to new foundations, approximately $20 billion is given to existing foundations.

- *Giving USA* reports the amount of giving to foundations using the Foundation Center's report of gifts received as listed on IRS Forms 990-PF. A foundation may receive announced gifts, as from an estate, many years after the initial announcement.

- In January 2006, the search tool FoundationSearch.com reported 1,624 foundations registered since January 2005 that had not yet filed their first IRS Form 990-PF.

- Foundation Center findings about gifts to foundations in 2005 will be released in the 2007 edition of *Foundation Growth and Giving Estimates*.

Giving USA: The Numbers

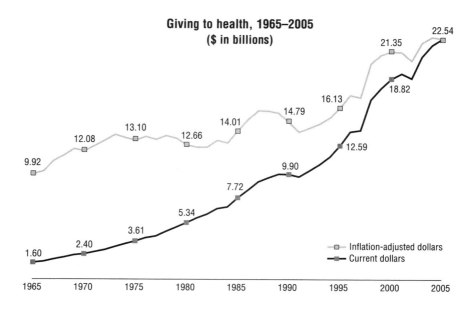

Giving to health, 1965–2005
($ in billions)

- Giving to organizations in the health subsector is estimated to be $22.54 billion in 2005. This is 8.7 percent of total estimated giving.

- In current dollars, giving to health rose by an estimated 2.7 percent in 2005. Adjusted for inflation, this is a decline of 0.7 percent, the first decline since 2002.

- Volunteers in the health professions and companies manufacturing health products organized countless formal (through an organization) and informal (direct to individuals) rescue and relief efforts after Hurricanes Katrina, Rita, and Wilma struck the Gulf Coast of the United States. No dollar value can be put on the total of volunteer hours and the donated medicines, supplies, and equipment.

- Health organizations also received contributions for needs that arose after the hurricanes. No total estimate was available in mid-2006. Examples include a $1 million foundation grant for health clinics and reported gifts from individuals to help provide continuing care for people with cancer, diabetes, arthritis, or other illnesses.

- Several major health-related organizations committed funds from their reserves or raised new funds to support relief and rebuilding efforts in the storm zone. These include the American Diabetes Association, the American Heart Association, the National Mental Health Association, Easter Seals, the Leukemia and Lymphoma Society, and more.

- In the *Giving USA* survey, large and medium-sized health charities reported increases in contributions received. Small health organizations reported a decline.

Giving USA: The Numbers

Giving to human services, 1965–2005
($ in billions)

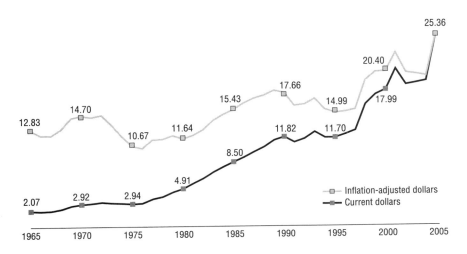

- Giving to organizations in the human services subsector is estimated to be $25.36 billion in 2005. This is 9.7 percent of total estimated giving.

- In current dollars, giving to human services organizations increased by an estimated 32.3 percent in 2005. Adjusted for inflation, this is growth of 28.0 percent. This is the highest rate of growth on record for this subsector.

- Only some of the growth in the human services subsector giving can be attributed to giving for disaster relief. The balance is from other changes. Before the disaster contribution amounts are added, there was growth of 15.0 percent (11.3 percent adjusted for inflation) in contributions reported by the organizations participating in the _Giving USA_ survey, reversing a three-year trend of inflation-adjusted declines in giving to organizations in this subsector.

- Survey responses about disaster relief contributions received were supplemented with public records from organizations not returning the survey. Disaster giving reached an estimated $3.31 billion for human services organizations. The largest single recipient was the American Red Cross, with an estimated $2.4 billion (72.5 percent) received for the three disasters: the Indian Ocean tsunami, the hurricanes in the Caribbean that struck the U.S. Gulf Coast, and the earthquake in the mountains of Pakistan.

Giving USA: The Numbers

Giving to public-society benefit, 1965–2005
($ in billions)

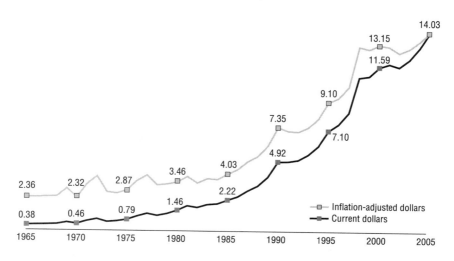

- Giving to organizations in the public-society benefit subsector is estimated to be $14.03 billion in 2005. This is 5.4 percent of total estimated giving.

- In current dollars, giving to public-society benefit organizations rose by an estimated 8.3 percent in 2005. Adjusted for inflation, this is an increase of 4.7 percent.

- Before disaster relief contributions are included, survey responses showed that giving was up 6.2 percent (2.8 percent adjusted for inflation) for all organizations combined.

- With disaster giving included, large organizations responding to the survey reported an average increase of $344,574 in contributions received. Medium-sized and small organizations in this subsector also reported increased contributions received in 2005.

- United Way of America reported that contributions for hurricane response reached $45 million by October 2005. The Bush-Clinton fund established for response to the tsunami was replicated for the Katrina response. Combined, the two funds raised more than $110 million in 2005. A number of other organizations in the public-society benefit subsector raised funds for disaster response. Not all amounts were available in mid-2006 to add to the estimate for giving to this subsector.

Giving USA: The Numbers

Giving to arts, culture, and humanities, 1965–2005
($ in billions)

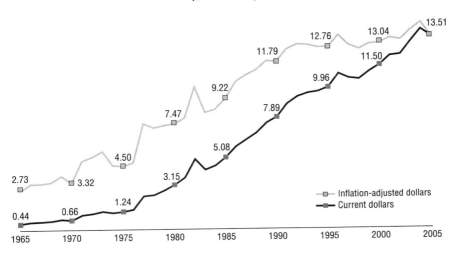

- Giving to organizations in the arts subsector declined in 2005, to $13.51 billion, a drop of 3.4 percent (-6.6 percent adjusted for inflation). This is the first decline before inflation found since 1998.

- Contributions to the arts, culture, and humanities subsector are 5.2 percent of total estimated giving.

- Among organizations responding to the *Giving USA* survey, large arts organizations and small arts organizations reported a decline in charitable gifts received; medium-sized organizations saw growth in giving.

- About 65 large arts organizations receive one-quarter of total contributions in the arts subsector, based on IRS Forms 990 filed in 2003. Changes in the large organizations heavily influence the direction of change for all organizations in arts giving.

- Several large donations to arts organizations announced in 2005 were in-kind gifts, including collections given to the Dallas Museum of Art, the Getty Museum, the Detroit Institute of Arts, the de Young Museum, and the Virginia Museum of Fine Arts. The value of in-kind contributions is not sought in the *Giving USA* survey. Donors of collections, however, are allowed by law to claim at least some portion of the value of the gift as a tax deduction. The amount that donors claim is in the estimates of giving by source but the value of the gift will not necessarily appear in the arts subsector. Instead, it forms a part of "unallocated giving."

Giving USA: The Numbers

Giving to environment and animals, 1987–2005
($ in billions)

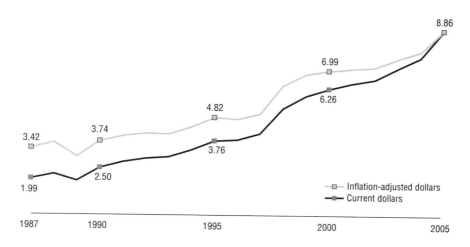

- Giving to organizations in the environment and animals subsector is estimated to be $8.86 billion in 2005. This is 3.4 percent of total estimated giving.

- In current dollars, giving to environment and animals organizations increased by an estimated 16.4 percent in 2005. Adjusted for inflation, this is an increase of 12.6 percent.

- The estimate of giving to this subsector rose in 2005 because 63 percent of organizations reported an increase in charitable revenue from 2004 to 2005. The increases were large, on average 26 percent more than the amount raised in 2004.

- Organizations in all three size groups (large, medium-sized, and small) reported growth in giving. The amount donated to all the large organizations providing data rose by 15 percent; medium-sized organizations received 14 percent more than in 2004; and gifts to small organizations rose by 28 percent.

- Animal rescue efforts in the aftermath of Hurricane Katrina received an estimated $29 million or more in donations, much of which was from online giving.

Giving USA: The Numbers

Giving to international affairs, 1987–2005
($ in billions)

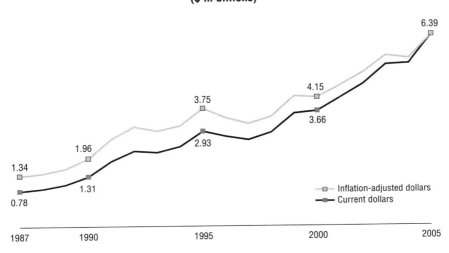

- Cash and in-kind giving to organizations in the international affairs subsector is estimated to be $6.39 billion in 2005, which includes at least $1.14 billion in gifts for relief work after the tsunami in December 2004 and after the October 2005 earthquake in Pakistan. International affairs organizations also reported gifts received for relief work after the hurricanes.

- International affairs giving is 2.5 percent of total estimated giving.

- In current dollars, giving to international affairs organizations grew by an estimated 19.4 percent in 2005. Adjusted for inflation, this is a change of 15.6 percent.

- The estimated $1.14 billion for natural disaster relief that went to organizations in the international affairs subsector is 17.8 percent of total estimated international affairs contributions in 2005.

- Calculated without the disaster giving, gifts to organizations in the international affairs subsector fell by 1.9 percent (to an estimated $5.25 billion in 2005). This would be an inflation-adjusted drop of 5.1 percent.

Giving USA: The Numbers

Giving by type of recipients, five-year spans (adjusted for inflation), 1965–2005

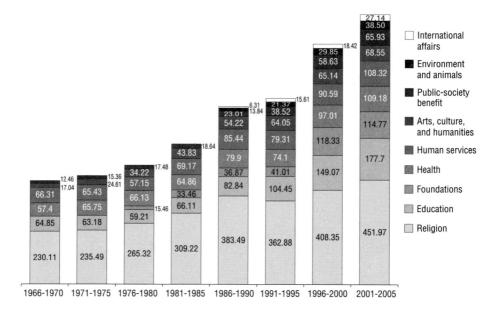

- Giving to religion has formed the largest share of total giving in all periods. The estimated gifts to religious organizations in the years 2001–2005 were $451.97 billion, growing by 96 percent since the 1966-1970 period.

- Educational organizations received $177.70 billion (adjusted for inflation) in the period from 2001–2005. This is a change of 174 percent since the 1966–1970 period.

- Giving to foundations has emerged recently as the third-largest type of charitable contribution. The inflation-adjusted $114.77 billion donated to foundations from 2001-2005 is 243 percent more than was reported for the 1986–1990 period (the first with five years of data). According to the Foundation Center, giving to foundations peaked in 1999, when the Gates Foundation received more than $11 billion.

- Health care organizations, which received $109.18 billion in the 2001-2005 period, have seen giving grow by 90 percent since the1966–1970 period.

- Giving for human services organizations has grown by 63 percent since the 1966–1970 period.

- Giving to organizations in the public-society benefit subsector rose by 429 percent between the 1966–1970 period and the 2001–2005 period.

- Giving for organizations in the arts, culture, and humanities subsector has increased by 302 percent since the 1966–1970 period. More recent years have seen much slower rates of growth (5 percent from the 1996–2000 period to the 2001–2005 period) than were observed in the earlier years (44 percent growth from 1966–1970 to 1971–1975).

- Giving to organizations in the environment and animals subsector began to be tracked separately in 1987. It has increased 178 percent since then.

- Giving to organizations in the international affairs subsector began to be tracked separately in 1987. From that first period to the 2001–2005 period, giving to this subsector increased an estimated 330 percent.

Giving USA: The Numbers

Giving by type of recipient as a percentage of total giving, 1966–2005
(Five-year spans; does not include "unallocated")

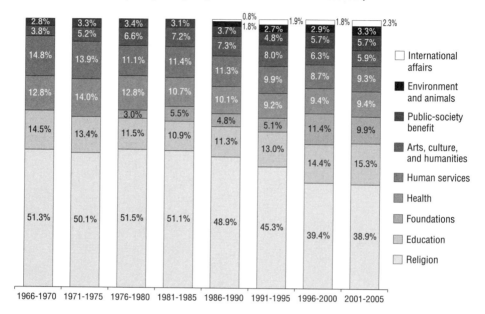

- Giving to religious organizations has increased in current dollars and in inflation-adjusted dollars since 1965. It has, however, declined as a percentage of the total as giving to other subsectors has risen.

- Giving to educational organizations reached 15.3 percent of the total in the most recent five-year period. This is the highest it has ever been as a share of all giving.

- Giving to foundations was 9.9 percent of giving in the period from 2001–2005. This is slightly less than in the preceding five years but a larger share than in all other five-year spans since it began to be tracked in 1978.

- Giving for health care organizations as a percentage of the total has remained around 9.2 to 9.4 percent of the total since 1991. It had previously been more than 10 percent.

- Giving for human services organizations, at 9.3 percent of the total in 2001–2005, is still much lower than the estimated 14.8 percent of the total reported for the period 1965–1970.

- As a percentage of total giving, gifts to organizations in the public-society benefit subsector have been gradually increasing since the 1981-1985 period.

Giving USA: The Numbers

- Contributions for arts, culture, and humanities organizations have been gradually declining as a share of the total since their peak of 8.0 percent in 1991–1995. For 2001–2005, this subsector received 5.9 percent of giving.

- Since it began to be tracked separately in 1987, giving to organizations in the subsector for the environment and animals has been a rising percentage of the total in each five-year period. For 2001–2005, it is an estimated 3.3 percent of giving.

- Contributions for organizations in the international affairs subsector began to be tracked separately in 1987. Since then, this subsector has received an increasing share in each of the five-year spans, ending with an estimated 2.3 percent of giving for the 2001–2005 period.

Giving USA: The Numbers

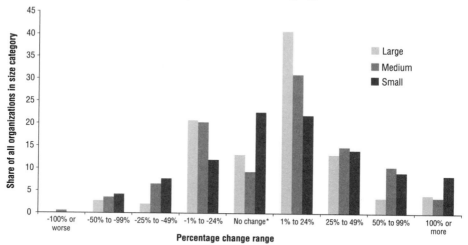

Distribution of levels of change in charitable revenue, 2004–2005
(By organizational size category)

*includes a change of less than 1 percent in either direction

- In the *Giving USA* survey for this edition, more organizations reported an increase in giving than a decrease. This was true for every size group: large, medium-sized, and small.

  - Large organizations:
    61 percent reported an increase
    13 percent reported "no change"
    26 percent reported a decrease

  - Medium-sized organizations:
    60 percent reported an increase
    9 percent reported no change
    31 percent reported a decrease

  - Small organizations:
    53 percent reported an increase
    23 percent reported no change
    24 percent reported a decrease

  - All organizations:
    59 percent reported an increase
    13 percent reported no change
    28 percent reported a decrease

- These percentages were little changed even when amounts reported as received for disaster relief were subtracted from charitable revenue received.

Giving USA: The Numbers

The number of 501(c)(3) organizations, 1995–2005

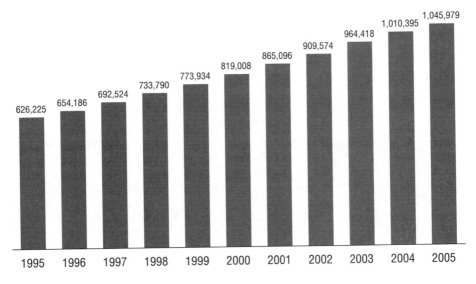

- The number of registered organizations under section 501(c)(3) of the Internal Revenue Code reached 1.05 million in 2005. This reflects an increase of 35,584 organizations compared with 2004. This is the smallest number of new organizations reported for any year since 1995.

- The number of registered charities rose by 3.5 percent between 2004 and 2005. This is the slowest rate of increase in the decade. Nonprofit creation averaged 5.5 percent a year from 1995 to 2004.

- The number of registered charities includes some, but not all, congregations. Some scholars estimate that there are 300,000 to 350,000 congregations in addition to registered charities, making an official count of the charitable subsector approximately 1.35 to 1.4 million entities.

- A study by Kirsten Grønbjerg at Indiana University found one-third more nonprofit organizations operating in the state of Indiana than were registered at the federal level. If the same is true for other states, the number of registered charities, congregations, and not-yet-registered charities could be as high as 1.7 to 1.8 million. Research in some other states is underway to determine whether Grønbjerg's findings hold in other parts of the United States.

Giving for disasters

- The total estimate of giving for disaster relief in 2005 is $7.37 billion. This estimate, which is based on the best available information as of early 2006, includes cash and in-kind giving from individuals, corporations, and foundations.

- Records kept by the Center on Philanthropy at Indiana University tally $5.34 billion in contributions received by various charitable organizations. The tally does not include many congregations or public agencies, such as schools or public hospitals, and may include values for corporate in-kind donations that exceeded allowed deductions.

- Individual donors contributed an estimated $5.83 billion for disaster relief, with most of that going for hurricane relief ($4.25 billion), followed by $1.54 billion contributed for tsunami relief in 2005, and a more typical disaster contribution of about $40 million for relief after the Pakistan earthquake of October 2005.

- Corporate donors gave an estimated $0.94 billion ($936 million) for relief after Hurricanes Katrina, Rita, and Wilma. Much of that amount was the value reported for in-kind donations and services. Corporate donors gave an estimated $0.34 billion ($344 million) for tsunami relief in 2005. They gave an estimated $0.10 billion ($100 million) in relief after the Pakistan earthquake.

- Foundation grantmaking for disasters is estimated to have been $0.16 billion ($160 million). Approximately $0.11 billion ($110 million) is thought to be grants paid in 2005 for relief work after the hurricanes and approximately $0.05 billion ($50 million) is thought to be grants paid in 2005 for tsunami relief in the Indian Ocean and for the earthquake in Pakistan. These are preliminary estimates based largely on publicly reported grant amounts. The Foundation Center will tabulate grants for relief purposes and release more information in 2007.

- In the wake of the Gulf Coast hurricanes, organizations in the human services subsector reported the highest share of the total received by organizations providing information.

- Gifts made in the wake of the tsunami went to organizations in the international subsector, the human services subsector, and the religion subsector.

Overview

The year 2005 had some of the most intense disasters ever, which led to an unusually large amount of charitable giving for rescue and relief work. A December 2004 earthquake and tsunami devastated areas of many nations bordering the Indian Ocean in Southeastern Asia. Nations throughout the world gathered together to help restore communities and livelihoods. Charitable aid agencies in the United States received donations of more than $1.76 billion in 2005 to aid tsunami victims and to provide a foundation for reconstruction.

Giving for disasters

Eight months later, in August 2005, Hurricane Katrina resulted in one of the most expensive disasters to date in the United States. However, Katrina was not the last force felt in 2005. Two more hurricanes—Rita and Wilma—struck Gulf states (largely in Texas and Florida) within two months of Katrina. In early October, a devastating earthquake shook Pakistan and neighboring nations.

For the three kinds of events—tsunami, hurricanes, and earthquake in Pakistan—an estimated $7.37 billion was reported as contributions by individuals, corporations, and foundations. More than $5.34 billion was collected by United States–based organizations that reported their receipts, which excludes most religious organizations that collected funds for relief work and a number of organizations that announced initiatives but did not provide dollar values for the gifts received.[1] Table 1 summarizes the amounts estimated by source of donation.

Table 1
Disaster relief donations in 2005 by source of contribution (estimates)
($ in billions)

	Individuals	Corporations	Foundations	Total
Katrina	4.25	0.94	0.11	5.30
Tsunami	1.54	0.34	0.04	1.92
Earthquake	0.04	0.10	0.01	0.15
Total	5.83	1.38	0.16	7.37

Despite the high amount contributed for relief work, $7.37 billion is just 2.8 percent of the total $260.28 billion estimated charitable giving in the United States for 2005. However, relief contributions were a far larger share of the giving for certain types of charities. Aid giving was concentrated in three subsectors: international, human services and public-society benefit. Preliminary estimates based on publicly reported amounts received and survey responses show:

- An estimated $3.31 billion contributed to human services organizations, which is approximately 13 percent of all estimated human services organization giving for 2005. Some aid for international relief also appears in the human services subsector (e.g., contributions to the Salvation Army, the American Red Cross, and other organizations).

- An estimated $1.14 billion for relief work was contributed to U.S.-based organizations in the international subsector. This is approximately 18 percent of total estimated giving to international organizations. Some international organizations also received support for relief work after Hurricane Katrina.

- An estimated $263 million contributed to United Ways and other collective fundraising entities for relief efforts is about 2 percent of total estimated giving to organizations in the public-society benefit subsector.

Table 2 summarizes estimated amounts received by type of charitable recipient. Data are incomplete, yet every effort has been made to collect information from the organizations widely recognized as the most likely to receive large amounts of relief donations.

Table 2
Gifts reported as received, by subsector, based on surveys and media records, 2005
($ in millions)

	Hurricane	Tsunami	Earthquake	Total
Religion	263.65	151.63	15.53	430.81
Education	10.42			10.42
Health	9.00			9.00
Human Services	2,700.17	592.75	15.00	3,307.92
Public-society benefit	248.86	11.96	2.00	262.82
Art	4.91	33.50		38.41
Environment	29.27			29.27
International affairs	140.29	965.14	36.82	1,142.25
Foundations	51.26			51.26
Unknown/other	1,837.35	165.01	80.65	2,083.00
Totals	5,295.17	1,919.99	160.00	7,365.16

Data: The Center on Philanthropy at Indiana University

Tsunami

The tsunami in the Indian Ocean struck on December 26, 2004. Images of the wave hitting numerous beach communities were broadcast on American news programs. Donations from individuals and corporations reached an estimated $400 million before the end of 2004 and continued into 2005. Congress passed legislation that permitted deductions on 2004 tax returns for gifts made through January 2005. By June 2005, total donations to U.S. charities reached an estimated $2 billion (including contributions to religious organizations responding to the *Giving USA* survey and not previously counted).

The American Red Cross's records of giving after international disasters help illustrate how exceptional the contributions for tsunami relief are in the context of U.S. giving. The American Red Cross is typically the organization that receives the single largest amount in relief contributions in national or international disasters. Figure 1 shows American Red Cross receipts after each of several disasters.

Figure 1
Donations to the American Red Cross for international crises
($ in millions)

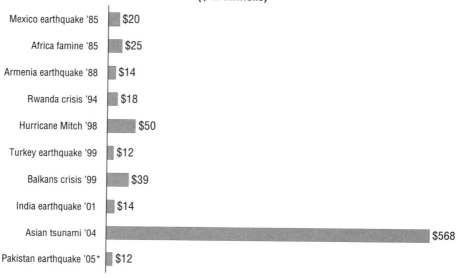

Mexico earthquake '85 $20
Africa famine '85 $25
Armenia earthquake '88 $14
Rwanda crisis '94 $18
Hurricane Mitch '98 $50
Turkey earthquake '99 $12
Balkans crisis '99 $39
India earthquake '01 $14
Asian tsunami '04 $568
Pakistan earthquake '05* $12

*Pakistan earthquake figure as of early January 2006.
Data: American Red Cross
Graphic: Center on Philanthropy at Indiana University

Caribbean hurricanes

Three Category 5 hurricanes struck the Caribbean and surrounding areas between late August and October 2005. The year 2005 marks the first time in recorded history that three Category 5 storms formed in the Atlantic Ocean in one year. Although much of the philanthropic response from donors in the United States focused on relief and recovery efforts in Louisiana, Alabama, Mississippi, and Florida, some donors contributed for relief work in Caribbean nations and in Mexico, where the hurricanes also devastated communities. *Giving USA* relies extensively on the reported contributions made to relief organizations and cannot separate the funding that supported efforts in the United States and funding for assistance offered in other countries.

Contributions for disaster relief and recovery

According to data collected by the Center on Philanthropy at Indiana University from more than 141 reporting organizations from the more than 300 that announced initiatives, the total amount received for relief and recovery from the hurricanes as of January 28, 2006, was $3.157 billion. This number represents the amount collected by organizations that shared information about contributions received. It does not include any estimates of contributions made by organizations working outside the relief sector (such as congregations, higher education institutions, health care organizations, and the like) that collected funds for various types of assistance they provided, such as sending volunteers, hosting displaced students at no cost, or shipping supplies. It also does not include incalculable amounts in "informal" giving, in which people or organizations gave money or assistance directly to survivors without going through a charity.

The largest recipient of donations for the relief work was the American Red Cross. As of February 2, 2006, the organization announced that it had raised $2.23 billion in response to Hurricanes Katrina, Rita, and Wilma. As a result, the American Red Cross stopped fundraising activities focused on hurricane relief. Additional money provided by the U.S. government is not included in this total. Even with the record-setting donations of 2005, the collected total is only a small fraction of the total cost of the damage caused by the storms.

Giving for hurricane relief reached $1 billion in less than three weeks. Figure 2 compares the amounts of disaster giving over time for relief efforts after the attacks of September 11, the 2004 tsunami, and the hurricanes of 2005.

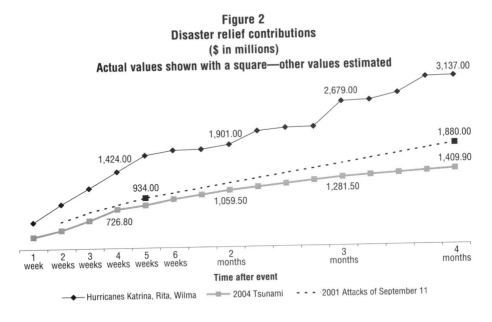

Figure 2
Disaster relief contributions
($ in millions)
Actual values shown with a square—other values estimated

Data: 9-11: Chronicle of Philanthropy
    Tsunami and hurricanes: Center on Philanthropy at Indiana University

Study of impact of the hurricanes on Louisiana charities

As of early 2006, no financial estimate was possible of the additional gifts received by charities in the hurricane areas to fund their work in recovery and rebuilding. *Giving USA* sent surveys to 198 charitable organizations in the three states most affected by the hurricanes—Louisiana, Mississippi, and Alabama. Thirteen could provide information about contributions received in 2005, which was not enough to analyze separately.

Just after the hurricane, the Center on Nonprofits and Philanthropy reported that in Louisiana alone, 3,200 charities had expenditures that totaled more than $8.7 billion.[2] These organizations included all "reporting charities" that file an IRS Form 990 (revenue of $25,000 or more and only those congregations that chose to file, because filing is not required for religious organizations). Of the 3,200 charities, 54 percent focused on providing health care and human services. In a separate study done in late 2005, 47 percent of health and human services nonprofits in southern Louisiana were operating, although many of them were offering limited services.[3] Among the health and human services organizations, just over half were receiving new funding since the hurricanes in the form of donations from individuals, corporations, or congregations. A smaller share was getting funding from foundations, and an even smaller share had financial support from state or federal government agencies.[4]

Recovery and review

By early 2006, much of the relief and recovery aid was distributed, and charities and governments began focusing on rebuilding.[5] Estimates are that rebuilding efforts will take many years. Fundraising continued in 2006, with many reports of fundraising events around the country where proceeds would be used to rebuild lives and structures in the hurricane-affected areas.

With the immediate relief and recovery past, numerous reviews were initiated. As always occurs in disaster situations with many survivors, there were cases of fraud,[6] concerns about the equity of the distribution of relief funding,[7] concern about mismanagement in large charitable organizations,[8] and instances in which beneficiaries of cash relief funds used money in ways that donors might not have selected. The reviews, including Congressional committee investigations and internal reviews at organizations, will continue.

Hurricane Katrina

In late August 2005, winds up to 175 mph created Hurricane Katrina, the sixth strongest storm ever experienced in the Atlantic. Efforts were made to evacuate New Orleans and other coastal regions in Louisiana, Mississippi, and Alabama. Thousands of people could not leave, and after the levees protecting New Orleans from Lake Pontchartrain and the Mississippi River broke, much of that city was submerged.[9] The severe flooding caused greater damage than the hurricane. The National Association of Home Builders estimated that 275,000 homes were destroyed. This number far exceeds the total of homes destroyed by all four Gulf hurricanes of 2004. Katrina is to date the most destructive and costly natural disaster ever for the United States.[10]

The American death toll from Hurricane Katrina was reported to be more than 1,300, mainly in Louisiana (1,079 victims). However, people whose bodies could not be recovered might not be included in that total.[11] In addition to the deaths, Hurricane Katrina displaced more than a million people and disrupted the economy. Estimates of damages of $200 billion made in September[12] far exceed the amount attributed to Hurricane Andrew ($25 billion),[13] which was previously the costliest disaster in the United States.

As a response to Katrina, charitable and religious organizations throughout the country quickly began collecting funds and initiating aid. Along with these charitable efforts, governmental agencies, such as the Coast Guard and the National Guard, were mobilized to help rescue survivors, provide additional security, and distribute supplies. With so many agencies and people involved in the rescue efforts, there were breakdowns in communications and transportation, and in the decision making needed to match resources to the most urgent needs.[14] Congressional investigations in late 2005 and early 2006 resulted in recommendations for reorganization of the federal government's disaster response and better advance preparation at charitable organizations responding to major disasters.[15]

The governments of more than 70 countries pledged to help in response to the disaster.[16] The single largest pledge came from Kuwait for a total of $500 million. Other nations aided America by sending relief personnel, helicopters, military ships, military equipment, food, bottled water, medical personnel, and multiple troops. Along with the help from governments throughout the world, charitable organizations sent funding and personnel to aid Katrina victims.

Hurricane Rita

Less than 30 days after Hurricane Katrina, another Category 5 storm headed toward the Caribbean, first crossing south Florida from the Atlantic and flooding the Florida Keys. A few days later, Hurricane Rita struck southeastern Texas and parts of Louisiana. The storm surge from Hurricane Rita broke open recently repaired levees in New Orleans, again flooding the lowest-lying areas of that city. Aid agencies extended their services to reach areas hit by Rita, opening shelters, offering lodging assistance, and operating hotlines to help family members reach loved ones. Total damages were estimated at $9 billion, and the hurricane directly caused 6 deaths and indirectly caused 119 more.[17]

Hurricane Wilma

In mid-October, less than 60 days after Hurricane Katrina, another Category 5 storm formed: Hurricane Wilma. Wilma hit with the most force on the Yucatan Peninsula in Mexico. As the storm veered, it struck south Florida on October 24 where intense winds caused severe damage and the storm surge again flooded the Florida Keys. Five deaths in the U.S. were reported directly attributable to Wilma, as victims were struck by falling trees or windblown debris. Total damages, including those to resorts and communities in Mexico and in Haiti, Cuba, and the Bahamas, were estimated at $20 billion.[18]

India-Pakistan earthquake

Hurricane Katrina was not the last major natural disaster of the year. On the morning of October 8, 2005, an earthquake with a magnitude of 7.6 struck a region on the India-Pakistan border. The earthquake was followed by more than 140 aftershocks that contributed to the damage in Pakistan, India, and Afghanistan.[19] The government of Pakistan announced the death toll from the earthquakes to be 47,700. However, this figure was estimated to climb to 75,000 to 80,000.[20] It is also estimated that in the aftermath nearly 2.5 million people were homeless in a mountainous region at the beginning of winter, with tens of thousands likely to die from malnutrition or exposure.[21]

As with the hurricanes and the tsunami, after the event itself, aid agencies and the American government sought to move quickly to provide water and sanitation to prevent disease. They also tried to provide urgently needed supplies, including clothing, shelter, food, and more. However, unlike the hurricane, the affected areas are located on some of the world's most rugged mountains, which made it difficult to locate survivors and distribute aid. American aid agencies reported receiving approximately $128 million in contributions from donors wanting to provide aid after the Pakistan border region earthquake.[22] This is far below the $1.8 billion contributed after the December 2004 tsunami, but it is in the same range as amounts contributed after other international natural disasters, such as an earthquake in India (2001), Hurricane Mitch (1998) in Central America, and an earthquake in Armenia (1988).

Countries, international organizations, and nongovernmental organizations offered immediate help for rescue throughout the affected areas and longer term help for rebuilding. It was estimated that by 2010, $5.2 billion would be needed for rebuilding the damaged cities as well as providing relief to survivors. Pakistan received pledges of $6.4 billion from international donor countries.[23]

Conclusion

The series of big disasters from December 2004 through fall 2005 affected the world. The media played an important role, not only in communicating the details of the tragedies but also in expressing the compelling need and taking the case for support to the American people. In the United States, hurricane relief grew to roughly $5.3 billion, which surpassed both the Asian earthquake relief and Indian Ocean tsunami relief combined. The United States raised about $150 million for the Asian earthquakes, with $12 million going to the American Red Cross by the end of 2005. Donations from the United States of $1.92 billion given in 2005 for relief after the tsunami were nearly 13 times the amount given for the Pakistan earthquake.

Giving for disasters

Hurricane relief funds for the U.S. came predominantly from U.S. donors. Other regions of the world contributed much more toward the other disasters because those disasters affected them more than the hurricanes did. Even though disaster relief was very prominent in 2005, it was only a fraction of the anticipated rebuilding costs in the Gulf Coast and in the nations around the Indian Ocean recovering from the tsunami.

1   The Center on Philanthropy at Indiana University: Tracking Crisis Giving, www.philanthropy.iupui. edu, consulted February 2, 2006. More than 240 organizations are listed as creating their own relief funds (e.g, Home Depot created its own relief fund and gave to it) or as receiving contributions from donors to established charities. Of the 246 who announced initiatives in the media, 114 provided financial information with a dollar value for cash gifts or gifts in kind.

2   Center on Nonprofits and Philanthropy, *State of the Nonprofit Sector in Louisiana*, September 2005, The Urban Institute, www.urban.org.

3   J. Auer and L. Lampkin, *Open and Operating? An Assessment of Louisiana Health and Human Services after Hurricanes Katrina and Rita*, February 2006, www.urban.org.

4   Auer and Lampkin, page 3. The graph on that page shows the source of new funding. It does not include the 39 percent of organizations that did not receive new funding. Thus, 85 percent of organizations getting new funding from individuals is 85 percent of the 61 percent that have any source of new funding at all.

5   J. Salmon and L. Smith, Two-thirds of Katrina donations exhausted, *Washington Post*, February 27, 2006, www.washingtonpost.com.

6   H. Hall, After hurricane, online charity scams grow in number and sophistication, *Chronicle of Philanthropy*, September 29, 2005, www.philanthropy.com.

7   Salmon and Smith.

8   I. Wilhelm, Fraud investigations raise new questions for beleaguered Red Cross, *Chronicle of Philanthropy*, April 6, 2006, www.philanthropy.com.

9   Hurricane Katrina, Wikipedia, wikipedia.org, consulted January 16, 2006.

10   Aon services, www.aon.com.

11   Katrina death toll unknown, February 10, 2006, www.foxnews.com.

12   D. Wyss, A second look at Katrina, *Business Week*, September 13, 2005, www.businessweek.com.

13   E. Rappaport, *Hurricane Andrew, 16-28 August 1992, Preliminary Report*, National Hurricane Center, December 10, 1993, www.publicaffairs.noaa.gov.

14   Hurricane Katrina entry, Wikipedia, http://en.wikipedia.org, consulted January 16, 2006.

15   Select Bipartisan Committee to Investigate the Preparation for and Response to Hurricane Katrina, http://katrina.house.gov/ and reported in N. Wallace, Red Cross gets chided by Congress, *Chronicle of Philanthropy*, February 23, 2006, www.philanthropy.com.

16   United States Diplomatic Mission to Germany: U.S. Policies & Issues, http://usembassy.state.gov/germany/hurricane_news.html, consulted January 18, 2006.

17   Hurricane Rita, Wikipedia, consulted February 16, 2006.

18   Hurricane Wilma, Wikipedia.org, consulted February 16, 2006.

19   Pakistan Earthquake 2005 [http://www.pakquake2005.com/], consulted February 20, 2006.

20   MSNBC, New figures put quake toll at more than 79,000, October 19, 2005, www.msnbc.msn.com.

21   CBC News, South Asian quake, In Depth, October 12, 2006, www.cbc.ca.

22   The Center on Philanthropy at Indiana University: Tracking Crisis Giving, release of late January 2006, www.philanthropy.iupui.edu.

23   Pakistan's earthquake survivors will receive more housing aid, January 31, 2006, www.bloomberg.com

Giving by individuals

- Charitable giving by individuals and households reached an estimated $199.07 billion in 2005, compared with a revised estimate of $187.11 billion for 2004. This is a growth of 6.4 percent (2.9 percent adjusted for inflation).

- This estimate includes a projection that households itemizing charitable deductions on their tax returns will claim gifts totaling $156.32 billion for 2005. For 2003, households itemized deductions for charitable gifts of $145.70 billion. This is the most recent data available in spring 2006.

- The estimate of giving by households that do not itemize charitable deductions is $36.92 billion, or an average of $551 in contributions from each of the 70 or so percent of households that do not itemize charitable deductions.

- Before adding disaster giving, individual giving is estimated to be $193.24 billion.

- Individual giving includes $5.83 billion in estimated contributions for disaster relief made in 2005. Most studies conducted suggest that almost all disaster relief giving by households was in addition to any other giving by those families.

- Individual giving is 76.5 percent of total giving for 2006.

- The Katrina Emergency Tax Relief Act (KETRA) may have stimulated some new giving, and it may have shifted some giving into 2005 that would have occurred in later years. With no data available in April 2006 about the extent of the impact of the KETRA provision, no adjustment has been made to the *Giving USA* estimate for individual giving in 2005. Please see the Legal/Legislative chapter for a discussion of the Act's provisions.

Findings from *Giving USA*

Giving USA estimates giving by using a model that takes into account the historical relationships between changes in giving and economic factors, such as inflation-adjusted changes in personal income, in the Standard & Poor's 500 Index, in the highest tax rate, and in giving from prior years.

For 2005, a 2.6 percent inflation-adjusted increase in personal income accounted for $3.5 billion (75 percent) of the estimated giving increase of $4.68 billion before disaster relief giving is added. The stock market stayed flat (increasing only 0.2 percent from the end of 2004 to the end of 2005) and had a negligible impact ($20 million) on the estimated change in giving in 2005. The combined impact of the other variables in the model is growth in giving of $1.16 billion in 2005.

To the change estimated by the modeling procedure, *Giving USA* added another $5.83 billion in estimated contributions in 2005 for disaster relief. This amount incorporates an estimate of $1.54 billion donated in 2005 by individuals after the tsunami and an estimate of $4.25 billion donated by individuals in 2005 for relief work after Hurricanes Katrina, Rita, and Wilma.[1]

Individual donations for disaster relief reach at least $5.83 billion

Many relief agencies increased their capacity to receive and process gifts made via the Internet, in part to accommodate the extraordinary response to the tsunami disaster. Americans have never before contributed such an amount (more than $1 billion) after a disaster elsewhere in the world. After Hurricane Katrina, donations to agencies such as the American Red Cross and others were made quickly online, to special established call centers, and through the mail.

The Center on Philanthropy at Indiana University developed household giving estimates for *Giving USA*, using survey replies from the Panel Study of Income Dynamics and the Conference Board. With data available in April 2005, the estimated household contributions for disaster relief in 2005 reached at least $5.83 billion. (The estimating procedure is explained briefly in note 1 and in greater detail in the complete methodology chapter available online at the site referenced at the front of this book.)

The estimated total disaster contribution from households is 2.9 percent of estimated household/individual giving for 2005. Prior research suggests that in response to a disaster, most households give a relatively small amount (less than $100) and that few households give for disaster relief instead of making other contributions. Instead, households give for disaster relief in addition to their other giving.[2]

KETRA reportedly stimulated additional giving in 2005

The Katrina Emergency Tax Relief Act (KETRA), which was in effect from August 28, 2005, through December 31, 2005, reportedly stimulated additional contributions. The act permitted individual taxpayers to claim as charitable deductions gifts up to 100 percent of their income, except for gifts to foundations, which were not included. It also exempted charitable gifts temporarily from the usual requirement that all deductions be reduced by 3 percent on tax returns with an income above a certain limit. Thus, married couples filing jointly with income of $145,950 or more in 2005 could claim 100 percent of their charitable deductions made in the period covered by KETRA instead of having to reduce the charitable gift amount by 3 percent.

Anecdotes suggest that giving rose because of (a) prepayment of pledges by donors who wanted to maximize the tax benefits of their commitment; (b) additional giving by some people; and (c) payment in 2005 of amounts intended to be given in 2006. There is no estimate by mid-2006 of how much individual giving in 2005 stemmed solely from the incentives in KETRA.

Chronicle of Philanthropy records top ten gifts for 2005

The most generous donors gave and pledged a total of $1.4 billion in 2005. This amount is down from a high of $4.12 billion in 2004. Bill and Melinda Gates made a commitment in 2004 to give $3.35 billion to the Bill & Melinda Gates Foundation,

Giving by individuals

which is included in the total for that year, although the payments did not all occur in 2004.

The Gates family and George Soros gave the two largest gifts in 2005. The Gates gave $320 million to the Bill & Melinda Gates Foundation, and Soros gave $206 million for the endowment at the Central European University (CEU) in Budapest, Hungary. David Rockefeller made a $100 million pledge to the Museum of Modern Art in New York City; and several other donors gave large contributions to higher education institutions, including Harvard, New York University, Arizona State University, and Tufts University. Table 1 shows the largest announced gifts, including pledges, from living individuals in 2005.

Table 1
Top eleven gifts announced by living donors, 2005
($ in millions)

Donor	Amount	Recipient
Bill and Melinda Gates	320	Bill & Melinda Gates Foundation
George Soros	206	Central European University (Budapest)
T. Boone Pickens	165	Oklahoma State University (announced in 2006)
Lawrence J. Ellison	115	Pledge to Harvard University
Jan and Marica Vilcek	105	Pledge to New York University School of Medicine
Pierre and Pam Omidyar	103	Tufts University
Peter B. Lewis	101	Yale University (announced in 2006)
Anonymous	100	Johns Hopkins University (announced in 2006)
Ira and Mary Lou Fulton	100	Pledge to Arizona State University
David Rockefeller	100	Pledge to the Museum of Modern Art
David Rockefeller	100	Pledge to Rockefeller University

Adapted from *The Chronicle of Philanthropy*, issues of January 1, 2006 and February 23, 2006.

Number of gifts on Million Dollar List rises 39 percent, but total dollars fall

Publicly announced gifts of $1 million or more from individuals (including couples and families) numbered 796 in 2005, according to the Center on Philanthropy's Million Dollar List.[3] This amount is a 39 percent increase over 574 such gifts announced in 2004. However, the total dollar amount announced in 2005 was lower because there were no gifts in 2005 of more than $1 billion, and there were three gifts or more of that size in 2004.

About 1 in 6 of all million-dollar donors is a woman

Each year since 2000, 55 to 58 percent of the donors listed on the Million Dollar List have been families, couples, or women alone. Women alone have averaged 16 percent of the donors listed on the Million Dollar List since 2000. Thomas J. Stanley, in his book *Millionaire Women Next Door*, found that female millionaires who earned their fortunes in business donate 7 percent of their income every year, on average.[4] This percentage is much higher than the 3 percent average for all U.S. donors and is higher than the 5.34 percent average found for male millionaires. Female millionaires donate $1 for every $14.62 of income, whereas male millionaires donate $1 for every $18.73 of income. Charities must often make special efforts to reach female millionaires, who are typically extremely busy.[5]

Direct mail fundraising shows unprecedented growth in 2005

Target Analysis Group, which represents many of the nation's largest direct mail fundraising programs, reported that growth in fundraising was seen in all subsectors throughout the year.[6] Relief and animal welfare groups saw median revenue increase by 44 percent and 39 percent, respectively. Most other subsectors saw median revenue increase between 3 and 6 percent. The health sector, however, which shows little change in *Giving USA*'s estimate, was "essentially flat, with a slight 1 percent decline in revenue" in the Target Analysis results. The Target Analysis report states that "...the tsunami and hurricane relief efforts only temporarily increased the proportion of income that people were willing to donate to nonprofits. But the unusually strong giving to relief organizations has not appeared to have depressed revenue for other sectors in a significant way." (p. 2)

Tax reform bills passed the Senate and are debated in the House

The Senate passed a bill to allow deductions on tax returns for charitable donations even among households that do not itemize other tax deductions. The House of Representatives did not pass the bill in 2005. This is the fourth year since 2001 in which Congress has considered legislation permitting tax filers who do not itemize other types of deductions to receive tax benefits for charitable gifts. Some nonprofit organizations such as the Direct Marketing Association Nonprofit Federation worry that, if passed, such legislation will reduce the number or amount of contributions. The United Way of America thinks that the bill may increase total donations by $1 billion dollars.[7]

Center on Philanthropy finds 67 percent of households contributed average of $1,872 in 2002

Using data collected in 2003 and released in late 2004, the Center on Philanthropy found that 67 percent of households contributed to charity in 2002—a year following a recession and after the attacks of September 11, 2001.[8] The percentage of households giving is slightly lower than a survey of the same people found for 2000, when 69 percent of households contributed to charity. In the 2002 findings, the average household contribution to charity was $1,872. After adjustment for inflation, the 2002 average contribution amount is 3.3 percent less than the average found for 2000. In 2002, household giving was allocated among the subsectors as shown in Figure 1.[9]

Giving by individuals

Figure 1
Distribution of total estimated household giving, 2002*

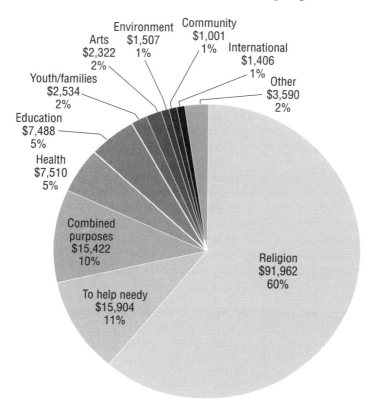

*In millions of dollars. Total estimated giving: $150.6 billion. The nation's wealthiest and highest-income households give a disproportionate share of all individual contributions and are not represented in the sample for this study at a level that permits inclusion of all of their giving.
Data Source: Center on Philanthropy Panel Study (COPPS) 2003 Wave, n=6,378 Weights applied.

Levels of Black philanthropy linked to income, wealth; philanthropic priorities may be shifting away from religion toward education in some Black communities

A special issue of *New Directions for Philanthropic Fundraising*, released by Jossey-Bass, focused on African American philanthropy. In that edition, John Havens and Paul Schervish of the Center on Wealth and Philanthropy at Boston College reported their findings that African American income, wealth, and charitable giving all increased from 1992 to 2001 after adjusting for inflation rates,[10] but all grew more slowly than the rates of growth found for other racial groups.

Giving by individuals

Richard Steinberg and Mark Wilhelm of Indiana University-Purdue University Indianapolis showed that African American giving patterns, in which it is perceived that members of minority groups "give less,"[11] are not due to race, but to other socio-economic factors.[12] Steinberg and Wilhelm used the Center on Philanthropy Panel Study (COPPS) data and found that the differences in giving among various ethnic groups are mostly because of the differences in donors' income, wealth, and education levels instead of racial and ethnic differences. In other words, the African American households that have the same level of income, wealth, and education levels give as much as other ethnic groups that have the same socio-economic background.

Felinda Mottino and Eugene Miller, both at City University of New York, conducted face-to-face interviews with 58 African American donors in New York City.[13] Sixty-six percent of the participants were born before the civil rights movement. These participants had all earned an undergraduate degree. Most of those born since the civil rights movement have obtained a graduate degree, primarily in business. Participants' household giving ranged from $200 to $40,000 in 1999. This study shows that the younger generation has a much broader understanding of community. They do support broad causes to promote "greater equality of opportunity." The top philanthropic priority for the older generation was church, which they saw as a religious organization and a community center. The top philanthropic priority for the younger generation was educational institutions or programs.

Nonprofit leaders' priorities do not match moderate donors' priorities

Research by the Public Agenda organization suggests that nonprofit leaders are concerned with management issues different from the ones that moderate donors take into account when considering whether to give to a nonprofit organization. The study included focus group discussions with donors who contributed more than $300 in 2004 and one-on-one interviews with nonprofit CEOs, CFOs, and program and development officers. The study included private and public charities and corporate and community foundations.[14]

The nonprofit leaders focused their attention on national public policy issues and overestimated the importance of such issues for moderate donors. Moderate donors trusted local nonprofit organizations.[15] They paid little attention to public policy issues or the level of government funding at a nonprofit.[16] Rather, they were concerned with the over-compensation of nonprofit employees and over-professionalization of fundraising techniques. Donors' concerns were barely mentioned by nonprofit leaders.

Donors hear about unusual compensation amounts from news reports and appear to extend the facts of a single case to the entire sector, whereas nonprofit leaders have knowledge of the range of compensation practices and standards that vary by organizational situation. Charity Navigator recommends that donors compare CEO compensation at one organization with similar organizations before drawing conclusions about whether a particular CEO is overcompensated.[17] In doing such comparisons, moderate donors would find that CEO compensation is mostly determined by the budget and staff size of the nonprofit organization, and, in some cases, by the reputation of the institution.[18]

These studies suggest that CEOs and moderate donors do not understand each other's priorities very well. Fundraisers need to understand these differences, so they can more effectively educate donors about the compensation structure and norms within the nonprofit sector and personalize their fundraising strategies.

Giving circles expand as donors collaborate in charity

Giving circles have become a more important giving trend since 2000. New Ventures in Philanthropy conducted national research on 61 giving circles selected from more than 200 identified nationwide.[19] These 61 circles have 5,300 dedicated donors, and they have collected nearly $32 million and distributed $23 million over the past several years. Giving circles often support causes that differ from those selected by traditional foundations. Giving circles focus more on youth development, women's and girls' issues, and mental health/crisis intervention; foundations tend to support education, health, and arts and culture.

According to this study, giving circles are mixed in gender and in ethnic background. Some giving circles are more formal than others. At one end, giving circles can simply be a circle of friends.[20] On the other end, giving circles can be as formal as a foundation. Giving circles often consider the cultivation of philanthropists as one of their core missions. They share a vision of transformational philanthropy, where the power of philanthropy lies jointly in its influence on recipients and in its capacity to transform the meaning of life for the donors.[21]

Rural philanthropy has increased through community foundations

Rural philanthropy, especially through community foundations, has grown dramatically in recent years. The Aspen Institute studied rural philanthropy in 2005 and looked at geographic component funds (GCF). A GCF is, "a fund (or collection of funds) established under the umbrella of a lead community foundation that is specified for a geographic area and governed in some way by people from that area."[22]

Most such ventures consciously use an inclusive strategy by treating everyone in the rural community as a prospective donor and a beneficiary.[23] In contrast, until the inclusive strategy was implemented, people in rural communities had relatively few local entities to support. They contributed to national nonprofit organizations and nonprofit organizations in urban areas that might or might not serve the needs of the rural community. The inclusive strategy renews the idea of rural philanthropy in which residents of an area give and help other residents of the area.

Research suggests improvements for fundraising practice

Academic fundraising research appearing in 2005 focused on how to increase response rate, how to increase the amount of contributions and how to maintain

Giving by individuals

long-term financial support. At least five studies offer specific fundraising suggestions based on their findings. Each is summarized briefly in the following sections.

Report prior (high) response rates to inspire more donations

Bruno Frey and Stephen Meier used a mail fundraising campaign at their university to examine whether telling letter recipients about a relatively high response rate from a previous campaign increases response rate in the current effort.[24] In this field experiment, half the students at the college received a letter telling them that 64 percent of students had previously contributed to a school program; the other half received a letter telling them that 46 percent of students had previously contributed. Both of these two pieces of information were true: 64 percent reported donations in a recent semester; 46 percent was the contribution rate over 10 years. There was no deception of potential donors in this study. The authors found a statistically significant higher response rate in the 64 percent group than in the 46 percent group after controlling for the previous contribution history of each respondent. Reporting relatively high response rates from previous campaigns is one way to increase future response rate with close to zero cost and with no deception, if administered appropriately.

Appeal to people with high levels of "social capital"

Other studies considered various different factors that play a role as donors determine how much to give to a cause. Arthur Brooks used data from the 2000 Social Capital Community Benchmark survey and found that donors with high levels of certain forms of "social capital," or connections to others, contribute more than people with lower levels.[25] Social capital in this study includes group involvement, level of social trust, and political activities. People give more when they are more involved in groups that engage others (through religion, youth programs, services for the elderly, etc.). Further, people give more when they have higher levels of social trust in other people, such as neighbors, co-workers, police, people of other races and people in general. In addition, people give more to charity when they are more politically engaged, such as belonging to a group involved in local action for reform, attending a political meeting, signing a petition, or participating in a political group or a demonstration. Fundraisers can work to identify prospective donors who are already "primed" to give through their current levels of involvement in groups that engage others.

Show prospective donors that their own financial security will not be diminished through their gift(s)

In a different study about donors' attitudes, Paul Schervish and his colleagues found that people who feel more financially secure give more. This psychological security is not the same as actual financial security. In other words, how much money people feel they have is more important than how much money people actually have.[26] Therefore, one strategy for more effective fundraising is to emphasize the reality that people will have enough money for their own security even after their donation. For example, fundraisers can draw analogies like this: Membership in this public radio station is the equivalent of only two fancy restaurant meals. This is better than saying public radio membership is only fifty cents a day, half the price of a morning coffee. People can comfortably "give up" fancy restaurant meals, but many will not cut out daily coffee (or some other beverage). Applying the Schervish finding, fundraising appeals that draw people's attention to their disposable income or luxury activities will be more successful than those that ask them to reduce their own psychological security about the future.

Provide a "benchmark" gift level that is bigger than 95 percent of all gifts in a prior, similar campaign
A study about donor motivations looked at creating some "benchmark" giving level as part of the request. Jen Shang and Rachel Croson found that telling committed donors how much another donor contributed in the past might increase contributions. The most effective contribution level to use when informing a committed (renewing) donor is the 95th percentile of the donations from a similar, prior fundraising campaign. For example, if a nonprofit collected 100 contributions in its last direct mail campaign, and the gifts were put in order from the smallest dollar amount to the largest, the gift at the 95th percentile is the 95th gift in the sequence. If the gift at the 95th percentile is $150, in the next direct mail campaign, the following sentence can be printed on the pledge form: "We invite you to join another donor who contributed $150 by making your contribution today!" Shang and Croson's research showed that the donors who read the 95th percentile information contributed more than people who read the following sentence: "We invite you to join another donor and make a contribution today!"[27]

Excellent stewardship is more important than frequency of requests, gifts
The preceding technique is designed to increase the level of one-time donations. The argument has been made that monthly donors may be more committed than one-time donors. Adrian Sargeant and Lucy Woodliffe found that a donor's level of commitment is not measured by the frequency of donation. People making monthly donations through a credit card are not the most committed donors. Instead, donors become committed after they are treated nicely by the fundraising teams and after they understand more about how the nonprofit has fulfilled its mission, regardless of whether the credit card transaction is yearly or monthly.[28] This study suggests that instead of focusing on the payment frequency, fundraisers who conduct excellent stewardship to keep donors informed are likely to see a larger increase in giving than those who set up monthly payment plans without focusing on stewardship.

Internet giving increasingly important, still small part of total
The number of online donors increased significantly in 2005. Thirteen million people donated online after Hurricanes Katrina and Rita. This represents 9 percent of Internet users in the United States.[29] There is a generational difference in online giving. A study by Craver, Mathews, Smith & Company and the Prime Group found that 29 percent of the post-boomers (born since 1964) had made an online contribution

Giving by individuals

by year-end, while only 13 percent of the baby boomers (born 1946 to 1964) had used online giving. Among post-boomers, 15 percent actually prefer e-mail appeals to direct mail appeals.[30]

The *Chronicle of Philanthropy* conducted a survey of online donations at the nation's largest charities in 2004. Two hundred and eleven organizations of 400 contacted responded to the survey.[31] One hundred and seventy-three organizations reported that they conducted online fundraising in 2004. The 164 organizations that responded to the survey in two consecutive years raised $166.2 million online in 2004. This is a 63.2 percent increase from $101.9 million raised by the same organizations online in 2003.[32] However, even if giving through the Internet is more than $2 billion, as was reported in 2004 by Kintera, Inc., it is just 1 percent of total estimated individual giving.

Online donation has shown an increasing success rate in soliciting funds compared to other traditional methods, according to the Philanthropic Giving Index, produced by the Center on Philanthropy at Indiana University.[33] According to this index, the success rate of Internet giving increased in 2005, while the success rates of telephone and direct mail declined. However, Internet giving is still the least used and least successful fundraising method of those studied.

In a survey about donor trends conducted by Craver, Mathews, Smith & Company and the Prime Group, 75 percent of respondents had never responded to an e-mail solicitation, whereas only 37 percent of them have never responded to direct mail.[34] This suggests that fundraisers should not abandon direct mail solicitation. However, thinking more creatively about how to use the Internet to help generate revenue is becoming more important as "post-boomers" play an increasing role as donors and as postage rates increased in 2006 by another 3 percent for nonprofit organizations.[35]

One method of revenue generation using the Internet has been online auctions. In 2005, eBay reported that in two years 60,000 items had been auctioned for 5,245 charities through its Giving Works division.[36] Charities also conduct "cause-related marketing" campaigns with commercial web sites. Typically a purchaser will buy something online and choose to have a percentage of the sale price of the item go to a charity.[37]

1   The tsunami giving estimate uses data collected in the Panel Study of Income Dynamics by the University of Michigan. That survey of more than 8,000 households found 30 percent of households reported a contribution around $75 each. With 125 million households, this results in donations of $1.88 billion for the tsunami. An estimated $300 million had been donated by January 1, 2005. The estimated amount for tsunami relief giving in 2005 is $1.58 billion. For giving after the hurricanes, *Giving USA* relies on data collected by the Conference Board in its survey of consumers. In that study, more than 5,000 households participated. At least 48 percent reported contributions for hurricane relief. The Conference Board provided the percentage of households that donated at each of several gift sizes (less than $25 up to more than $500). Using these figures, *Giving USA* estimates an average gift per donor household of $72 and a total estimate of $4.25 billion. Note that these average gift amounts are very close to amounts found for donations after the attacks of September 11, when 65 percent of households said they gave and the most frequent donation amount was less than $75.

2   K. Steinberg and P. Rooney, America Gives: A survey of Americans' generosity after September 11, *Nonprofit and Voluntary Sector Quarterly*, March 2005.

3   Center on Philanthropy Million Dollar List, www.philanthropy.iupui.edu.

4   T. Stanley, *Millionaire Women Next Door: The Many Journeys of Successful American Businesswomen*, Kansas City, Missouri, Andrews McMell Publishing, 2004.

5   H. Hall, Women's funds step up efforts to win support from female donors, *Chronicle of Philanthropy*, February 17, 2005, www.philanthropy.com.

6   Quarter 4 2005 Index of National Fundraising Performance, Target Analysis Group, www.targetanalysis.com.

7   Senate's Effort to Change Charity Tax Breaks Provokes Controversy, *Chronicle of Philanthropy*, December 8, 2005, www.philanthropy.com.

8   *Average and Median Amounts of Household Giving and Volunteering in 2002*, The Center on Philanthropy at Indiana University, released March 2006, www.philanthropy.iupui.edu.

9   *Distribution of Household Giving by Type of Recipient, 2002*, The Center on Philanthropy at Indiana University, released March 2006, www.philanthropy.iupui.edu.

10 J. Havens and P. Schervish, Wealth transfer estimates for African American households, *New Directions for Philanthropic Fundraising: Exploring Black Philanthropy*, 48.

11 See, for example, *Giving and Volunteering in the United States, 2001*, page 132. Independent Sector, www.independentsector.com.

12 R. Steinberg and M. Wilhelm, Religion and secular giving, by race and ethnicity, *New Directions for Philanthropic Fundraising: Exploring Black Philanthropy*, 48.

13 F. Mottino and E. Miller, Philanthropy among African American donors in the New York metropolitan region. *New Directions for Philanthropic Fundraising: Exploring Black Philanthropy*, 48.

14 A. M. Arumi, R. Wooden, J. Johnson, S. Farkas, A. Duffett, and A. Ott, *The Charitable Impulse*. A Report from Public Agenda for the Kettering Foundation and INDEPENDENT SECTOR, 2005.

15 B. Jensen, New findings show philanthropic efforts are growing in rural areas, *Chronicle of Philanthropy*, September 15, 2005, www.philanthropy.com.

16 C. Horne, J. Johnson, and D. Van Slyke, Do charitable donors know enough–and care enough–about government subsidies to affect private giving to nonprofit organizations? *Nonprofit and Voluntary Sector Quarterly* 34(1), 2005.

17 Charity Navigator, CEO compensation study, August 8, 2005, www.charitynavigator.org.

18 J. O'Connell, Administrative Compensation in Private Nonprofits: The Case of Liberal Arts Colleges. *Quarterly Journal of Business and Economics* 44(1/2). 2005.

19 T. Rutnik and J. Bearman, *Giving Together: A National Scan of Giving Circles and Shared Giving*, Forum of Regional Associations of Grantmakers, 2005, www.givingforum.org.

20 J. Zaslow, Moving on: You don't have a choice: How to ask friends for a charitable donation. March 3, 2005, *Wall Street Journal*. http://online.wsj.com.

21 J. Hodge, Transformational Philanthropy. A presentation made at Indiana University in Fall, 2005.

22 Community Strategies Group from The Aspen Institute, *Growing Local Philanthropy: The Role and Reach of Community Foundations*, 2005, www.aspencsg.org.

Giving by individuals

23   Al. McGregor and B. Chaney, from New Ventures in Philanthropy, The Power of Rural
      Philanthropy, www.givingforum.org.
24   B. Frey and S. Meier, Public goods & cooperative games, *American Economic Review*, 45(5), 1717-
      1722.
25   A. Brooks, Does Social Capital Make You Generous? *Social Science Quarterly*, 86(1).
26   P. Schervish, G. Whitaker, J. Havens, Philanthropy's Indispensable Ally. *Philanthropy Magazine*
      19(3). 2005.
27   J. Shang and R. Croson. The Impact of Social Comparisons on Nonprofit Fundraising. *Research
      in Experimental Economics*, 2006.
28   A. Sargeant and L. Woodliffe, The antecedents of donor commitment to voluntary organizations.
      Nonprofit Management & Leadership, Fall, 2005.
29   J. Horrigan and S. Morrise, Relief donations after Hurricanes Katrina and Rita and use of
      the Internet to get disaster news. November, 2005. Pew Internet & American Life Project.
      www.pewinternet.org.
30   A Donor Trend® Executive Summary by Craver, Mathews, Smith & Company and the Prime Group,
      Boomers! Navigating the generational divide in fundraising & advocacy, 2005,
      http://cms.convio.net.
31   C. Moore, The online-donations survey: How it was done, *Chronicle of Philanthropy*, June 9,
      2005, www.philanthropy.com. The results of the survey are available in tables under the title: Online
      Fund Raising: How Much Big Charities Are Raising. www.philanthropy.com.
32   N. Wallace, A surge in online giving: Internet donations doubled at many big charities. *Chronicle
      of Philanthropy*, June 9, 2005, www.philanthropy.com.
33   Philanthropic Giving Index, December 2005, The Center on Philanthropy at Indiana University,
      www.philanthropy.iupui.edu.
34   A Donor Trend®. See note 30.
35   C. Preston, New postal rates for charities to take effect in January, Chronicle of Philanthropy,
      November 24, 2005, www.philanthropy.com.
36   L. Kerkman, Highest bidder: from glitzy to garage-sale, online auctions net big returns for
      many charities, *Chronicle of Philanthropy*, June 9, 2005, www.philanthropy.com.
37   J. Borzo, Buying and giving: Charities have figured out a way to get their little piece of the
      e-commerce boom. March 21, 2005, *Wall Street Journal*, http://online.wsj.com.

Giving by bequest

- Charitable bequests in 2005 reached an estimated $17.44 billion. This is a decrease of 5.5 percent compared with the revised estimate of $18.47 billion for 2004. Adjusted for inflation, the decline is 8.6 percent.

- Charitable bequests accounted for approximately 6.7 percent of total estimated charitable giving in 2005.

- Charitable bequests are dropping at least in part because of a decrease in the number of people dying. The National Center for Health Statistics office reported a decline of 50,000 in the number of deaths in 2004, compared to 2003, the sharpest decline in 70 years.

- Another contributing factor to the decline in charitable bequests in recent years is very slow growth in household assets from 1999 through 2004. John Havens of the Boston College Center on Wealth and Philanthropy reports that, adjusted for inflation, in those years total household wealth held by all families grew by just 0.2 percent.

- Researchers at the Federal Reserve Board released an analysis of the 2004 Survey of Consumer Finances, which shows that for people age 65 and above, on average, net worth fell between 2001 and 2004. Lower net worth means lower charitable bequests.

Giving USA analysis of charitable bequests

Each year, *Giving USA* sends a survey to more than 7,000 nonprofit organizations representing the charitable sector (other than congregations and foundations). Charities that return the survey report their bequest receipts as well as other information about charitable revenue and total revenue. Using this information, *Giving USA* can present some averages and medians for bequest receipts by different types and sizes of charitable organizations. *Giving USA* includes only realized bequests in its estimates, not planned commitments. The survey results are not used to develop the estimates of charitable bequests.

For the estimates of giving by bequest, *Giving USA* relies on federal reports of charitable bequests claimed on estate tax returns and on estimates for estates that fall below the federal filing threshold. The estimates for giving by estates below the federal estate tax filing threshold rely on:

- Data obtained from the U.S. Treasury's analysis of estate tax returns showing the percentage of net estate value donated by donor estates, which increases with the age at death;

- IRS income tax return data for the percentage of estates that make charitable contributions (4.6 percent in 2004, the most recent year for which this analysis is available); and

- Estimates of household net worth by age, developed by the Federal Reserve Board.

Giving by bequest

In this analysis, giving by estates below the federal filing threshold is up to 17 percent of the total estimate.

Giving USA 2006 survey

Table 1 summarizes findings from the 2006 survey of nonprofits, which asked about realized bequests. In most subsectors, among large organizations 43 to 80 percent of the responding organizations reported bequest receipts. Among medium-sized organizations, 24 to 62 percent reported bequest receipts. In most subsectors, less than 10 percent of small organizations received bequest gifts. On average, the largest amount per bequest was for large arts organizations. The largest average number of bequests was received at health-related charities.

Table 1
Organizations that reported bequest receipts, by size and subsector, 2005

	Large			Medium			Small		
	Percent-age of organi-zations	Average no. of bequests	Average amount per bequest ($)	Percent-age of organi-zations	Average no. of bequests	Average amount per bequest ($)	Percent-age of organi-zations	Average no. of bequests	Average amount per bequest ($)
Arts	43	18	2,067,765	34	5	157,320	11	1	17,460
Education	80	64	138,345	38	6	97,667	21	7	60,763
Environment	75	71	52,548	54	11	35,147	7	1	5,806
Health	59	233	91,610	62	16	48,558	4	5	10,551
Human services	45	65	46,682	25	8	35,319	5	1	100
International	65	93	23,638	24	4	21,200	7	1	12,000
Public-society benefit*	55	53	35,203	25	3	134,631	None reported in survey		

*Includes United Ways, Jewish federations, and large community foundations, but not private foundations

Planned commitments are not included in estimates of giving by bequest. Assets in a planned commitment that are claimed as a deduction by a living donor appear in the estimate of giving by individuals.

Charitable bequests reported to Giving USA do not always match date of charitable deductions claimed on estate tax returns

Estate tax returns, on which the IRS data are based, are filed for the year in which an estate is closed. That is, for 2004 returns, the returns might be for individuals who died much earlier (as is likely the case for people of great wealth) or for people who died in 2004 (which is more likely for relatively small estates).

Estate tax returns, however, do not tell us when the bequest was actually distributed to the recipient, only when it was reported to the Internal Revenue Service. *Giving USA*'s survey of nonprofit organizations tracks when organizations receive the gifts. Some distributions are made far in advance of the date of filing the estate tax return.

Giving by bequest

Because of these differences in timing between payment of the gift and reporting of the gift, there will sometimes be a discrepancy between *Giving USA*'s estimate of gifts by charitable bequest in a given year and the amount reported later in estate tax returns.

Giving USA *is investigating alternatives to IRS data as a way of generating future estimates*
As the filing threshold rises through 2009 and fewer estates are required to file tax returns, it becomes increasingly important to find alternative methods of estimating giving by bequest. Since 2000, *Giving USA* has tracked the percentage of organizations reporting bequest receipts and the average amount received through bequest by like organizations (small arts; big education; medium-sized international, etc.). With these data, which rely extensively on the return rates for the *Giving USA* survey, estimates of charitable bequests can be developed in parallel with the current methods used, which are based on IRS reports and an estimate of giving by estates below the IRS filing threshold. A paper discussing this issue and presenting some alternatives for estimating charitable bequests is posted on the Giving Institute/Giving USA Foundation website for *Giving USA 2006*.

No billion dollar or more bequests announced in 2005
The year 2005 is the first year since 2002 without an announced charitable bequest of $1 billion or more. Using the Million Dollar List maintained at the Center on Philanthropy at Indiana University, 109 bequest contributions could be identified for 2004, totaling more than $3.72 billion. In 2005, the same source compiled a list of 115 bequest contributions, totaling $1.05 billion.

Federal estate tax filing threshold in 2005 was $1.5 million; largest estates account for more than 40 percent of charitable bequest dollars
For 2005, the federal estate tax filing threshold was $1,500,000 and the tax rate on estates was 47 percent. There has been a great deal of concern that increasing filing thresholds will reduce total contributions through bequest. Historically, estates valued at $20 million or more account for less than one-half of one percent of estate tax returns each year, yet provide more than 40 percent of the total dollar value of charitable bequests. Thus, the bequest total fluctuates dramatically depending on a relatively small number of estates.

More than 4,000 organizations issue gift annuities
The American Council on Gift Annuities released a report in spring 2005 estimating that 4,000 or more charities issue gift annuities.[1] The report, through a survey of charities with gift annuity programs, found that one-quarter of the organizations had started a gift annuity program since 1999 (the date of the prior survey by the same organization). The survey found that the average number of new annuities issued in 2004 (or the nearest fiscal year) was 17.5, and the median was 5 because some organizations with established programs generated a high number of new annuities. Religious organizations issued, on average, more annuities than other types of

charities. Donors creating immediate gift annuities averaged 78 years of age, whereas those creating deferred gift annuities were, on average, age 60. For most types of organizations, the median amount for a gift annuity falls near $30,000, plus or minus $5,000. However, organizations classified as a "public college/university" reported a median of $50,000, and social service organizations had a median of $24,633.

Philanthropy and voluntarism remains single largest type of recipient for charitable bequests claimed on estate tax returns, 2004

David Joulfaian, a researcher at the U.S. Department of the Treasury, analyzed the types of recipients of charitable bequests reported on estate tax returns for 2004. Philanthropy and voluntarism, which includes private foundations, community foundations, Jewish federations, and United Ways, received 43 percent of the total dollar amount claimed. Figure 1 shows the distribution of dollars claimed as deductions for charitable bequests on estate tax returns.

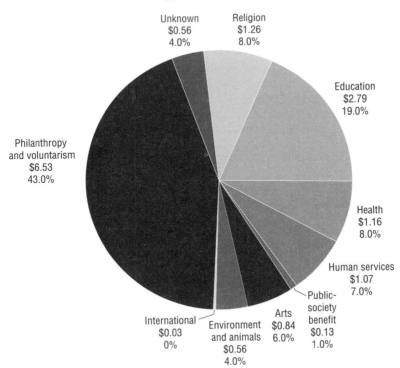

Figure 1
Bequest Contributions, Estate Tax Returns, 2004
$14.97 billion total
($ in billions)

Unknown
$0.56
4.0%

Religion
$1.26
8.0%

Education
$2.79
19.0%

Philanthropy
and voluntarism
$6.53
43.0%

Health
$1.16
8.0%

Human services
$1.07
7.0%

Public-
society
benefit
$0.13
1.0%

Arts
$0.84
6.0%

Environment
and animals
$0.56
4.0%

International
$0.03
0%

Data: David Joulfaian, *Basic facts about charitable giving*, U.S. Department of the Treasury, May 2006. Mimeo.

Giving by bequest

Dr. Joulfaian found $14.97 billion in deductions claimed on estate tax returns for 2004, an increase of 1.4 percent over the amount claimed in 2003. More estates claimed charitable bequests as deductions in 2003, but the average bequest amount that year was $1.10 million, less than the average of $1.26 million per estate reporting a bequest in 2004.

Just under one-third (32.2 percent) of the estates claiming deductions for charitable bequests were from decedents with a surviving spouse. The dollars reported in charitable bequests by estates of people with a surviving spouse were just less than one-quarter (24.8 percent) of the total dollars claimed as deductions. Bequests from these estates went to philanthropy and voluntarism (68 percent); arts, culture, and humanities (10.7 percent); education (8.7 percent); recreation-sports-athletics (3.6 percent), and religion (2.2 percent). The remaining 6.8 percent was distributed among all the other types of recipients.

Data released in 2005 provides more information about charitable bequests in 2001

Data released in mid-2005 by the Internal Revenue Service summarized findings about charitable bequests reported on estate tax returns filed for people who died in 2001.[2] In 2001, estates had to file a federal estate tax return if their gross estate value was more than $675,000. Estate tax returns for 2001 represented only 108,000 (or 5 percent) of the 2.1 million adult deaths that year. That filing level has increased since then to $1.5 million in 2005 and $2.0 million in 2006.

Among estate tax returns filed for people who died in 2001, 17.2 percent included a charitable deduction. Of the men who died, 12.8 percent included a charitable deduction. Among women, who tend to be the sole survivor of a marriage and more likely to leave a charitable gift from a final estate, 22.1 percent left a charitable bequest. Of the estates leaving charitable bequests:

- A higher percentage of women left bequests for:
    Religion (61 percent compared with 55 percent of men)
    Health (33 percent compared with 24 percent of men)
    Human services (31 percent compared with 27 percent of men)
    Environment (11 percent compared with 7 percent of men)

- About the same percentage of men and women left bequests for
    Art (10 percent of women, 9 percent of men)
    International affairs (1 percent of each)
    Other (14 percent of women, 13 percent of men)

- A higher percentage of men left bequests for
    Public-society benefit (22 percent of men compared with 17 percent of women)
    Education (36 percent of men compared with 32 percent of women)

Giving by bequest

Giving USA has used the 2005 IRS report to compare charitable bequests by men and women whose estates filed estate tax returns. The dollar distribution by type of recipient varies largely because women left more to charity (because more women left gifts). Figure 2 illustrates the distribution of charitable bequest amounts and percentage of total by subsector.

Figure 2
Bequest gift distribution by subsector,
Federal estate tax returns filed for 2001 decedents
($ in billions)

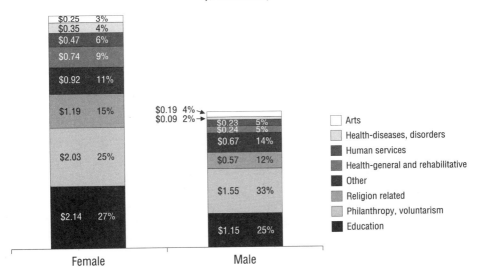

The three most important differences in the dollar distribution are:

- the higher percentage of charitable dollars distributed to philanthropy and voluntarism by men (33 percent compared with 25 percent from women),

- the higher percentage distributed by women to general health (9 percent compared with 5 percent for men), and

- the higher percentage distributed by women to religion (15 percent compared with 12 percent from men).

Similar data released in 2002 about 1998 estate tax returns permits comparison of the two years (1998 and 2001). In that period, there was little change in the gender breakdown and marital status of decedents leaving bequests (see Figure 3).

Giving by bequest

Figure 3
Share of estate tax returns that included a charitable bequest,
by gender and marital status, 1998 and 2001

■ 1998 Women   ■ 2001 Women   ▨ 1998 Men   ▨ 2001 Men

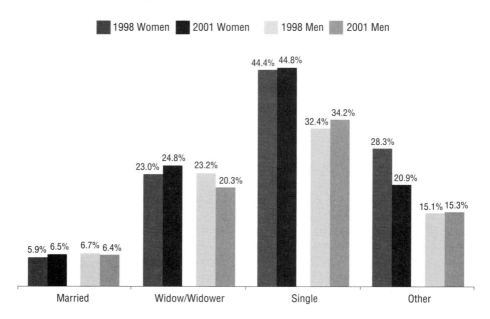

The percentage of all estate tax returns that made any charitable bequest remained relatively constant from 1998 to 2001. Similarly, the percentage of all estates that gave to each subsector also remained fairly stable in the period (see Figure 4). The one area of noticeable change was an increase in the percentage of estates—both men and women—that contributed to public-society benefit (a subsector that includes foundations, United Ways, and other combined fundraising efforts that redistribute funds to charities).

Giving by bequest

Figure 4
Percentage of all estate tax returns that included a charitable bequest for a subsector, by gender, 1998 and 2001

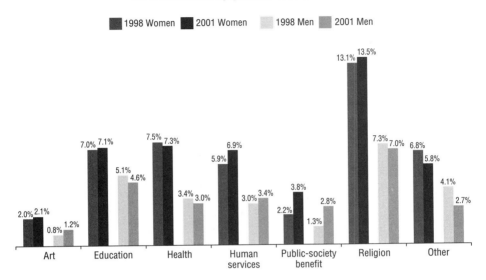

■ 1998 Women ■ 2001 Women ▨ 1998 Men ▨ 2001 Men

Reports appearing annually, summarized

Key findings of the most recent data available from annual studies are summarized in Table 1. These include data about planned gift instruments other than charitable bequests. *Giving USA* provides the web site addresses to help readers more easily access the complete reports.

Table 1
Key findings from studies of bequest and deferred giving

Internal Revenue Service		
Estate tax returns filed, data available at www.irs.gov		
	2002	2003	2004
Total number of estate tax returns filed	98,359	66,044	62,718
Number with charitable deduction (from analysis by U.S. Department of the Treasury)	16,105	13,400	11,861
Charitable deductions itemized on returns (from analysis by U.S. Department of the Treasury) (in billions)	$17.83	$14.77	$14.97

Giving by bequest

Charitable remainder unitrust Tax returns filed Data available at www.irs.gov			
	2002	2003	2004
Number	89,874	91,371	93,329
Assets (per Form 5227, book value, in billions)	$84.28	$81.56	$77.37
Assets (year-end, estimated fair market value, in billions)	$100.27	$84.70	$89.57

Charitable remainder annuity trust Tax returns filed Data available at www.irs.gov			
	2002	2003	2004
Number	22,958	22,783	22,626
Assets (book value, in billions)	$10.18	$9.60	$9.46

Charitable lead trusts Tax returns filed Data available at www.irs.gov			
	2002	2003	2004
Number	5,292	5,481	5,658
Assets (book value, in billions)	$15.08	$12.78	$12.32

1   *Reports and Comments on the American Council of Gift Annuities 2004 Survey of Charitable Gift Annuities*, April 2005, www.acga-web.org.
2   M. Britton Eller, Which estates are affected by the federal estate tax? An examination of the filing population for Year-of-Death 2001, *Statistics of Income Bulletin*, Summer 2005. www.irs.gov.

Giving by foundations

The Foundation Center estimated $30.00 billion in giving in 2005 by independent, community, and operating foundations. This is a 5.6 percent increase in grantmaking by these types of foundations (2.1 percent adjusted for inflation) compared with the final amount of $28.41 billion for 2004.

The Foundation Center summarized the following trends as important to foundation grantmaking in 2005:

- Growth in foundation assets in 2004
- New gifts to existing foundations
- Creation of new foundations in 2004 and 2005

The Foundation Center notes that growth in grantmaking in 2005 was lower than the percentage increase in assets in 2004. For independent, community, and operating foundations, grantmaking rose by 5.6 percent and asset values (including new gifts to existing foundations, investment yields, and assets of newly created foundations) rose by 7.1 percent. Grantmaking budgets in 2005 may reflect grantmaker caution in light of a two-year decline in assets from 2000 to 2002 and the practice at many large foundations of basing grantmaking on an average of asset values calculated over several years. Added to these factors was the relatively lackluster performance of the stock market in 2005.

Foundation grantmaking represented 11.5 percent of all estimated contributions in 2005, which is near the all-time high of 11.8 percent in 2001.

Foundation grantmaking in 2005

Giving USA reports the Foundation Center's estimates of foundation grantmaking for the year just concluded.[1] The Foundation Center figure of $33.6 billion is adjusted by *Giving USA* to move $3.6 billion of corporate foundation grantmaking to the corporate giving estimate for *Giving USA*. The estimate here for 2005 is for grantmaking by independent, community, and operating foundations. It includes grants paid in 2005 for disaster relief.

Foundation response to the Gulf Coast hurricanes

The Foundation Center released a summary in February 2006 presenting the initial response from independent, community, and corporate foundations to the Gulf Coast hurricanes of 2005.[2] The tabulation of reported commitments included more than $350 million from corporate foundations, which is included in the estimate in the *Giving USA* chapter for giving by corporations. Independent and family foundations had announced grants of $118 million by mid-November 2005, with $5 million in commitments from community foundations and $16 million committed by public foundations, such as the Pew Charitable Trusts, the McCormick Tribune Foundation, and the Missouri Foundation for Health (among others). The *Giving USA* estimate of $110 million in grants paid in 2005 for hurricane relief reflects the knowledge that some of the announced $139 million in commitments will be paid in 2006 and not count toward grantmaking in 2005.

The largest foundation commitment was $30 million from Lilly Endowment Inc. to be divided among the American Red Cross, the Salvation Army, and United Way of America. The W.K. Kellogg Foundation announced a $15 million commitment to support various relief efforts. The Ford Foundation provided $10 million for organizations meeting the immediate needs in communities struck by the hurricanes, and the Andrew W. Mellon Foundation announced funding of $10 million directed to affected educational institutions.

Survey finds majority of funders projected increase in 2005 giving

The Foundation Center's survey conducted in early 2005 asked funders to indicate the likely direction of change in their grantmaking during the year. Fifty-five percent reported planning to increase giving in 2005; one-quarter (25 percent) projected a decline in giving; and one-fifth (20 percent) anticipated no change.[3] Those projecting an increase were most likely to say that giving would rise between 1 and 5 percent, with fewer anticipating growth of more than 5 percent. With the planned increases relatively low, the Foundation Center wrote that giving would increase but at a more modest rate than was seen between 2003 and 2004. In fact, grantmaking grew slightly more than foundations predicted at the beginning of 2005, with an increase of 6.6 percent. The 6.6 percent change from 2004 to 2005 outpaced the 4.8 percent growth reported for 2003 to 2004.

Foundation giving rises in 2004 among largest foundations studied

The Foundation Center reported that in 2004, for the first time since 2001, overall giving by the largest private and community foundations increased, growing by 8.1 percent over the prior year. Grantees in most subsectors saw growth in foundation grantmaking, according to the study, which included 1,172 larger foundations and represented about half of the overall foundation giving for 2004. Figure 1 shows the dollar amounts and percentages of grant dollars supporting different areas in 2004 as reported by the participating foundations.[4]

Giving USA finds that, compared with 2001, foundation grantmaking priorities in 2004 as studied by the Foundation Center shifted slightly toward arts and public-society benefit and away from education and environmental causes. Figure 2 compares grantmaking as a percentage of dollars awarded by foundations sampled in the 2001 and 2004 grant years, based on the Foundation Center's study. The year 2001 is selected because the Gates Foundation, which was funded in 1999 and 2000, began its major grantmaking efforts that year. The Gates Foundation's focus on global health issues pushed health giving up considerably between 2000 and 2001. It has remained a major health funder since 2001.

Giving by foundations

Figure 1
Foundation funding priorities, 2004
($ in millions)

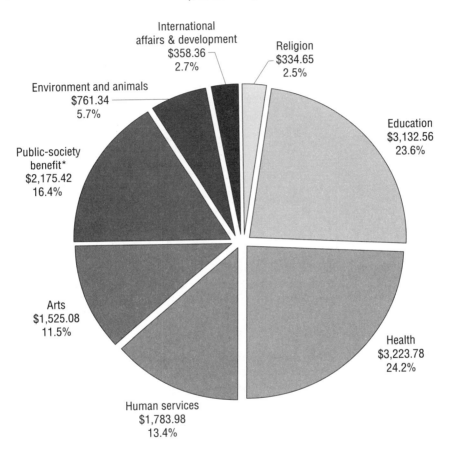

International affairs & development
$358.36
2.7%

Religion
$334.65
2.5%

Environment and animals
$761.34
5.7%

Education
$3,132.56
23.6%

Public-society benefit*
$2,175.42
16.4%

Arts
$1,525.08
11.5%

Health
$3,223.78
24.2%

Human services
$1,783.98
13.4%

*Includes amounts for science and technology and for social science, reported separately by The Foundation Center.
Data: The Foundation Center, *Foundation Giving Trends*, 2006 edition, page 73. Based on a sample of foundations.

Figure 2
Foundation grantmaking priorities, 2001 and 2004

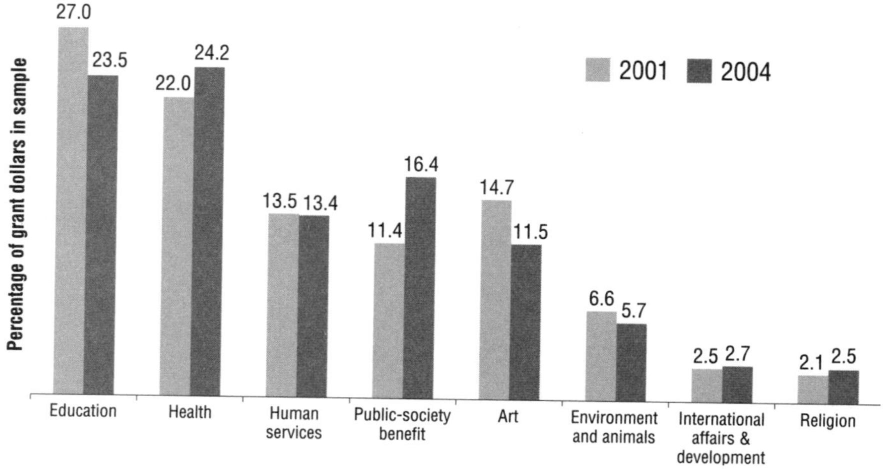

Family foundations number more than 33,100

According to the Foundation Center, family foundations represent more than one-half of all independent foundations and account for $12.67 billion in grantmaking, which is just under one-half of the dollars granted in 2004 by independent foundations.[5] In an earlier study about family foundations, the Foundation Center found that in 1998, family foundations were 43 percent of all independent foundations and accounted for about 48 percent of all independent foundation giving.[6]

A foundation is considered a family foundation if it reports itself as such on a Foundation Center survey, uses the word "family" or "families" in its name, has a living donor whose surname matches the foundation name, or has at least two trustees who share the donor's surname.

For the study released in early 2006, and using data for 31,347 family foundations that made grants in 2004, the Foundation Center found that many family foundations are comparatively small: 36 percent of family foundations had assets of less than $250,000, and 63 percent had assets less than $1 million. Most family foundations (65 percent) gave less than $100,000 in 2004. Only 5 percent gave more than $1 million in 2004.

Paid staff is the most significant cost for foundation operations

In recent years, media reports and Congressional and Internal Revenue Service investigations spurred interest in examining the expenses (other than grantmaking) of foundations. One concern was that at least some foundations spend "too much" on operations, and not enough money is distributed in grants. A study released in 2006 found that most foundations—in fact, nearly all studied—spend a very small percentage of their budget on operations.[7]

Giving by foundations

The study of the 10,000 largest independent foundations was conducted by the Foundation Center and the Urban Institute in collaboration with Philanthropic Research (which operates Guidestar.org). It reported that nearly three-quarters of independent foundations (72 percent, or 6,361 foundations) did not have any paid staff. At foundations with no staff, operating expenses and administrative expenses were typically less than 1 percent of qualifying distributions, that is, grantmaking and expenses related to grantmaking.

Less than one-quarter of the independent foundations in the study had paid staff (2,327 foundations). Of those staffed foundations, more than 60 percent had operating and administrative expenses that were less than 10 percent of their qualifying distributions. Among all the foundations studied, operating and administrative expenses ranged from 5 percent or less of qualifying distributions (at about 950 foundations) to 20 percent or more (at 325 foundations).

Foundations with operating costs that were a larger share of qualifying distributions were likely to be small (less than $1 million in assets); or have international grantmaking programs; or conduct direct charitable activities (such as research or fellowship programs, technical assistance for grantees, or conferences); or make grants to individuals.

For this study, the researchers compiled and analyzed data from IRS forms 990-PF filed for 2001. These foundations accounted for 78 percent of the dollar amount in foundation grantmaking and 77 percent of foundation assets of the nearly 62,000 active foundations in 2001.

Grantmaking to Native American causes rising slowly

Sarah Hicks and Miriam Jorgensen, researchers at Harvard University, released a study in 2005 that found grantmaking by the largest foundations for Native American causes and concerns increased from $32.9 million in 1989 (adjusted for inflation to 2002 values) to $91.9 million in 2002,[8] a growth of 179 percent. However, overall grantmaking by all independent and community foundations in the same period rose slightly more, by 184 percent.[9] Grants for Native American causes from the nation's largest foundations remained less than 0.3 percent of those foundations' overall grantmaking in 2002, about the same as in 1989. The American Indian, Alaska Native, and Hawaii Native population (including people who report more than one ethnic or racial origin) is approximately 1.5 percent of the entire U.S. population.[10]

From 1996 to 2002, grantmaking for Native American causes was concentrated on Indian education (26 percent); arts, culture, and humanities issues (16 percent); community improvement and development (10 percent); and health issues (8 percent). Recipients tended to be large institutions, including the American Indian College Fund, several economic development and empowerment efforts, colleges and universities, various museums, two tribes, and one regranting entity.

Key findings from other studies summarized

Table 1 presents three years of findings from studies released annually about foundations. Web site addresses are provided to help readers get access to the full report.

Table 1
Key findings from other studies

Foundation Yearbook, 2004, 2005 and 2006 editions The Foundation Center, www.fdncenter.org			
	2002	2003	2004
Number of active independent and community grantmaking foundations	58,495	59,690	60,731
Number of all active grantmaking foundations (including corporate and operating)	64,843	66,398	67,736
Assets in independent and community foundations	$393.91 billion	$400.00 billion	$463.89 billion

Foundation Giving Trends, 2004, 2005 and 2006 editions The Foundation Center, www.fdncenter.org			
	2002	2003	2004
Average grant amount, surveyed foundations	$124,678	$118,649	$122,355
Median grant amount, surveyed foundations	$25,000	$25,000	$25,000

Columbus Foundation Survey of Community Foundations 2004, 2005 and 2006 editions Columbus Foundation, www.columbusfoundation.org			
	2002	2003	2004
Number of community foundations	650	645	636
Assets in community foundations	$29.7 billion	$34.9 billion	$39.4 billion
Grants made	$2.55 billion	$2.60 billion	$2.97 billion

1   L. Renz, S. Lawrence and J. Atienza, *Foundation Growth and Giving Estimates: Current Outlook*, 2006, www.fdncenter.org.

2   S. Lawrence, *Snapshot of Philanthropy's Response to the Gulf Coast Hurricanes*, February 2006, www.fdncenter.org.

3   L. Renz and S. Lawrence, 2005 foundation giving forecast, *Foundation Growth and Giving Estimates: 2004 Preview*, 2005, pp. 2-3, www.fdncenter.org.

4   J. Atienza and J. Altman, *Foundation Giving Trends: Preview*, released in December 2005 with 2004 data, The Foundation Center, www.fdncenter.org.

5   S. Lawrence, *Key Facts on Family Foundations*, The Foundation Center, released January 2006 with data for 2004, www.fdncenter.org.

6   *Family Foundations*, The Foundation Center, released in 2000 with data for 1998, www.fdncenter.org.

7   E. Boris, L. Renz, et al., *Foundation Expenses & Compensation: How Operating Characteristics Influence Spending*, 2006, The Urban Institute, The Foundation Center, and Philanthropic Research, Inc, www.urban.org, www.fdncenter.org, and www.guidestar.org.

8   S. Hicks and M. Jorgensen, *Large Foundations' Grantmaking to Native America*, September 2005, Harvard Project on American Indian Economic Development.

9   *Giving USA* calculation.

10 *Giving USA* calculation, February 2006, using data from the 2003 Data Profile, General Demographic Characteristics at www.census.gov.

Giving by corporations

- Corporate contributions rose to an estimated $13.77 billion in 2005, an increase of 22.5 percent (18.5 percent adjusted for inflation) compared with the revised estimate of $11.24 billion for 2004.

- Corporate charitable contributions are 5.3 percent of total estimated giving in 2005.

- The growth in corporate giving in 2005 reflects:
  - An estimated $1.38 billion in donations for disaster relief with $84 million removed from that total as potentially double-counted corporate foundation grants.
  - An estimated increase of more than $1 billion associated with changes in gross domestic product and corporate profits.
  - Corporate foundation grantmaking of an estimated $3.6 billion, using data collected by the Foundation Center.
  - Subtraction of corporate gifts of an estimated $3.4 billion made to corporate foundations, based on the past three years of corporate giving to fund corporate foundations and including the creation of the Google Foundation with a gift of $90 million.

- Corporate giving is associated with changes in corporate profits. One profit measure, the Bureau of Economic Analysis's report of corporate profits before tax, showed a very high rate of growth in 2005, which at least partially reflected tax law changes for 2002 through 2005 that affect depreciation. *Giving USA* developed an estimate with an adjusted level of profits to try to take into account the portion of the profit increase attributable to depreciation. The resulting estimate of corporate giving for 2005 was $13.76 billion instead of $13.77.

- The Committee to Encourage Corporate Philanthropy (CECP) collected data from more than 100 of the country's largest firms and, collectively, those companies reported a 15 percent increase in tax-deductible charitable contributions for 2005, including cash and noncash contributions. CECP's survey respondents have, in the past, accounted for about one-third to 40 percent of corporate giving claimed on tax returns.

Giving USA Findings

The year 2005 was remarkable for a number of reasons, including the occurrence of major natural disasters and the corporate response to these. For example, the Asian tsunami that hit in December 2004 led American corporations to contribute in record amounts for an international crisis, an estimated total $0.34 billion contributed in 2005.[1] Contributions in response to the tsunami were eclipsed only by the $750 million donated following the September 11, 2001, attacks on New York City and Washington, D.C.[2] Corporations also gave a significant portion (approximately one-fifth) of the $5.3 billion raised for immediate relief work after Hurricanes Katrina,

Giving by corporations

Rita, and Wilma struck the U.S. Gulf Coast. The generous responses to disasters are an estimated 10 percent of all corporate giving in 2005.

As *Giving USA* has previously reported, corporate giving tends to rise and fall based upon many factors, with profitability and a history of giving being chief among them. Other factors include gross domestic product (GDP), prior giving levels, and corporate tax rates.[3] In 2005, America's economy continued to rebound and its GDP surpassed $13 trillion.[4] Government estimates about profitability are supported by reports from corporations themselves. Nearly half of the executives in one survey reported that their company's 2005 financial performance had improved over 2004.[5] A number of sources report variations of this fact: profitability among America's corporations substantially improved in 2005.[6]

There is no single way to track giving by an individual firm. Corporate giving programs are not required to file government documents about their contributions. Company foundations do file an IRS Form 990-PF, and their giving is public information.[7] Information about an individual firm's giving may be collected from media reports or the firm's own statements. Sometimes, however, there are differences among the various reports and the amount claimed for a tax deduction, which the firm might report in a survey, such as that of the Conference Board. *Giving USA*'s estimates use the figures reported by the IRS as the total claimed in charitable deductions on corporate tax returns.

Corporate profits were very strong in 2005

Corporate profits in 2005 rose by 35.8 percent, according to the U.S. Bureau of Economic Analysis. This marks the third year in a row in which there was an increase.[8] Many corporate donors reported that giving in 2005 was based upon the profitability of the previous year.[9] Profitability is considered in the model used by *Giving USA* to estimate itemized corporate charitable deductions as part of the estimate of corporate giving.

For the estimate of giving in 2005, growth in gross domestic product plays an important role. Three years of inflation-adjusted growth in GDP of 2.8 percent or more, combined with corporate profit increases, boosted estimated itemized deductions for corporate charitable contributions in 2005 by $0.79 billion. This change is before any adjustments for disaster relief giving or corporate foundation giving. Growth in corporate charitable contributions of $0.79 billion is inflation-adjusted growth of 6.6 percent, the highest estimated rate of increase in corporate charitable contributions since 1999 and significantly above the 40-year average growth of 4.6 percent.

Foundation Center estimated $3.6 billion in corporate foundation giving for 2005

Based on survey responses received early in 2006, the Foundation Center released an estimate that corporate foundations paid grants of $3.6 billion in 2005, including payment of disaster relief grants. This amount is added to the *Giving USA* estimate of itemized corporate charitable contributions. *Giving USA* subtracted an estimate of $3.4 billion given to corporate foundations by their corporate donors to avoid double-counting gifts. Without this adjustment, gifts to the corporate foundation would be counted once when they are claimed as deductions by corporations and once again in the amount of corporate foundation grants paid. While some corporate foundations are endowed and make grants from interest earnings, most are "pass through" funders, receiving funds and paying grants from that amount within the same year or so.

Major donations in 2005 from consumer-based companies

Following its multibillion-dollar initial public stock offering, search-engine giant Google announced that $265 million of the dollars raised would go to philanthropy. The company created the Google Foundation with a gift of $90 million and pledged $175 million in charitable gifts to be made over two to three years.[10] This level of commitment puts the Silicon Valley-based firm in the top ranks of U.S. corporate donors for 2005 when measured by amount donated.

Wal-Mart reported that it donated more than $200 million in 2005.[11] Wal-Mart has been the company with the largest amount of cash donations at least since 2000, according to the *Chronicle of Philanthropy*'s annual survey.

Tsunami relief aid tops all prior disaster relief giving

While *Giving USA* reported early tsunami-related contributions in its 2005 edition (which covered 2004), corporate donors gave a reported total (including cash, in-kind, and noncategorized gifts but excluding customer contributions) of $493 million by June of 2005.[12] The U.S. Chamber of Commerce reported that tsunami relief contributions formed the largest international corporate aid effort since records were first kept following Hurricane Mitch in 1998. The total of $493 million includes an estimated $153 million in gifts in late 2004 and values for in-kind products and services, not all of which will appear as deductions on corporate tax returns.

Johnson & Johnson gave the largest corporate donation to relief efforts: $10 million in cash and $80 million in products. Other super-sized donations came from Pfizer ($10.6 million in cash and $40 million in products), Coca-Cola ($17.3 million in cash and $2.5 million in products), and Chevron ($12 million in cash).[13]

Hurricane relief giving breaks records

In August 2005, Hurricane Katrina slammed into the southeastern United States. Just a few weeks later, in September 2005, Hurricane Rita hit major areas of the Gulf Coast, including some areas that Katrina had damaged. By some measures, Rita was even more powerful than Katrina, but ultimately caused less damage in terms of lives and dollars. In October, Hurricane Wilma hit southern Florida, flooding the Keys and damaging homes and businesses.

Giving by corporations

Black Enterprise magazine (BE) reported that African-American businesses felt especially compelled to donate to the hurricane-ravaged Gulf Coast.[15] Among the businesses responding: Thompson Hospitality, a food service company that is 23rd on the BE list of the 100 largest African-American businesses, offered a free meal plan for the academic year to any student who had to relocate to another college or university because of Hurricane Katrina. H.J. Russell & Co. (13th on the BE list) created a fund to help meet the immediate needs of approximately 185 evacuees who were relatives of Russell employees.

Earthquake relief in Pakistan

In October 2005, five corporate leaders and their companies created the South Asia Earthquake Relief Fund (SAERF), with backing from President Bush. SAERF's leaders said they were committed to raising "awareness and resources to help survivors of the South Asia earthquake rebuild their lives and communities."[16] SAERF issued a press release stating that the fund was donating $2.5 million in grants to five nonprofit agencies for earthquake relief: the Aga Khan Foundation, Catholic Relief Services, International Rescue Committee, Mercy Corps, and Save the Children. *Giving USA* estimates that American companies contributed about $100 million ($0.1 billion) by year-end for earthquake relief, including outright company donations and matching gifts for employee donations.

A word about differing measurements of corporate donations

More than one-third (and up to one-half, in some studies) of corporate giving is in-kind. The U.S. tax code permits corporations a "limited deduction for charitable contributions made in cash or other property." Noncash donations are often reported in the media at fair market value, but the amount allowed as a deduction is fair market value minus the income and capital gains that would be earned if the product were sold at fair market value. In effect, this means that the corporation can deduct its cost for purchasing or manufacturing the asset. These two different methods lead to differences between corporations' valuations of product donations for their tax returns, which *Giving USA* uses for its estimates, and amounts reported by companies responding to some surveys. For example, in-kind values from the U.S. Chamber of Commerce, the Committee to Encourage Corporate Philanthropy, and the *Chronicle of Philanthropy* may include the fair market value of product donations rather than what the firm will be able to claim as a deductible gift for tax purposes.

In-kind donations have a value to the recipient charity that is whatever the charity saves by receiving an item that it would otherwise pay for. Charities receive other types of support from companies that matter for the charitable budget but are not always tracked as charitable contributions in the tax code. *Giving USA* also does not estimate the value of other forms of corporate support, including expenditures from a marketing budget for activities such as advertising or sponsorship that benefit a charity, time volunteered by company employees, or services provided at a discount.

Corporate donors for 2004 ranked by amount and by percentage of profits donated

Depending on how donations are calculated, Wal-Mart is either the number-one or the number-five corporate contributor in the U.S. The *Chronicle of Philanthropy* ranks it first for cash donations. However, the Taft Group listed Wal-Mart as the fifth highest corporate philanthropy contributor in the latest edition of its corporate giving directory.[17] The Taft Group includes in-kind donations in its rankings and places Wal-Mart behind Merck Co./Merck Foundation, Pfizer Inc./Pfizer Foundation, Eli Lilly & Co./Eli Lilly Foundation, and Microsoft Corporation, all of which are known for large in-kind donations.[18]

When giving is measured as a percentage of profits, *Business Week* ranked Biogen IDEC at the top. The firm reportedly gave $8.3 million or 13 percent of pretax profits in cash donations in 2004.[19] The company is an international biotechnology firm that creates, manufactures, and distributes medicines for serious illnesses, such as various cancers and multiple sclerosis.[20] Following Biogen IDEC were Kroger Stores (12.2 percent of pretax profits donated); Tiffany (5.5 percent); and technology firm Advanced Micro Devices (5.4 percent). On the list of donors who gave a high percentage of profits, the largest AMOUNT contributed was from Target Corp., which had cash donations of $107.8 million in 2004, or 3.6 percent of pretax profits.[21]

The Conference Board survey finds 21.8 percent increase in giving for 2004

In its 2005 *Corporate Contributions Report*, the Conference Board released findings about 189 companies that it surveyed regarding their 2004 giving. The firms responding to the survey are among the country's largest and reported giving to United States-based charities of $6.4 billion,[22] or 61 percent of the estimated $11.24 billion estimated by *Giving USA* for corporate giving in 2004.

Among the 133 companies participating in the 2003 and 2004 surveys of the Conference Board, giving rose in 2004 by 21.8 percent. This far surpasses *Giving USA*'s estimate of an increase of 1.6 percent for all corporate giving in 2004. The Conference Board respondents reported a 24 percent increase in 2003, far exceeding the 2.5 percent increase found when claimed deductions on tax returns and corporate foundation giving are calculated to develop an estimate of all giving by corporations for the year.

As has been the case in the past, the Conference Board found that corporations favored giving to health and human services (one category in the Conference Board study) and to education. Combined, these domestic programs received 58 percent of the reported dollar value of corporate contributions. Gifts for international recipients, at $1.45 billion, were 19 percent of the total. Figure 1 shows the allocation of corporate giving priorities in 2004 based on the Conference Board's survey. The total, because it includes international giving, is $7.85 billion (more than the $6.40 billion in estimated giving to U.S. recipients).

Giving by corporations

Figure 1
Corporate Funding Priorities, 2004
($ in billions)

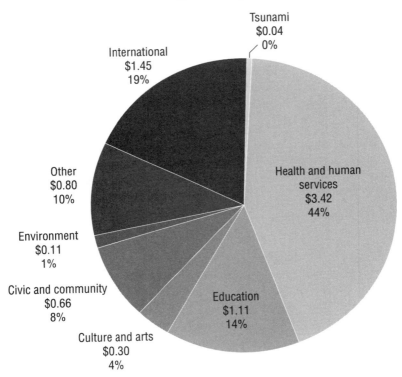

Data: The Conference Board, 2005 *Corporate Contributions Report*, page 8.

Most firms that made gifts for tsunami relief made those commitments in the first two months of 2005. Firms responding to the Conference Board survey reported total contributions for the tsunami of $260 million (including contributions in 2004 of $30.9 million in cash and $5.9 million in noncash donations). The U.S. Chamber of Commerce estimated total corporate giving for tsunami relief as of June 2005 to have been $566 million. Among the Conference Board participants, 65 percent of their tsunami relief giving was in cash. The noncash gifts were most likely to have been contributed by manufacturing firms. Tsunami giving did not affect other contributions in 2005 at 67 percent of the firms participating in the Conference Board study. Fifty-nine percent of those giving for tsunami relief said the contributions to that purpose were in addition to a preexisting budget; only 19 percent reported reallocating funds from a preexisting budget.

Giving by corporations

Chronicle of Philanthropy reports growth in corporate giving in 2004

In its now-annual survey of major corporations, the *Chronicle of Philanthropy* compiled responses from 94 firms about their giving in 2004 and plans for giving in 2005.[23] Among the responding companies, giving in 2004 rose a median of 5.5 percent (half the firms reported a change below 5.5 percent; half reported a change in giving that exceeded 5.5 percent). This is also far different from the Conference Board findings and closer to the *Giving USA* finding that corporate giving, including corporate foundation grants paid, rose 1.6 percent in 2004 for all 5 million corporations in the United States.

One firm in the *Chronicle*'s poll, Pfizer, reported cash and in-kind donations in 2004 of more than $1 billion, the first time any firm in the *Chronicle*'s poll has met that level of giving. The *Chronicle* poll asks firms to report noncash donations at fair market value, which typically exceeds the deduction at basis (the cost of production) permitted for a tax deduction. The Pfizer value included a significant portion (92 percent) attributable to medicines manufactured by the company.

General Motors, through both corporate giving and corporate foundation grantmaking, reported the highest amount of cash giving, at $207.6 million.

Corporate foundation grantmaking priorities, 2004

The Foundation Center surveys corporate foundations annually and gathers information about the purposes for which grant dollars are paid. Figure 2 shows the allocation of corporate foundation funding for 2004.

IRS report on corporate donations, 2003

The Internal Revenue Service analyzes tax returns and releases aggregate (summary) data periodically. The most recent corporate tax data available in early 2006 is the preliminary information from tax returns filed for 2003. *Giving USA* has calculated the amount of itemized charitable deductions claimed by industry sector as a percentage of all profits subject to tax from firms in that sector. Not all firms contribute, so the giving is from donor firms only, and the income is from all companies. Overall, donor firms claimed deductions for contributions that were 1.5 percent of all income subject to tax. The industries where giving was the highest percentage of income were arts, entertainment and recreation (2.8 percent) and "other services" (2.4 percent). The industries with the lowest percentages were educational services (0.8 percent) and finance and insurance (1.1 percent). Table 1 shows the results for all industry sectors and major industrial categories.

Giving by corporations

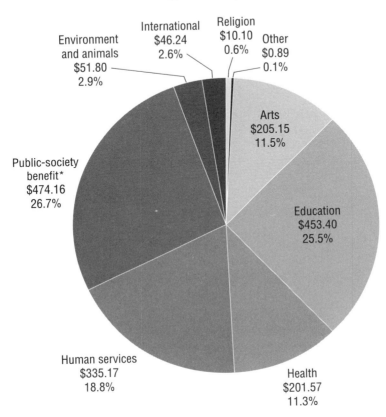

**Figure 2
Corporate Foundation Funding Priorities, 2004
($ in millions)**

International $46.24 2.6%

Religion $10.10 0.6%

Other $0.89 0.1%

Environment and animals $51.80 2.9%

Arts $205.15 11.5%

Public-society benefit* $474.16 26.7%

Education $453.40 25.5%

Human services $335.17 18.8%

Health $201.57 11.3%

Data: The Foundation Center, *Foundation Giving Trends*, 2006. Based on grants of $10,000 or more awarded by a sample of U.S. corporate foundations.
*Includes civil rights and social action, community improvement and development, philanthropy and voluntarism, public affairs, science and technology, and social sciences.

Giving by corporations

Table 1
Charitable contributions deduction as a percentage of income subject to tax, by corporate sector, 2003
(Based on IRS preliminary summary data for corporate tax returns as released March 2005)

All sectors	1.5%
Resource use	
Agriculture, forestry, fishing and hunting	1.8%
Mining	1.3%
Utilities	2.2%
Building and manufacturing	
Construction	1.6%
Manufacturing	1.8%
Trade	
Wholesale trade	2.2%
Retail trade	1.6%
Services	
Transportation and warehousing	1.5%
Information	1.3%
Finance and insurance	1.1%
Professional, scientific, and technical services	2.0%
Management of companies (holding companies)	1.2%
Administrative and support and waste management and remediation services	1.3%
Educational services	0.8%
Health care and social assistance	2.2%
Arts, entertainment and recreation	2.8%
Accommodation and food services	2.1%
Other services	2.4%

U.S. Treasury researchers find that corporate giving is closely linked to advertising expenditures

In the first-ever study to use firm-level data to explore corporate giving, David Joulfaian and Robert Carroll, both scholars working at the U.S. Department of the Treasury, found that a given firm's likelihood of giving and amount of giving rose with income, with tax rates, and with the amount the firm spent on advertising.[24] That is, firms earning more were more likely to give at all and to give more when they did give.

Firms facing high tax rates were more likely to give and give more than comparable firms with the same revenues but different expenses. The first two findings are consistent with work done for *Giving USA* estimates of corporate giving. Because they had access to tax return information specific to each firm in the analysis, Joulfaian and Carroll could also examine variables that could be linked to giving that cannot be explored at the aggregate level with all firms considered at once. They found that firms spending higher amounts on advertising were more likely than firms comparable in other ways to be donors and to give more than like firms. Table 2 summarizes this finding.

Table 2
Percentage of firms giving and advertising, by type of firm and by asset size, 1991 data

C corporations (many shareholders)

Firm assets, billions	<$0.05	>$0.05 <$1.0	>$1.0
Percentage of firms that give	51	62	77
Of those that give, percentage that advertise	85	85	94
Among nondonors, percentage that advertise	64	54	33

S corporations (income and deductions pass through to the few shareholders)

Firm assets, billions	<$0.05	>$0.05 <$1.0	>$1.0
Percentage of firms that give	6	9	–
Of those that give, percentage that advertise	86	86	
Among nondonors, percentage that advertise	67	64	

Source: D. Joulfaian and R. Carroll, May 2005, adapted from their Table 2.

Key findings from annual studies summarized
Table 3 summarizes key findings from studies that appear annually. Three years of data are presented, the most recent available. Web site addresses are provided to help readers get access to the full reports.

Table 3
Key findings from annual studies about corporate giving

$5 Million Dollar List Center on Philanthropy at Indiana University, www.philanthropy.iupui.edu			
	2003	2004	2005
Largest publicized corporate gift	$1 billion over 5 years, Microsoft Corporation for its Unlimited Potential program	$208 million, from PACE, the Partners for the Advancement of Collaborative Engineering Education, consortium of four firms, to Georgia Institute of Technology	$265 million, Google to its foundation ($90 million) and other to-be-named nonprofit groups ($175 million)

Giving by corporations

The Corporate Contributions Report
The Conference Board, www.conference-board.org

	2002	2003	2004
Percentage growth in giving over prior year among firms that responded two years in a row to the survey	13.7 111 firms	24 134 firms	21.8 133 firms
U.S. contributions as a percentage of U.S. pretax income (median)	1.6	1.7	1.6
U.S. contributions as a percentage of consolidated (U.S. and international operations) pretax income (median)	1.0	0.90	0.85
Donations per employee, worldwide (median)	$291	$360	$392
Share from corporate cash	31	24	23
Share in-kind	35	49	54
Share from foundation grants	34	27	23

Foundation Center report about corporate foundations
Foundation Yearbook, various editions
The Foundation Center, www.fdncenter.org

	2002	2003	2004
Number of corporate foundations	2,362	2,549	2,596
New gifts received	$3.00 billion	$3.23 billion	$3.667 billion
Grants made	$3.46 billion	$3.47 billion	$3.443 billion

Charitable giving at major corporations, July 24, 2003, August 5, 2004 and August 4, 2005
Chronicle of Philanthropy, www.philanthropy.com
(Note: 2005 data not available in April 2006)

	2002	2003	2004
Corporate donor identified as largest cash donor and amount contributed in cash	Wal-Mart $136 million	Wal-Mart $153 million	Wal-Mart $198 million
Company reported with the highest amount in cash and product donations	Merck & Company $633 million	Merck & Company $843 million	Pfizer $1.26 billion

Giving by corporations

Business Committee for the Arts, Inc. survey of corporate arts funders Poll of 100 or more prominent corporate funders of the arts Fall surveys project direction of change in giving for the next year, www.bcainc.org (Note: 2006 report not yet available)			
	2003	2004	2005
Percentage who expected their arts giving to:			
Remain stable	58	67	70
Increase	8	13	19
Decrease	19	11	5
Don't know	15	9	6

Sponsorships (includes for-profit and nonprofit) IEG Sponsorship Report, www.sponsorship.com $ in billions (% change)			
	2003	2004	2005
Sports	7.08 (9.3)	7.67 (8.3)	8.30 (8.3)
Entertainment	0.87 (-2.4)	1.06 (21.7)	1.17 (10.4)
Fairs, events, festivals	0.77 (-8.5)	0.48 (n/a)	0.52 (7.9)
Causes	0.92 (10.4)	0.99 (7.2)	1.11 (12.3)
Arts	0.61 (0.8)	0.61 (0.3)	.65 (6.4)
Associations/membership groups		0.31 (n/a)	.34 (11.1)

Note: Associations and membership groups were separated in 2004 from fairs, events, and festivals; n/a indicates that percentage change cannot be calculated for 2004.

1 Data about corporate giving following the tsunami were collected and tabulated by the U.S. Chamber of Commerce through its Business Civic Leadership Center. Total corporate giving for tsunami relief (excluding customer contributions made through corporate collection efforts) was reported at $493 million, including $140 million in in-kind products and services, $273 million in cash contributions (including an estimated $84 million from corporate foundations), and $79 million in corporate matching gifts for employee contributions. *Giving USA* adjusted the corporate cash contributions amount to subtract $32.8 million, or 12 percent, following the Conference Board's finding covered later in this chapter, that 12 percent of corporate cash donations were made in 2004. This leaves a cash contribution amount of $240.74 million, to which was added matching gifts of $79.31 million to yield $320.05 million in cash donations in 2005. To that was added 15 percent of the reported value of in-kind donations and services (0.15 x $140.39 million = $21.06 million) for a total in 2005 of $341.11 million, or $0.34 billion.

2 Data from the U.S. Chamber of Commerce, as reported on the web site of the Committee to Encourage Corporate Philanthropy.

3 W. Chin, M. Brown, and P. Rooney, Estimating corporate giving for *Giving USA*, working paper available from the Center on Philanthropy at Indiana University upon request. E-mail msbrown@iupui.edu.

4   See the March 30, 2006, release about gross domestic product at the Bureau of Economic Analysis, U.S. Department of Commerce, www.bea.gov.

5   Data from "The State of Corporate Citizenship in the U.S.", published by the Center for Corporate Citizenship at Boston College.

6   See the March 30, 2006, release about corporate profits from the U.S. Bureau of Economic Analysis, www.bea.gov, which reports that corporate profits before taxes rose by 35.8 percent. A portion of this increase is attributed to different methods of claiming deductions for depreciation. Nonetheless, corporate revenues from operations also increased.

7   The Taft Group's Corporate Giving Directory, 27th edition.

8   Bureau of Economic Analysis, U.S. Department of Commerce, www.bea.gov.

9   I. Wilhelm, Corporate giving rebounds, *Chronicle of Philanthropy*, August 8, 2005, www.philanthropy.com.

10 S. Hansell, Google earmarks $265 million for charity and social causes, *New York Times*, October 12, 2005. Accessed at www.lexis-nexis.com.

11 Wal-Mart web site, http://www.walmartfacts.com/community/walmart-foundation.aspx, viewed February 13, 2006

12 Tsunami relief giving and reconstruction: The private sector response, U.S. Chamber of Commerce, August 29, 2005, www.uschamber.com.

13 *Chronicle of Philanthropy*, January 23, 2006. http://philanthropy.com.

14 *Chronicle of Philanthropy*, as in note 9.

15 *Black Enterprise*, "BE100s Support Hurricane Victims," September 12, 2005.

16 Information published on the SAERF web site, www.southasiaearthquakerelief.org.

17 *Corporate Giving Directory*. 27th ed. Edited by Laurie J. Fundukian. Detroit, MI: The Taft Group, 2005. 1,568 p.

18 N. Byrnes, Smarter corporate giving: Targeted donations, support for volunteers, and consumer awareness ads are paying off, *Business Week*, November 28, 2005, www.businessweek.com.

19 Ibid.

20 Biogen web site, http://www.biogenidec.com/site/home.html, viewed April 28, 2006.

21 N. Byrnes, *Business Week* as in note 18.

22 S. Muirhead, *The 2005 Corporate Contributions Report*, The Conference Board, www.conference-board.org.

23 *Chronicle of Philanthropy*, August 8, 2005, issue.

24 D. Joulfaian and R. Carroll, Corporate taxes and giving to charity, *Public Finance Review*, May 2005.

Giving to religion

- Giving to religious organizations increased by 5.9 percent (2.5 percent adjusted for inflation), reaching an estimated $93.18 billion in 2005.[1]

- Giving to religious organizations represented 35.8 percent of total estimated charitable contributions in the United States in 2005.

- Religious organizations received contributions of more than $430 million for disaster relief.[2] Giving USA does not count the thousands of volunteer hours contributed by members of congregations or the household items collected by congregations to give directly to survivors of natural disasters.

Giving USA findings benchmark giving to religion, 2005

The 2005 *Giving USA* estimate of giving to religion includes contributions to religious congregations; giving to national or regional offices of faith groups; missionary societies; religious media (including print and broadcast); and other organizations formed for religious fellowship, worship, or evangelism (Young Life, Campus Crusade for Christ, and so on). The 2005 estimate is based on data from 31 religious congregations reporting contributions to the National Council of Churches' *Yearbook on American and Canadian Churches*. It also includes religious organizations found on the *Chronicle of Philanthropy*'s list of "The Philanthropy 400," released in fall 2005 for contributions in 2004. The estimate also includes financial information from 54 additional large religious organizations, including some religious denominations whose contribution information is publicly available through the Evangelical Council for Financial Accountability.

This estimate does not include contributions to nondenominational mega-churches and separately incorporated organizations, even when faith-based, that provide education, health care, or other services. Thus, giving to St. Elizabeth's Hospital, the Reform Jewish Academy, or Lutheran Social Services and similar organizations appears in health, education, and human services, respectively.

Factors that may have influenced giving to religion in 2005

This section summarizes key information that may inform our understanding of the estimated changes in giving to religious organizations in 2005. These include the following:

- Religious organizations raising millions of dollars for relief and recovery efforts after the Asian tsunami, the Gulf Coast hurricanes, and the Pakistan earthquake (see Table 1);

- New analysis indicating that nearly one-fifth of all new charities are religious organizations; further study also found that religious radio was the fastest growing type of nonprofit from 1999 to 2003;

Giving to religion

- New research on total membership that found that there are 176.48 million adult Americans who indicate membership in faith groups;

- A report that shows those of Jewish faith was recalculated to a total of 4.5 million, up from 3.9 million originally estimated in 2000;

- Projections that the number of Catholic Americans is expected to reach 82 million by 2025;

- Findings that only 20 percent of adult Americans attend religious services weekly; and

- A report showing that the proportion of Americans who are Protestant may be below 50 percent for the first time in history.

Table 1
Charitable contributions to disaster relief in 2005 by U.S. religious and faith-based organizations, partial tally based on information available as of April 2006 (millions of dollars)

	U.S. religious organizations		U.S. faith-based organizations not in religion subsector	
	Documented contributions for the disaster*	Percentage of overall total contributed	Documented contributions for the disaster*	Percentage of overall total contributed
Asian tsunami	151.63	8%	441.74	23%
Gulf Coast hurricanes	263.65	5%	451.51	9%
Pakistan earthquake	15.53	10%	10.45	7%
Total	$430.81	6%	$903.70	12%

*Includes cash and some in-kind donations.
Source: Center on Philanthropy at Indiana University, www.philanthropy.iupui.edu

Religous nonprofits raise millions for victims of disasters

Following the Asian tsunami, the Gulf Coast hurricanes, and the Pakistan earthquake, many religious organizations began raising funds for relief and recovery. According to data collected by the Center on Philanthropy at Indiana University, religious organizations contributed more than $430 million in cash and some in-kind donations to aid victims of disasters in 2005. This estimate includes only contributions to organizations formed for the purpose of religious fellowship, worship, or evangelism, such as the Evangelical Lutheran Church of America or the Southern Baptist Convention, as two examples among many. It includes reported values of giving by more than 1,200 Southern Baptist churches that committed to give 12 to 24 months of assistance to destroyed or damaged Southern Baptist churches through an Adopt a Church program.[3]

More than $904 million in cash and in-kind donations were raised by faith-based organizations that are not actually congregations or affiliations of congregations. These include charitable organizations with religious affiliations, such as Food for the Poor, the Salvation Army, World Vision, and many others.

According to the Center on Philanthropy researchers, the documented giving is a low estimate because it does not include informal donations, such as those churches that adopted pastors and paid their salaries for a period of time, or in-kind donations of food and clothing that were collected at thousands of churches across the country and delivered to regions affected by the disasters. Nor do the estimates include donations by churches that housed and fed hundreds, or perhaps thousands, of people in response to the disasters of 2005, nor the volunteer time contributed by members of congregations.[4]

More than one-fifth of all new charities are religious organizations
More than 35,000 new religious nonprofit organizations were registered with the Internal Revenue Service (IRS) between 1999 and 2003, accounting for more than one-fifth of all new charities during the same time period,[5] according to an analysis of IRS databases conducted by the *Chronicle of Philanthropy* and the National Center for Charitable Statistics at the Urban Institute in Washington, DC. According to the analysis, the nation is experiencing an unparalleled growth in nonprofit organizations. Nearly 40 percent of the nation's charities (more than 300,000 organizations) received tax-exempt status in the past decade. Religious organizations are reported by the study's authors to be experiencing the highest rate of growth. Almost half of the newly registered organizations are considered Christian, but the number of Buddhist and Islamic organizations nearly tripled, to 1,000 charities.

Religious radio was the fastest growing type of nonprofit organization
The number of newly registered charities with the IRS classified as religious radio grew from 46 to 201 between 1999 and 2003, or by 336.9 percent—making it the fastest growing type of nonprofit organization.[6] The analysis of IRS data was conducted by the *Chronicle of Philanthropy* and the Urban Institute in Washington. The increase in religious radio organizations contrasts with a new report by the Barna Group, which reported a decline in the total audience for Christian radio.[7] The research further showed that the decline in listeners to Christian radio has mostly been the result of fewer non-Christians listening. The increase in religious radio organizations is mirrored by a more general growth in newly registered religious media organizations, which include radio, television, and other publishers of religious material, as well as the explosion of religion on the Internet. The number of religious media organizations registered with the IRS grew by 272.4 percent (from 308 organizations in 1999 to 1,147 organizations in 2003).

Researchers recalculate American membership in religious congregations
Dissatisfied with estimations done in 2000 that undercounted traditionally African-

Giving to religion

American churches and many denominations, researchers Roger Finke and Christopher Scheitle recalculated the number of religious adherents or those who hold membership in local synagogues, congregations, temples, or mosques in America.[8] According to Finke and Scheitle, there are 176.48 million adherents, or 62.7 percent of the United States population (see Figure 1). This percentage is significantly higher than the 50 percent estimated by the 2000 Religious Congregations and Membership Study, the study used by the researchers before adding uncounted population groups. In addition to corrections made to some religious denominations, the new estimate includes more than 1 million Hindus, 2 million Buddhists, and 562,844 Americans of other non-Christian religions. The estimate also includes more than 4 million Jewish adherents or those of Jewish affiliation who attend worship services. The rate of adherence to faith groups differs by region. The Northeast has the highest adherence rate at 70.6 percent, whereas the West's adherence rate is the lowest in the nation at 50.6 percent. The Midwest's adherence rate is 60.7 percent, and South's rate is 62.9 percent.

The study also analyzed the percentage of membership in a faith group by the total population of the state. Louisiana and Utah have the highest percentages of their population as members of a faith group: 84.9 percent and 82.9 percent, respectively. Oregon and Washington, on the other hand, have the lowest adherence rate to a faith group of all states: 35.0 percent and 37.3 percent, respectively.

Figure 1
Percentage of adult population who are members of a faith group by region

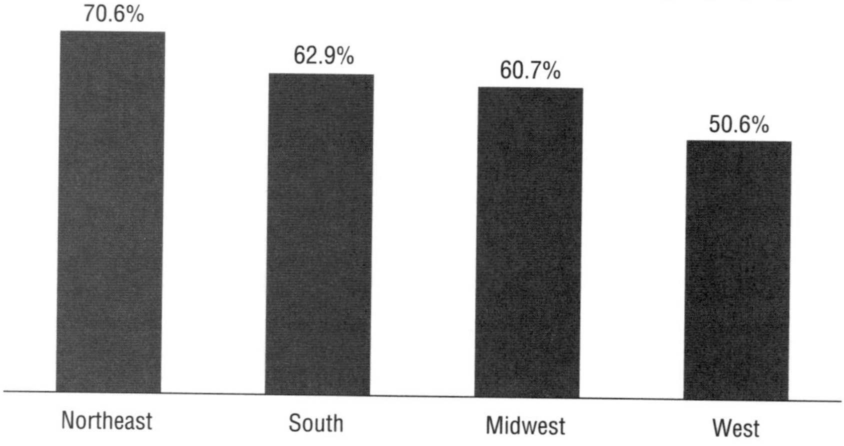

Northeast	South	Midwest	West
70.6%	62.9%	60.7%	50.6%

Sources: Roger Finke and Christopher Scheitle, *Review of Religious Research*, Vol. 47, No. 1, 2005

Giving to religion

Table 2
Percentage of the state population who are members of a faith group

Highest states		Lowest states	
Louisiana	84.9%	Oregon	35.0%
Utah	82.9%	Washington	37.3%
Mississippi	81.8%	Alaska	39.2%
North Dakota	81.0%	Nevada	39.6%
New York	75.7%	Maine	40.1%

Source: Roger Finke and Christopher Scheitle, Pennsylvania State University

4.5 million Americans identify themselves as Jewish by religion

A study released at the inaugural conference of the Steinhardt Social Research Institute at Brandeis University in 2005 reported that the number of Americans identifying themselves as Jewish by religion is 4.5 million.[9] Approximately 6.5 million Americans identify themselves as Jewish more broadly. The National Jewish Population Survey 2000–01 estimated the population to be 3.9 million Jewish Americans by religion and 5.3 million using broader cultural criteria. The American Jewish population figure is expected to decline to between 5 million and 3.6 million by 2051. This is according to Sergio Della Pergola's research, titled *Community Implications of U.S. Jewish Population Change, 2001–2051*, also reported on at the conference.

The U.S. Catholic Church in 2025 will include 17 million more members

Pope John Paul II died in April 2005 after 26 years as the head of the Roman Catholic Church. According to researcher Joseph Harris, Pope Benedict XVI can expect the U.S. Catholic Church to experience an increase in members by 2025.[10] The Catholic population is expected to increase by 17.4 million to 82.7 million (Table 3). Harris estimates approximately four out of five new Catholics will be Latino. The Latino Catholic population as a percentage of the total U.S. Catholic church membership will increase from 38 percent in 2005 to 48 percent by 2025.

Table 3
Projected growth and decline of U.S. Catholic population by 2025

Projected growth	Number of Catholics
• Infant baptisms	19,400,645
• Adult conversions	3,503,524
• International migration	4,553,429
Projected decrease	
• Funerals	−10,015,371
Gain in Catholic membership before estimates of people leaving this faith	17,442,227

Source: Joseph Harris, sharris7@earthlink.net

Giving to religion

Only 20 percent of Americans attend weekly religious services
Researchers C. Kirk Hadaway and Penny Long Marler have developed a strategy
for measuring weekly attendance rates at religious services in the United States.[11]
Their new estimates suggest that only 20.4 percent of the American population
over the age of five attends weekly religious services. This estimate is significantly
lower than that commonly reported in polls.

As shown in Table 4, the weekly attendance rate of Orthodox/other Catholic
congregants is highest at 35.9 percent, whereas the proportion of conservative/
evangelical Protestants attending weekly worship services is 25.4 percent.
Approximately 19.4 percent of all mainline Protestant Americans can be found
worshiping each week. The average weekly attendance for Roman Catholics is
25.4 percent or 16.7 million persons over the age of five.

Table 4
Estimated U.S. attendance at religious services by religious tradition, 2000

Religious tradition	Number of congregations	Average weekly attendance per congregation	Estimated attendees	Percentage of constituent population age 5+
Mainline Protestant	82,183	109.8	9,023,693	19.4
Conservative/evangelical Protestant	178,672	124.4	22,233,944	25.4
Roman Catholic	19,544	853.5	16,680,804	25.4
Orthodox/other Catholic	2,431	193.8	471,128	35.9
Other Christian	36,450	97.9	3,568,455	25.2
Non-Christian	11,720	138.7	1,625,564	18.2
Total	331,000	161.9	53,603,588	20.4

Source: Hadaway and Marler, *Journal for the Scientific Study of Religion* Vol. 44, No. 3, 2005, page 316.

The study also indicated a significant concentration of conservative/evangelical
Protestants in the South and high levels of non-Christians in the Northeast (see
Table 5).

Giving to religion

Table 5
Distribution of U.S. congregations by type of religious tradition, 2000

Religious tradition	Northeast (%)	South (%)	Midwest (%)	West (%)	Estimated total U.S. congregations	Distribution of U.S. congregations
Mainline Protestant	34.5	20.9	31.3	16.0	82,183	24.8
Conservative/evangelical Protestant	34.1	65.5	47.2	52.6	178,672	54.0
Catholic/Orthodox	14.3	2.9	8.3	7.8	21,975	6.6
Other Christian	9.8	9.0	10.7	17.0	36,450	11.0
Non-Christian	7.3	1.7	2.5	6.6	11,720	3.5
Total*	99.9	100.0	100.0	100.0	331,000	99.9

*May not equal 100 due to rounding.
Source: As for Table 4, pages 310 and 312.

The percentage of Protestants in the U.S. declining significantly
Although Protestant congregations are numerous, they tend to be smaller than Catholic parishes, and Protestantism is a declining percentage of the population overall. New research suggests that in the past decade the percentage of Americans identifying themselves as Protestant has declined by 10.7 percentage points.[12] Researchers also found that the proportion of Americans who are Protestants may be less than 50 percent for the first time in U.S. history. Researchers Tom W. Smith and Seokho Kim found that between 1972 and 1993 the percentage of Protestants did not differ significantly, but started a sharp decline mid-1990s. This decline resulted partially from the declining rate of Americans being raised Protestant, which decreased from 75 percent for people born pre-1919 to 49 percent for people born since 1980. In addition, immigration and the increasing share of people identifying themselves as Catholic, nondenominational Christians, or having no religion, may have contributed to the shift.

Other studies of giving to religion released in 2005
A number of reports were released in 2005 by scholars and others examining giving to religion. Those reports include an annual report on Catholic giving; an analysis of welfare spending in one denomination; regional differences in giving to religious organizations; a study of Indiana's giving patterns; the annual release of the State of Church Giving report by empty tomb, inc.; a study of church giving in relation to attendance at religious services; and a look at differences in giving patterns by strict and nonstrict congregations.

Giving to religion

Catholic giving grows in 2004

The International Catholic Stewardship Council (ICSC) continued a multiyear research program on Catholic giving to parishes and dioceses. The Center for Applied Research in the Apostolate (CARA) at Georgetown University annually surveys members of the ICSC on levels of Catholic giving. The ICSC data for 2004 contained replies from 54 percent of the dioceses and archdioceses in the 50 states and the District of Columbia. Joseph Claude Harris, an independent research analyst, used the ICSC data to create an estimate of giving to all parishes in the country. His analysis was prepared for *Giving USA* and contains comparisons between 2003 and 2004, a period that includes the continuing tragedy of scandals resulting from abuse by priests.

Catholics continued to give more money to support parish programs in 2004. Total Catholic offertory collections increased by $227 million, or 3.7 percent between 2003 and 2004. Collections increased by $258 million between 2002 and 2003. The increased funding likely came from two sources: Catholic parishes registered an additional 190,000 households, and the average gift increased from $375 to $384.

Table 6 summarizes parish offertory collections by region. Average household donations were lowest in the Pacific ($184) and Northeast ($290) regions. These two areas had the largest number of households per parish of any region in the country. The Midwest, with the smallest average number of households (344), had the largest average household donation of $885. These data underscore the finding that the cost of operating a parish does not increase when more Catholics register as members.

Welfare spending impacts the charitable spending of Presbyterian churches, but not charitable donations

A study of the Presbyterian Church (USA) from 1994 to 2000 by researcher Daniel Hungerman of Duke University suggests that government spending does not affect church donations, but it does affect the level of charitable spending of congregations in the community.[13] A dollar decrease in nationwide per-capita welfare spending by the government is associated with an average 40 cent increase in per-member spending by Presbyterian congregations in the community. The study also found that higher nationwide unemployment is associated with increased church spending, but not increased charitable contributions. Having a high percentage of individuals in the congregation between the ages of 50 and 64 had the greatest impact on donations to the church, whereas a high percentage of individuals over the age of 84 increased the amount of charitable spending by the church. In communities with higher incomes, congregations had higher levels of donations, but not necessarily higher levels of charitable spending. Finally, smaller churches tended to have higher levels of per-member charitable donations and spending.

Giving to religion

Table 6
Estimated offertory collections for the Roman Catholic Church, 2004

Region	Number of parishes	Total offertory collection ($ in millions)	Registered households	Average household donation ($)	Average parish collection ($)	Average households per parish	Percentage of dioceses reporting
Northeast	5,074	$1,519	5,235,069	$290	$299,369	1,032	53%
South Atlantic	1,499	$825	1,342,639	$614	$550,195	896	56%
South	2,477	$862	2,142,395	$402	$347,945	865	44%
Great Lakes	3,976	$1,405	2,716,524	$517	$353,250	683	66%
Midwest	2,766	$842	950,850	$885	$304,266	344	64%
Mountain	869	$262	795,308	$329	$301,063	915	33%
Pacific	1,634	$595	3,232,333	$184	$364,335	1,978	57%
Total	18,295	$5,310	16,415,118	$384	$344,830	897	54%

Northeast	Connecticut, Maine, Massachusetts, New Hampshire, New York, New Jersey, Pennsylvania, Rhode Island, Vermont
South Atlantic	Delaware, District of Columbia, Florida, Georgia, Maryland, North Carolina, South Carolina, Virginia, West Virginia
South	Alabama, Arkansas, Kentucky, Louisiana, Mississippi, Oklahoma, Tennessee, Texas
Great Lakes	Illinois, Indiana, Michigan, Ohio, Wisconsin
Midwest	Iowa, Kansas, Nebraska, Minnesota, Missouri, North Dakota, South Dakota
Mountain	Arizona, Colorado, Idaho, Montana, Nevada, New Mexico, Utah, Wyoming
Pacific	Alaska, California, Hawaii, Oregon, Washington

Data from: Joseph Claude Harris, sharris7@earthlink.net

Recent release of data indicates regional differences in giving to religious organizations

Households in the Pacific region that donated to religious organizations in 2002 gave, on average, $2,221 to religion. This was a higher average amount than any other region (as shown in Figure 2). This is according to a recent release of data from the Center on Philanthropy Panel Study (COPPS).[14] Of those households that donated to religion in New England, the average amount contributed to religion was $918, the lowest average of all U.S. regions. However, New England households gave, on average, more to secular causes than any other region: $1,190.

Giving to religion

Figure 2
Average total amount contributed per donor household; religious versus secular giving by census region, 2002

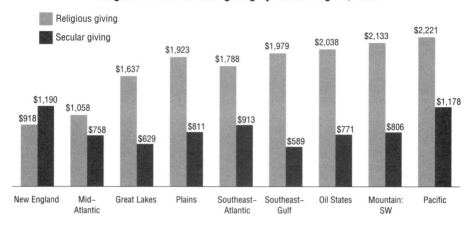

Data Source: Center on Philanthropy Panel Study (COPPS) 2003 Wave

New England	Connecticut, Maine, Massachusetts, New Hampshire, Rhode Island, Vermont
Mid-Atlantic	New York, New Jersey, Pennsylvania
Great Lakes	Illinois, Indiana, Michigan, Ohio, Wisconsin
Plains	Iowa, Kansas, Nebraska, Minnesota, Missouri, North Dakota, South Dakota
Southeast Atlantic	Delaware, District of Columbia, Florida, Georgia, Maryland, North Carolina, South Carolina, Virginia, West Virginia
Southeast Gulf	Alabama, Kentucky, Mississippi, Tennessee
Oil States	Arkansas, Louisiana, Oklahoma, Texas
Mountain and Southwest	Arizona, Colorado, Idaho, Montana, Nevada, New Mexico, Utah, Wyoming
Pacific	Alaska, California, Hawaii, Oregon, Washington

Researchers also noted that in four regions—New England, Mid-Atlantic, Great Lakes, and the Pacific—the percentage of total religious contributions was lower than the percentage of household income in the United States, as shown in Figure 3. In contrast, 10.1 percent of U.S. household income is earned by families in the Oil States region, but the region gives an estimated 14.0 percent of the nation's total contributions to religious organizations.

Giving to religion

Figure 3
Percentage of total US household income and percentage of total US donations to religion by census region, 2002

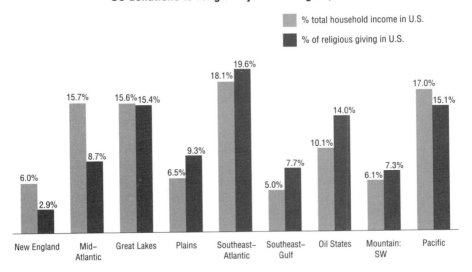

Legend:
- % total household income in U.S.
- % of religious giving in U.S.

Data by region:
- New England: 6.0%, 2.9%
- Mid-Atlantic: 15.7%, 8.7%
- Great Lakes: 15.6%, 15.4%
- Plains: 6.5%, 9.3%
- Southeast-Atlantic: 18.1%, 19.6%
- Southeast-Gulf: 5.0%, 7.7%
- Oil States: 10.1%, 14.0%
- Mountain: SW: 6.1%, 7.3%
- Pacific: 17.0%, 15.1%

Data Source: Center on Philanthropy Panel Study (COPPS) 2003 Wave
For a definition of regions, see Figure 2.

More New England households give to religion, but give a lower amount
A study titled A Closer Look at New England Giving was released in November 2005 by six regional grantmaking associations and community foundations in the New England region.[15] The study found that nearly 49 percent of New Englanders give to religious organizations, compared with 45 percent of all households in the United States. However, the average total contributed to religious organizations by New England households is 47 percent less than the average U.S. total ($918 by New Englanders versus $1,743 nationally). In addition, New Englanders give a much smaller share of income to religious organizations (0.6% versus 2.1% nationally).

New study released on giving in Indiana
Religious organizations received the largest share of total giving to charity (39.5 percent) by Indiana households, corporations, and foundations in 2003. This is according to a study called *Indiana Gives 2004*, released in 2005 by the Center on Philanthropy at Indiana University.[16] This study indicates that 97 percent of those contributions to religious causes came from Indiana households, 1 percent from Indiana corporations and corporate foundations, and 2 percent from Indiana private and community foundations. More than 60 percent of Indiana households reported giving to religion in 2003, with an average gift from those donors of $1,561. Just

over one in five businesses in the *Indiana Gives* survey reported making, on average, a $25,317 gift to religious organizations (23 of 103). Family-owned businesses were most likely to report donating to religious organizations. Of the foundations in the study, 23 percent contributed to religious organizations, with an average gift of $561,672. However, the median foundation grant amount to religion was $13,271. Excluding the Lilly Endowment, the average total granted in 2003 to religion by Indiana foundations in the *Indiana Gives* study was $54,101, and the median was $13,225.

Protestant congregants are giving a smaller percentage of their income to church, 2003

Per-member giving to Protestant religious congregations declined from 3.1 percent of disposable personal income in 1968 to 2.59 percent in 2003, according to the *State of Church Giving Through 2003*, an annual report released by empty tomb, inc.[17] Although total contributions to Protestant congregations have increased by 76 percent since 1968, per-capita disposable income has increased by 111 percent. The report also noted a 42 percent decrease in per-member giving to benevolences from 0.7 percent of total contributions in 1968 to 0.4 percent in 2003. The study is largely based on an analysis of 31 Protestant denominations obtained through the *Yearbook of American and Canadian Churches* and compares the Protestant contributions to per-capita disposable income for all U.S. households.

Changes in giving to religious organizations is reflected in changes in attendance at religious services

A study completed in June 2005 by researchers Mark Wilhelm, Patrick Rooney, and Eugene Tempel found that changes in giving to religious organizations may be due at least in part to generational differences in religious involvement.[18] Using the Center on Philanthropy Panel Study (COPPS), the researchers looked at patterns of giving to religious organizations and religious attendance with both the prewar (born 1924–1938) and baby boomer (born 1951–1965) generations over the course of their lives. The study found that baby boomers give less than expected to religious organizations and attend less. Specifically, the pattern is most noticeable among Catholic baby boomers as opposed to Protestant boomers. The researchers argue that changes in giving to religious organizations may reflect changes in religious involvement.

Conservative congregations have a higher average level of giving

A study of churches' giving patterns from five denominations has found that strict, conservative congregations, such as those in the Assembly of God and Southern Baptist denominations, have a higher average giving level and have fewer congregants giving smaller donations or not giving at all to their church (also called cheap- or free-riding).[19] Researchers Daniel Olson and Paul Perl note that the cause is not due to a few generous donors or because each member is giving more. Rather, they suggest that a combination of strict rules and/or conservative theology limits the number of free- or cheap-riders by encouraging low-end givers to increase their giving or by discouraging those who would free-ride from participating in church at all. In general, the average amounts contributed are higher at strict congregations than at nonstrict congregations ($2,627 versus $1,582). Strict congregations have only one-half to two-thirds as many of their contributions below $1,000 per year. In addition, strict congregations have twice as many contributions at levels higher than $2,500 per year. For instance, the highest 2.5 percent of givers in strict congregations give, on average, $9,500 per year versus $7,000 per year in nonstrict congregations.

---

1   The *Giving USA* estimate for giving to religion in 2005 includes a revised estimate for giving to religion in 2004. New data from the National Council of Churches about giving to Protestant churches in 2004 and data on Catholic parish and other Catholic giving in 2004 were incorporated to form the revised estimate. Additional data on contributions to other religious organizations, such as media ministries, were also included. The revised estimate for giving for religion in 2004 is $87.95 billion or a growth rate of 4.0 percent from 2003 to 2004.

2   Estimated total from the Center on Philanthropy at Indiana University, January 2006, www.philanthropy.iupui.edu/Hurricane_Katrina.html.

3   Anthony K. Valley, 1,200-plus churches vow to adopt damaged churches on Gulf, *In The Faith–A Chronicle of the Christian Faith*, September 28, 2005, www.inthefaith.com.

4   See J. Price, Keep the faith, and they will come; Religious folk step forward to clean up after Katrina, *Washington Times*, October 27, 2005 and M. Noah, Project HOAH to draw thousands of Baptists to New Orleans to rebuild homes, churches, North American Mission Board, www.namb.net, for some examples.

5   Harvy Lipman, Religion and Education Groups Grew the Most, *Chronicle of Philanthropy*, January 6, 2005, www.philanthropy.com.

6   Ian Wilhelm, Religious Radio: Spreading the Word, *Chronicle of Philanthropy*, January 6, 2005, www.philanthropy.com.

7   More People Use Christian Media than Attend Church, *The Barna Group*, March 14, 2005, www.barna.org/FlexPage.aspx?PageCMD=Print.

8   Roger Finke and Christopher Scheitle, Accounting for the Uncounted: Computing Correctives for the 2000 RCMS Data, *Review of Religious Research*, Vol. 47, No. 1, 2005, http://rra.hartsem.edu/finkescheitlearticle.htm.

9   Richard Asinof, Counting American Jews, *Focus on Issues*, Brandeis University, November 8, 2005.

10   Joseph Claude Harris, The Catholic Church is Not Foundering: More Members, More Money, More Ministers, 2005, sharris7@earthlink.net.

11   C. Kirk Hadaway and Penny Long Marler, How Many Americans Attend Worship Each Week? An Alternative Approach to Measurement, *Journal for the Scientific Study of Religion*, Vol. 44, No. 3, 2005.

12   Tom W. Smith and Seokho Kim, The Vanishing Protestant Majority, *Journal for the Scientific Study of Religion*, Vol. 44, No. 2, 2005.

13   Daniel M. Hungerman, Are Church and State Substitutes? Evidence from the 1996 Welfare Reform, *Journal of Public Economics*, Vol. 89 No 11–12, December 2005.

14   Source of data, the Center on Philanthropy Panel Study (COPPS) 2003, data analyzed by researchers at the Center on Philanthropy at Indiana University.

15   A Closer Look at New England Giving, sponsored by: Associated Grant Makers, Connecticut Council for Philanthropy, Main Philanthropy Center, New Hampshire Charitable Foundation, The Rhode Island Foundation, and the Vermont Community Foundation, prepared by the Center on Philanthropy at Indiana University, November 2005, www.nhcf.org/images/Regional_differences_in_Giving._Nov_08_05.pdf.

Giving to religion

16   *Indiana Gives 2004*, the Center on Philanthropy at Indiana University, www.philanthorpy.iupui.edu/.

17   John L. and Sylvia Ronsvalle, *The State of Church Giving Through 2003*: 15th edition, empty tomb, inc., 2005.

18   Mark Wilhelm, Patrick Rooney, and Eugene Tempel, Changes in Religious Giving Reflect Changes in Involvement: Life-Cycle and Cross-Cohort Evidence on Religious Giving, Secular Giving, and Attendance, *Working Paper, Center on Philanthropy at Indiana University*, June 2005, www.philanthropy.iupui.edu/working_papers.html.

19   Daniel V.A. Olson and Paul Perl, Free and Cheap Riding in Strict, Conservative Churches, *Journal for the Scientific Study of Religion*, 44(2), 2005.

Giving to education

- Charitable gifts to educational organizations reached an estimated $38.56 billion in 2005, an increase of 13.1 percent compared with 2004 (9.4 percent adjusted for inflation).

- Educational organizations received 14.8 percent of estimated total giving.

- The increase was driven by large organizations, most of which are colleges and universities. Among the large institutions that responded to the *Giving USA* survey, nearly two-thirds (64 percent) reported an increase averaging $11 million. All sizes of educational organizations in the *Giving USA* survey reported growth in charitable receipts in 2005.

- Anecdotal reports suggest that at least part of the increase seen in giving to educational institutions in 2005 is attributable to the fact that donors prepaid pledges to benefit from the tax advantages available in the Katrina Emergency Tax Relief Act. This parallels the 14.9 percent increase in giving to education in 1986, when donors made gifts before tax rate changes for 1987 reduced the tax benefit for contributions itemized as tax deductions.

- Donations to educational institutions after Hurricane Katrina included funding for institutions in New Orleans to defray the costs of rebuilding, contributions toward tuition for students relocating to other schools, and a major gift of $50 million for rebuilding public schools in Mississippi.

Giving USA survey findings

The education subsector includes colleges and universities, scholarship funds such as the United Negro College Fund and Scholarship America, private schools for grades kindergarten through high school, tutoring programs, private libraries, supporting organizations raising funds for public libraries or public schools, vocational institutes, organizations formed to provide adult continuing education, and educational service organizations, including the foundations formed by fraternities and sororities. Educational organizations are in section B of the National Taxonomy of Exempt Entities. The *Giving USA* estimate includes funds given to public higher education, thanks to the estimates created by the Council for Aid to Education.

As with all *Giving USA* estimates, the amount estimated in giving to educational organizations includes gifts received of cash, cash equivalents (securities), and in-kind gifts (artwork, patents, real estate, and other items of value). *Giving USA* tries to exclude from its estimates the value of deferred or planned gift commitments and new pledges.

Tables 1 through 3 summarize key findings from the *Giving USA* survey.[1] Table 1 shows that in all sizes of organizations in the education subsector, average and median amounts received in charitable gifts increased in 2005 compared with 2004.

Giving to education

Table 1
Charitable revenue received by educational organizations in 2004 and 2005 by organizational size

Organizational size	Number of completed surveys	2004 average ($)	2004 median ($)	2005 average ($)	2005 median ($)
Large	44	65,102,647	41,853,531	69,841,957	49,761,380
Medium	51	2,568,274	1,573,659	2,764,853	1,635,100
Small	13	308,385	40,602	377,166	42,400

Large denotes organizations that receive $20 million or more in charitable revenue; *medium* is used for organizations having revenue between $1 million and $19.99 million, and *small* is for organizations that have charitable revenue of less than $1 million.

Table 2 summarizes the average and median increases or decreases in charitable revenue reported for 2005 by organizational size.

Table 2
Increases or decreases in charitable revenue of educational organizations, 2005

Organizational size	Number	Percentage of organizations in size group	Average change ($)	Average change (%)	Median change ($)	Median change (%)
Large						
Increase	28	64	11,118,288	26	6,012,493	15
Decrease	14	32	-7,216,095	-17	-4,229,924	-7
No change	2	5	-885,536	<1	-885,536	<1
Total	44	101*				
All large organizations			4,739,310	11	1,564,355	7
Medium						
Increase	29	57	921,709	73	323,303	26
Decrease	7	33	-981,480	-34	-440,982	-24
No change	5	10	-3,768	<1	0	0
Total	51	100				
All medium organizations			196,580	30	68,619	8
Small						
Increase	13	100	68,782	67	16,160	25
Decrease	0	–	–	–	–	–
No change	0	–	–	–	–	–
Total	13	100				
All small organizations			68,782	67	16,150	25

*Total does not equal 100 due to rounding.

Table 3 shows bequest receipts by organizational size. Although large organizations reported an increase in average bequest amounts received in 2005 compared with 2004, the median declined. Half the bequest gift amounts received are below the median. In medium-sized organizations, the average and the median dropped in 2005.

Table 3
Bequest receipts by organizational size, 2005

Organizational size	Percentage with bequest revenues	2004 average ($)	2004 median ($)	2005 average ($)	2005 median ($)
Large	87	8,790,550	8,046,945	9,228,795	7,124,789
Medium	43	595,768	313,942	546,262	185,658
Small*	23	405,087	30,000	525,992	525,992

*For 2005, only a few small educational organizations provided bequest information. The values are reported here although the number of responses is too low to use in making statistical inferences about all small educational organizations.

2005 sees a major increase in number of announced gifts to education
In 2005, the Center on Philanthropy found 213 gifts of $5 million or more for educational institutions, including higher education and K-12 education. The announced gifts (some of which were pledges) totaled approximately $3.8 billion. In 2004, there were 149 such gifts totaling $2.6 billion. The figures are indications but not proof of the change in education giving. The number of announced gifts rose by 34 percent and the amount increased by 46 percent. Among the largest education gifts announced in 2005 were:

- $202 million from George Soros, a financier in New York, to the Central European University;[2]

- $169 million, in kind, to the University of Texas at El Paso from General Motors, EDS, Sun Microsystems and UGS;[3]

- $103 million to Tufts University from Pierre and Pam Omidyar, co-founders of e-Bay, to create a micro-finance loan program;[4] and

- $100 million to Arizona State University from Ira and Mary Lou Fulton, regional real estate developers, for the College of Education.[5]

Some gifts reportedly made at the end of 2005 were not announced formally until 2006, including a contribution of $165 million to Oklahoma State University from T. Boone Pickens, a gift of $101 million to Princeton University from Peter Lewis; and an anonymous donation of $100 million to Johns Hopkins University.[6]

Giving to university-based hospitals or schools of medicine included in giving to education

Gifts to universities and colleges are recorded in the education sector, yet a substantial percentage are for health-related purposes, whether for research or patient care. The largest such gifts in 2005 are as follows:

- Larry Ellison, founder of Oracle Corporation, announced a gift of $115 million to Harvard University for a program to analyze global health spending;[7]

- Jan Vilcek, a microbiology professor and inventor, pledged $105 million to New York University School of Medicine to recruit scientists and upgrade laboratories;[8]

- The Broad Institute of MIT and Harvard received $100 million from the Los Angeles-based Broad Foundation to support the institute's research in genomic medicine;[9] and

- The University of Texas Southwestern Medical Center received $50 million from Harold Simmons, a Dallas investor, and his wife Annette. The funding is for cancer research and treatment.[10]

Katrina Emergency Tax Relief Act stimulated some giving to education, other subsectors, but total impact cannot yet be evaluated

Lorry I. Lokey, founder of Business Wire, a company that distributes news releases, credited the Katrina Emergency Tax Relief Act (KETRA) with spurring some of his gifts in 2005. Mr. Lokey paid the last half of his $20 million gift to Stanford University for a science building ahead of schedule in part because of the tax benefits of the act. [11] The *Chronicle of Philanthropy* reported an estimate that an additional $220 million was donated to 150 charities working with the Sharpe Group, a fundraising consulting firm.[12] Robert F. Sharpe, Jr., head of that firm, was quoted as estimating the total impact of KETRA in the billions of dollars. A summary of the charitable giving provision of the tax relief act is in the legal-legislative chapter of this book.

There are no data to permit national estimates of how many donors took advantage of the additional tax benefits nor of how much these donors contributed in 2005. The situation is somewhat like an earlier time when at least some donors pre-paid gifts in 1986 to maximize the tax benefits of giving before an announced reduction in tax rates took place in 1987. With the prepayment in 1986, individual charitable giving rose because the tax rate was higher (and the corresponding tax benefit for a charitable gift deduction was higher). The following year, in 1987 after the tax rate dropped, individual charitable giving fell below the levels it might have reached.[13]

Model document released to aid public higher education institutions and the foundations created to raise money for them

Many public colleges and universities (as well as public school systems, public hospitals, and other public organizations) are funded in part through gifts made to an

Giving to education

affiliated foundation that was founded as a private, 501(c)(3) nonprofit corporation with the purpose of raising and managing private support for the designated partner institution. The Council for Advancement and Support of Education (CASE) and the Association of Governing Boards (AGB) collaborated to release the "AGB-CASE Illustrative Memorandum of Understanding Between a Foundation and Host Institution or System."[14] The language in the illustrative document outlines possible relationships between the foundation and the institution; foundation responsibilities, including fund raising and asset management; funding and administration of the foundation, including responsibilities for data and records management and office expenses; and terms of the agreement, including a process for ending it.

The Center on Philanthropy finds 15 percent of households give to education; the average gift is $416 a year

The Center on Philanthropy analyzed data collected in 2003 about giving in 2002 based on a survey of more than 8,000 households. Limiting the analysis to a section of the survey that contains a nationally representative sample of families, the Center found that 15 percent of households reported gifts to education and that among those who gave for this cause, the average total amount contributed was $416. Education giving accounted for approximately 5 percent of household contributions.[15]

This study did not reach a large number of families with the nation's top two percent of wealth, and *Giving USA* estimates that the highest-wealth families may account for more than 40 percent of household or individual giving. Higher education is frequently the top recipient subsector of contributions from these households. The Center on Philanthropy's list of announced gifts of $5 million and above shows that nearly one-half of the dollar value donated by individuals and families goes to higher education institutions ($3.6 billion in 2005 to higher education out of a total value for all gifts on the list of $7.5 billion, or 48 percent). More about the panel study findings and methods can be found in the Overview section of this book.

Council for Aid to Education finds growth in gifts to higher education in 2004-2005 fiscal year

The Council for Aid to Education reported an increase of 4.9 percent in contributions to colleges and universities in the United States between 2003-2004 and 2004-2005.[16] Total higher education giving reached an estimated $25.6 billion in 2004-2005. Figure 1 shows trends in giving by different types of donors for higher education. The increase reported for 2004-2005 was driven in part by gifts from alumni, whose giving rose by 6 percent in 2004-2005. Foundation grants and gifts from other supporting organizations also rose. Corporate charitable support, however, did not increase in 2005. Gifts from other individuals, a highly variable source of contributions, fell in 2004-2005 compared with the prior year.

Giving to education

Figure 1
Sources of voluntary support of higher education, 1994-1995 to 2004-2005
($ in billions)

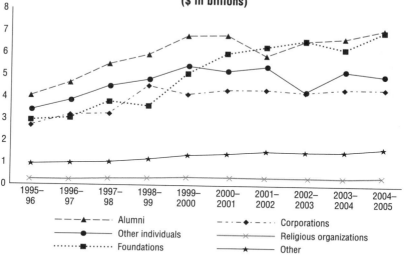

Source: Council for Aid to Education

$1 billion or more higher education campaigns closed or announced in 2005

Universities use campaigns to raise billions for facilities, faculty recruitment, scholarships, medical research, and more. In 2005, at least six institutions announced the conclusion of a campaign with a goal of at least $1 billion. One institution announced the opening of the public phase of a $1 billion campaign. Table 4 summarizes reported campaigns in 2005.

Table 4
Education fundraising campaigns of $1 billion or more closed or announced in 2005
($ in billions)

Campaigns closed

Institution	Announced	Closed	Goal ($)	Raised ($)	Source	As of
U. of California at Los Angeles	May 1997	Dec. 2005	2.4	3.053	www.ucla.edu	2/16/06
U. of Iowa	June 2002	Dec. 2005	1.0	1.058	www.uiowa.edu	2/6/06
U. of California at San Francisco	July 1998	June 2005	1.4	1.665	http://insider.ucsf.edu	7/05
U. of Arizona	Oct. 2001	June 2005	1.4	1.196	http://uanews.org	11/23/05
U. of Arkansas	Oct. 2001	June 2005	1.0	1.046	http://dailyheadlines.uark.edu	9/13/05
Stanford U.	Oct. 2000	Dec. 2005	1.0	1.135	www.stanford.edu	1/10/06

Campaigns announced

Institution	Announced	Closed	Goal ($)	Raised ($)	Source	As of
North Carolina State U.	Sept. 2005	June 2008	1.0	0.900	http://campaign.ncsu.edu	5/16/06

Giving to education

Target Analysis group tracks direct mail results for 77 universities; finds growth in 2003-2004 fiscal year compared with 2002-2003

In an "Index of University Fundraising," Target Analysis Group presented findings based on actual donations made in response to direct mail solicitations sent by 77 participating universities and colleges.[17] These donations came to about $470 million, or 2 percent of the Council for Aid to Education's total estimated giving to higher education in 2003-2004.

Key data from annual studies summarized

Table 5 presents three years of data from several studies appearing annually about giving to education. Web site addresses are provided so readers can access the full reports.

Table 5
Key findings from other studies

$5 million dollar list, gifts from individuals to education Center on Philanthropy at Indiana University, www.philanthropy.iupui.edu			
	2003	2004	2005
Number, higher education	100	145	204
Largest gift, higher education	$100 million from Irwin & Joan Jacobs to University of California at San Diego	$300 million from Wisconsin United for Health Foundation, one gift each of that amount to Medical College of Wisconsin and to University of Wisconsin Medical School	$165 million to Oklahoma State University for the athletics program from T. Boone Pickens, announced in early 2006 as made in the last days of 2005
Dollars to higher education as percentage of all gifts on list	45 percent	21.5 percent (54.7 percent, an unusually high amount, was given to private foundations)	47.5 percent
Number, K–12 education	9	4	9
Largest gift, K–12 education	$18 million, estate of Maude Woods Wodehouse to Seabury Hall	$45 million, a group of anonymous donors to Jewish day schools in Boston	$50 million to public schools in Mississippi from James Barksdale
Dollars to K–12 education as a percentage of all gifts on list	4 percent	0.9 percent	2.4 percent

Giving to education

Foundation Giving Trends: Update on Funding Priorities
Grants to education
Foundation Center, www.fdncenter.org

	2002	2003	2004
Median grant amount	$25,000	$28,000	$30,000
Average grant amount	$158,903	$142,910	$141,128
Education funding as a percentage of grant dollars	26.4 percent	24.5 percent	23.4 percent

CASE Report of Educational Fundraising Campaigns
Council for Advancement and Support of Education, www.case.org

From all reporting institutions	2002–2003	2003-2004	2004-2005
Percentage of goal received from top 10 percent of donors	89	87	72
Percentage of goal received from top 1 percent of donors	75	66	54
Mean percentage of alumni who gave to campaign	27	29	Not available as of April 2006
Planned (deferred) commitments as percent of total (present value)	10	10	Not available as of April 2006

National Independent School Facts at a Glance
National Association of Independent Schools
Taken from reports dated 2003–2004; 2004–2005, and 2005-2006 www.nais.org

	2002–2003	2003-2004	2004-2005
Average annual giving per student	$1,348	$1,489	$1,588
Average endowment per student	$29,246	$33,668	$33,639
Giving by alumni Average gift Participation	$276 20.7%	$302 20.9%	$358 16%
Giving by current parents Average gift Participation	$859 62.3%	$975 64.1%	$1,039 63%
Giving by trustees Average gift Participation	$4,334 92.2%	$4,867 93.1%	$5,150 93%

Giving to education

IRS tax-exempt Organizations in Education Charities and Other Tax-exempt Organizations, 2002, 2003, and 2004 *Statistics of Income Bulletin*, www.irs.gov			
	2002	2003	2004
Number of organizations	38,629	41,153	45,163
Charitable revenue*	$51.92 billion	$52.47 billion	$54.73 billion

*Includes direct public support (from individuals, foundations, and corporations, as in *Giving USA*) and indirect public support (transfers from other nonprofits, such as United Way, or a membership association or other collective funding source).

1   *Giving USA* sent surveys to 1,402 educational organizations, including every organization that raised $20 million or more in charitable gifts in 2003 or 2004 and a random sample of medium-sized and small organizations. Responses came from 131 organizations (a return rate of 9.3 percent). Not all responses were complete, leaving 108 that could be analyzed. One-quarter of the large organizations responded. Large organizations account for one-quarter of all giving to education. The sample was selected based on charitable revenue received circa 2003 (includes some organizations that reported only in 2002 or only in 2001) supplemented with information appearing on the *Chronicle of Philanthropy* list of the 400 charities receiving the most charitable revenue in 2004. Many studies of nonprofit organizations receive a response rate of around 10 percent. *Giving USA* has analyzed the responses of "early responders" and "late responders" and found no statistically significant difference in the amount of change reported by these two groups. If nonresponders are similar to early or late responders in the amount of change they experience in charitable revenue, the low response rate will not materially affect the estimated rate of change.

2   George Soros pledges $202.4 million to Central European University, Central European University press release, June 16, 2005. Viewed at *Philanthropy News Digest*, http://fdncenter.org.

3   Partnership makes multimillion dollar donation to UTEP engineering programs, General Motors press release, April 18, 2005, www.gm.com.

4   K. Arenson, Tufts is getting gift of $100 million, with rare strings, *New York Times*, November 4, 2005.

5   Ira A. and Mary Lou Fulton give Arizona State University $100 million for Christmas, Arizona State University press release, December 24, 2005, www.asu.edu.

6   All three of these gifts are mentioned in the February 23, 2006, issue of the *Chronicle of Philanthropy* as among the donations made in 2005. Media reports begin for these gifts in late January or early February.

7   D. Bank, Oracle's Ellison gives $115 million to Harvard study, *Wall Street Journal*, June 30, 2005, www.wsj.com.

8   R. Perez-Pena, Research scientist's $105 million is a way to give back to NYU, *New York Times*, August 12, 2005.

9   Broad Foundation awards $100 million to Broad Institute of MIT, Harvard, press release, December 1, 2005. Viewed at *Philanthropy News Digest*, http://fdncenter.org.

10   Simmons family donates $50 million to Dallas medical school, Associated Press, November 2, 2005. Viewed at www.lexis-nexis.com.

11   M. Di Mento, N. Lewis, How the wealthy give: List of generous donors in 2005 includes some little-known names, *Chronicle of Philanthropy*, February 23, 2006, www.philanthropy.com.

12   H. Hall, A special Katrina-inspired tax break produced mixed results for charities, *Chronicle of Philanthropy*, January 26, 2006, www.philanthropy.iupui.edu.

Giving to education

13   The Tax Reform Act of 1986 lowered the tax advantages for giving for contributions after January 1, 1987. The law's provisions were well-publicized, and deductions claimed in 1986 were up 12.2 percent. The following year, in contrast, saw an 8.8 percent decrease (all before adjustment for inflation). Scholars attribute some of the rise in 1986 and the following year's decline to "pre-paid" gifts made in 1986 rather than to the stock market decline in October 1987.

14   CASE, AGB develop model agreement between educational institutions and affiliated foundations, Council for Advancement and Support of Education press release, March 24, 2005, www.case.org.

15   Findings from the Center on Philanthropy Panel Study are available at www.philanthropy.iupui.edu.

16   Contributions to colleges and universities up by 4.9% to $25.6 billion, Council for Aid to Education press release, February 16, 2006, www.cae.org.

17   See report at www.targetanalysis.com.

Giving to foundations

- The Foundation Center estimates approximately $21.70 billion in gifts to foundations in 2005. This represents approximately 8.3 percent of all giving in 2005.

- The Foundation Center tracks active, grantmaking foundations and reports a total of 65,140 foundations in 2004. The figure for 2005 from the Foundation Center will be released in early 2007.

- In prior years, the Foundation Center has found that for every $1 billion given to new foundations, approximately $20 billion is given to existing foundations.

- *Giving USA* reports the amount of giving to foundations using the Foundation Center's report of gifts received as listed on IRS Forms 990-PF. A foundation may receive announced gifts, as from an estate, many years after the initial announcement.

- In January 2006, the search tool FoundationSearch.com reported 1,624 foundations registered since January 2005 that had not yet filed their first IRS Form 990-PF.

- Foundation Center findings about gifts to foundations in 2005 will be released in the 2007 edition of *Foundation Growth and Giving Estimates*.

No $1 billion bequests to foundations announced in 2005

Since 2001, charitable bequests to "philanthropy and voluntarism" organizations, which include foundations, have averaged 34 percent of all giving to foundations.[1] Very few large donations to foundations were announced from estates in 2005. In 2005, the largest estate gift announced to a foundation was $25 million from the estate of Madeleine and Thomas Schneider of Ohio to the Findlay-Hancock County Community Foundation in that state.[2] This follows several years in which announced gifts to foundations included bequests of $1 billion or more from the estates of Susan Buffett (2004), Walter Annenberg (2002), William Hewlett (2001), and William Daniels (2000).[3]

Data about giving to foundations is compiled by the Foundation Center using IRS forms 990-PF. For large charitable bequests, it can take several years for assets to transfer from the estate to the named beneficiary. The Foundation Center releases its *Foundation Yearbook* in summer and reports its findings for the year that ended 18 months earlier (in summer 2006, the yearbook about 2004 will be available).

Foundation Center report of foundations ranked by value of gifts received, 2004

The Foundation Center posts online lists ranking foundations on various criteria.[4] Data for 2004 are the most recent available in spring 2006. In 2004, 10 independent foundations accounted for 15 percent ($2.0 billion) of the $13.37 billion received by all independent foundations that year. Table 1 summarizes the findings about the

Giving to foundations

independent foundations in 2004 that received the largest amounts in gifts. Data for 2005 will be released by the Foundation Center in mid- to late 2007.

Table 1
Top ten independent foundations, by gift amount received, 2004
($ in millions)

Foundation	Total Received
Bill & Melinda Gates Foundation	627.00
Walton Family Foundation	492.03
W.K. Kellogg Foundation	198.73
Cummings Foundation	125.07
William K Bowes, Jr. Foundation	114.42
Howard G. Buffett Foundation	101.40
E.M. Lynn Foundation	101.20
Welborn Baptist Foundation	90.87
Wallace Global Fund	86.50
AVI CHAI Foundation	86.00
Total	2,023.22

Source: Source: The Foundation Center, FC Stats: 50 Largest Foundations by Gifts Received, 2004, www.fdncenter.org.

Foundation Center reports $1.2 billion in gifts to new foundations, 2003

The Foundation Center's *Foundation Yearbook* of 2005 reported 1,555 more active grantmaking foundations in 2003 compared with 2002.[5] These new foundations received $1.2 billion in gifts in 2003.[6] Total giving to community foundations, independent foundations, and operating foundations in 2003 was $21.62 billion.[7] This means that newly formed foundations received about 6 percent of dollars donated to foundations in 2003.

Research done at FoundationSearch.com, an online resource from Metasoft, showed that 1,624 foundations were registered with the Internal Revenue Service between January 2005 and January 2006.[8] These foundations had not filed IRS Form 990-PF as of early 2006. Some may become active grantmaking foundations and be included in the Foundation Center data for 2005, to be released in 2007.

Five large operating foundations received $1.63 billion in 2004

Among the 50 foundations receiving the highest amount of gifts in 2004 were five operating foundations accounting for $1.63 billion of the $2.8 billion total received by operating foundations that year. All of the foundations classified as operating foundations are structured by their corporate donors as programs for giving pharmaceutical products. Table 2 shows the operating foundations and the amounts reported by the Foundation Center as gifts received.

Giving to foundations

Table 2
Top five operating foundations, by gift amount received, 2004
($ in millions)

Foundation	Total Received
Merk Patient Assistance Program	520.04
Bristol-Myers Squibb Patient Assistance Foundation	516.94
Janssen Ortho Patient Assistance Foundation	323.75
Roche Patient Assistance Foundation	173.80
Boehringer Ingelheim Cares Foundation	98.68
Total	1,633.21

Source: Source: The Foundation Center, FC Stats: 50 Largest Foundations
by Gifts Received, 2004, www.fdncenter.org.

Community Foundation survey for 2004 puts Tulsa Community Foundation at top of list for new gifts received

Each year, the Columbus Foundation surveys community foundations in the United States and reports their total gifts received, total assets, and total grantmaking. For 2004, this study reported 636 community foundations receiving $4.2 billion in new gifts. The top ten recipients account for $1.25 billion, or 30 percent of the total. The top 10 gift recipients are shown in Table 3.

Table 3
Top ten community foundations in the United States, by gift amount received, 2004
($ in millions)

Community foundation	Total Received
Tulsa Community Foundation OK	$271.58
Peninsula Community Foundation CA	156.27
Community Foundation Silicon Valley CA	137.17
California Community Foundation	132.07
Greater Kansas City Community Foundation MO	131.19
The Seattle Foundation WA	101.12
Community Foundation for Greater Atlanta GA	83.81
New York Community Trust	83.44
Foundation for the National Capital Region DC	77.85
Communities Foundation of Texas	77.54
Total	$1,252.04

Source: Community Foundation Survey, www.columbusfoundation.org.

Key findings from other studies

To permit readers to compare findings over time, *Giving USA* presents some key data points from the Foundation Center and the Community Foundation studies from 2002 through 2004 in Table 4. Web site addresses are provided to help readers quickly access the original reports.

Table 4
Key findings from other studies

Gifts to foundations* *Foundation Yearbook*, 2004, 2005 editions and *Foundation Growth and Giving Estimates*, 2006 www.fdncenter.org			
	2002	2003	2004
Independent foundations, new gifts received	$13.95 billion	$15.85 billion	$13.65 billion
Community foundations	$ 3.18 billion	$ 3.48 billion	$3.86 billion
Operating foundations	$ 2.03 billion	$ 2.30 billion	$2.81 billion
Total for these three types of foundation	$19.16 billion	$21.63 billion	$20.32 billion

*Data for 2005 will be available from the Foundation Center in 2007.

Gifts to community foundations, including inactive ones Survey of community foundations Columbus Foundation, www.columbusfoundation.org			
	2002	2003	2004
New gifts received	$3.25 billion	$3.80 billion	$4.20 billion

1   *Giving USA* calculation using data from the U.S. Department of the Treasury for charitable bequests by type of recipient and data from the Foundation Center for total giving to foundations.
2   Center on Philanthropy, Million Dollar List, 2005, www.philanthropy.iupui.edu.
3   Compiled from lists of gifts of $5 million and above printed in *Giving USA*, editions of 2002 through 2005.
4   The Foundation Center, Researching philanthropy, Grantmaker Stats, www.fdncenter.org.
5   S. Lawrence, J. Atienza, A. Barve, *Foundation Yearbook*, 2005, see Table 2, page 8. Foundation Center. www.fdncenter.org
6   Ibid., p. 13.
7   L. Renz and S. Lawrence, *Foundation Growth and Giving Estimates: 2004 Preview*, The Foundation Center, 2005, p. 5, wwwfdncenter.org.
8   *Giving USA* staff calculation based on listings obtained in January 2006 for new foundations registered in the prior 12 months.

Giving to health

- Giving to organizations in the health subsector is estimated to be $22.54 billion in 2005. This is 8.7 percent of total estimated giving.

- In current dollars, giving to health rose by an estimated 2.7 percent in 2005. Adjusted for inflation, this is a decline of 0.7 percent, the first decline since 2002.

- Volunteers in the health professions and from companies manufacturing health products organized countless formal (through an organization) and informal (direct to individuals) rescue and relief efforts after the hurricanes struck the Gulf Coast of the United States in 2005. No dollar value can be put on the total of volunteer hours and the donated medicines, supplies, and equipment.

- Health organizations also received contributions for needs that arose after the hurricanes. No total estimate was available in mid-2006. Examples include a $1 million foundation grant for health clinics and reported gifts from individuals to help provide continuing care for people with cancer, diabetes, arthritis, or other illnesses.

- Several major health-related organizations committed funds from their reserves or raised new funds to support relief and rebuilding efforts in the storm zone. These organizations include the American Diabetes Association, the American Heart Association, the National Mental Health Association, Easter Seals, the Leukemia and Lymphoma Society, and more.

- In the *Giving USA* survey, large health charities and medium-sized health charities reported increases in contributions received. On average, small health charities reported a decline.

Giving USA findings for benchmarking giving to health, 2005

Giving to health-related institutions includes contributions to nonprofit organizations providing health care services; mental health care and crisis intervention; or education, treatment, research, or support for specific disorders and diseases. Gifts to medical schools and to university health training programs appear in education, even when for medical research projects. The health subsector is in NTEE codes E, F, G, and H.

As with all *Giving USA* estimates, the amount estimated in giving to health-related organizations includes gifts received of cash, cash equivalents (securities), and in-kind gifts (art work, patents, real estate, and other items of value). *Giving USA* tries to exclude from its estimates the value of deferred or planned gift commitments and new pledges.

Table 1 summarizes the average and median amounts raised by health-related institutions in 2004 and 2005 based on organizational size.[1] Overall, large and

Giving to health

medium-sized organizations saw increases in the dollar value of gifts received and small organizations saw a drop.

Table 1
Charitable revenue received by health-related organizations in 2004 and 2005, by organizational size

Organizational size	Number of completed surveys	2004 average ($)	2004 median ($)	2005 average ($)	2005 median ($)
Large	19	84,550,820	42,583,950	91,018,672	57,022,702
Medium	50	3,448,564	2,040,275	3,958,431	2,176,287
Small	18	187,095	25,000	154,555	23,082

Large denotes organizations that receive $20 million or more in charitable revenue; medium is used for organizations having revenue between $1 million and $19.99 million, and small is for organizations that have charitable revenue of less than $1 million.

Table 2 summarizes the average and median increases or decreases in charitable revenue reported for 2005 by organizational size. In all size groups, a majority of organizations responding to the *Giving USA* survey reported an increase in charitable gifts received.

Table 2
Increases or decreases in charitable revenue of health-related organizations, 2005

Organizational size	Number	Percentage of organizations in size group	Average change ($)	Average change (%)	Median change ($)	Median change (%)
Large						
Increase	12	63	956,483	32	623,660	17
Decrease	4	21	-1,121,890	-8	-1,115,117	-8
No change	3	16	30,189	<1	0	0
Total	19	100				
All large organizations			6,467,852	12	1,980,872	4
Medium						
Increase	32	64	392,239	21	290,868	21
Decrease	10	20	-709,389	-24	-411,906	-17
No change	8	16	3,254	<1	0	0
Total	50	100				
All medium organizations			509,867	11	181,159	12

Giving to health

Organizational size	Number	Percentage of organizations in size group	Average change ($)	Average change (%)	Median change ($)	Median change (%)
Small						
Increase	10	56	79,622	38	11,161	30
Decrease	3	17	-77,732	-33	-59,000	-27
No change	5	28	0	0	0	0
Total	18	101*				
All small organizations			32,540	17	0	0

*Total does not equal 100 due to rounding.

Table 3 shows bequest receipts by organizational size. The average and the median increased in large organizations and medium-sized organizations. With only two small organizations reporting bequest revenue, there are not enough data to report a change.

Table 3
Bequest receipts by organizational size, 2005

Organizational size	Percentage with bequest revenues	2004 average ($)	2004 median ($)	2005 average ($)	2005 median ($)
Large	65	21,387,453	2,995,747	22,279,847	4,563,249
Medium	64	773,587	127,615	871,582	241,587
Small*	8	52,757	52,757	760,387	760,387

*The values are reported here, although the number of responses is too low to use in making statistical inferences about all small health organizations.

Giving to university-based hospitals or schools of medicine is not in health estimate

Gifts to universities and colleges are recorded in the education sector, yet a substantial percentage are for health-related purposes, whether for research or patient care. The larger such gifts in 2005 are reported in the education chapter.

Individual major gifts for health increase significantly in number

In 2005, more than 30 gifts of $5 million or more each for health were announced, including those for community hospitals, major institutions providing specialty research or care, and regional health systems. The gifts appear in the Center on Philanthropy's Million Dollar List and total more than $463 million. In each of the past two years (2003 and 2004), there were about 20 gifts to health causes made by individuals reported at $5 million or more. Announced gifts are often pledges that are paid in future years. The Million Dollar List does not record whether an institution received the funds in the year of the announcement.

The largest single health gift announced from an individual (or family) donor in 2005 was $70 million for the Cleveland Clinic given by Sydell Miller. Other gifts included $50 million announced by the Saddleback (Arizona) Memorial Medical Center from Bill and Louise Meiklejohn and $25 million announced by New York Presbyterian Hospital given by David and Phyllis Komansky. The individual gifts compiled for the Center's $5 million and above list appear in a separate section of this book.

Major foundation grants announced for global health

The Bill & Melinda Gates Foundation continued its commitment to world health and made major grants that far surpassed any other single donor's philanthropic support for the subsector. Total giving to Global Health Programs since the inception of the grant program exceeds $5.8 billion. Among the Gates Foundation's grants announced in 2005 were the following three:

- $107.6 million to Program for Appropriate Technology in Health (PATH) for clinical development leading to licensure and introduction of a malaria vaccine currently under development by the Malaria Vaccine Initiative;

- $25 million to the World Health Organization to support the eradication of polio; and

- $24.3 million to the Seattle, Washington, Program for Appropriate Technology in Health (PATH) to test and demonstrate a model of direct financial and technical resources at the community level to save newborn lives and reduce maternal mortality and morbidity in India.[2]

The Gates Foundation plays an important role in funding research for global health. The Ellison Medical Foundation, a project funded by Larry Ellison, has undertaken to tabulate and eventually evaluate some of the impact of foundation funding for global health initiatives. The Virginia-based Research!America (sic), with funding from the Ellison Medical Foundation, reported in 2005 that an analysis of grants awarded in 2003 showed private foundation funding of $505 million devoted to research and development projects to improve health in developing countries.[3]

Increasing funding for obesity prevention and wellness programs

With the 2005 publication *Preventing Childhood Obesity: Health in the Balance* by the Institute of Medicine,[4] programs to prevent and combat obesity came to the forefront of health funding. Announced funding included the following:

- Kaiser Permanente grants totaling $1.08 million to community health centers. The funded programs emphasize health promotion, physical activity, nutrition, and wellness for vulnerable populations;[5]

- The California Endowment grants totaling $11 million to six community partnerships throughout California as part of its four-year Healthy Eating, Active Communities initiative;[6] and

- The National Collaboration to Reduce Hunger and Improve Nutrition, with grants of $2 million from the UPS Foundation to eight organizations.[7]

Foundations seek to improve health care access and quality

The Colorado Trust began an initiative to reduce racial and ethnic disparities by addressing equality in medical services, access to care, environmental conditions, and healthy behaviors. Funding for this initiative, titled the Equality in Health Initiative, totals $13 million.[8]

Quality of care has been in the spotlight for the past several years. The Physicians' Foundation for Health Systems Excellence was founded by funds from an antiracketeering lawsuit settled in 2004. The foundation awarded its first round of grants totaling $16 million in 2005. These grants to nonprofits throughout the country are dedicated to improving health care quality.[9] The Robert Wood Johnson Foundation launched the Interdisciplinary Nursing Quality Research Initiative, a five-year, $10 million program to improve the quality of care provided in hospitals. This project will support teams of scholars from nursing and other fields, such as economics, sociology, engineering, and political science, to address gaps in knowledge about the relationship between nursing and health care quality. [10]

Center on Philanthropy Panel Study finds that 21 percent of households give an average of $298 for health-related causes, 2002

The Center on Philanthropy at Indiana University surveyed more than 7,800 households about their charitable giving and volunteering in 2002 and can use the results to develop national estimates. Among the respondents, 21 percent of households contributed to health-related causes. The average contribution amount from donor households was $298.[11] More findings from the Center on Philanthropy Panel Study appear in other chapters of this book, including the "Overview," the chapter on giving by individuals, and in chapters for other types of recipients of charitable gifts.

Association for Healthcare Philanthropy estimates $4.1 billion donated in cash contributions to member institutions in the United States, 2004

Health care institutions or organizations in the United States that are members of the Association for Healthcare Philanthropy (AHP) provided that organization with data about fundraising in 2004 in the annual AHP survey. Reported cash contributions totaled an estimated $4.1 billion (67 percent of all commitments).[12] Securities were an estimated $310.8 million or 7.6 percent of the cash total. Figure 1 illustrates the types of funding for health care organizations in the AHP.

Giving to health

Figure 1
Types of philanthropic support, Association for Healthcare Philanthropy, 2004 survey
total = $6.1 billion
($ in billions)

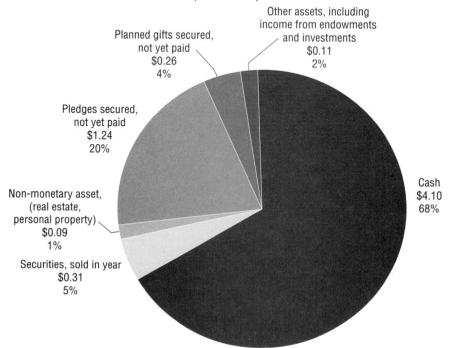

Data: Association for Healthcare Philanthropy, November 2005, www.ahp.org.

Survey respondents reported a 2.7 percent growth in the number of donors in 2004 and a 5 percent increase in the dollar amount received. *Giving USA* found a 5.1 percent increase in contributions to health between 2003 and 2004. Table 4 summarizes the sources of funding by type, in percentages of the number of donors and the amount of dollars raised based on the AHP study.

Giving to health

Table 4
Association for Healthcare Philanthropy findings about health care funding by donor type

Donor type	Percentage of dollars from type	Percentage of number of donors from type
Individuals, including estates of individuals	60	84
Individuals by relationship to institution		
Board members		44
Patients		6
Employees	Not available	13
Physicians		5
Other		16
Corporations, including corporate foundations	19	11
Independent, community, operating foundations	12	3
Other (auxiliaries, civic groups, etc.)	8	3

Data: Association for Healthcare Philanthropy, November 28, 2005, www.ahg.org.

Key findings from annual studies summarized

Table 5 presents three years of findings from studies released annually about giving for health care and health-related causes. Web site addresses are provided to help readers find the complete reports.

Table 5
Key findings from other studies

$5 million dollar list, gifts from individuals to health (does not include gifts to foundations) Center on Philanthropy at Indiana University, www.philanthropy.iupui.edu			
	2003	2004	2005
Number of health gifts	20	22	33
Largest gift to health	$50 million from Morris Silverman for the International Center for Nursing	$17.2 million from Earl and Doris Bakken to the Cleveland Clinic	$70 million from Sydell Miller to the Cleveland Clinic
Health dollars given as percentage of all individual gifts on list of $5 million and above	7.4 percent	1.9 percent*	7.9 percent

*This is unusually low due to an announced gift of $3 billion on the $5 Million Dollar List for 2004.

Giving to health

Foundation Giving Trends: Update on Funding Priorities Grants to health Foundation Center, www.fdncenter.org			
	2002	2003	2004
Median grant amount	35,000	36,000	35,000
Average grant amount	192,261	191,596	212,685
Health funding as a percentage of grant dollars (surveyed foundations, including corporate foundations)	18.3	19.5	22.3

Report on Giving FY 2002, 2003, and 2004 Association for Healthcare Philanthropy, www.ahp.org			
	2002	2003	2004
Estimated total giving to member organizations (approximately 3,400)	$5.53 billion	$5.89 billion	$6.1 billion
Estimated cash contributions	$3.6 billion	$4.1 billion	$4.1 billion
Median return on $1 spent for fundraising, all institutions	$5.51	$3.87	not reported
Median amount raised per bed, all types of institutions	$4,133	$4,782	not reported

IRS tax-exempt organizations in health category Charities and other tax-exempt organizations, 2000, 2001, 2002 Statistics of Income Bulletin, www.irs.gov			
	2000	2001	2002
Number	31,548	32,195	34,138
Charitable revenue*	$36.20 billion	$39.62 billion	$40.60 billion

*Charitable revenue includes gifts and foundation grants (which is comparable to what *Giving USA* tracks) as well as government grants and allocations from other nonprofit agencies, such as United Way and United Jewish Communities (which are not included in *Giving USA* estimates for contributions).

1   *Giving USA* sent surveys to 1,172 organizations in the health subsector. Responses from 108 organizations (9.2 percent) form the basis for this analysis, but not all responses were complete. The response rate was 26 percent for large organizations, which accounts for about 37 percent of all contributions received in the health section. The sample was selected based on charitable revenue received circa 2003 (includes some organizations that reported only in 2002 or only in 2001) supplemented with information appearing on the *Chronicle of Philanthropy* list of the 400 charities receiving the most charitable revenue in 2004. Many studies of nonprofit organizations receive a response rate of around 10 percent. *Giving USA* has analyzed the responses of "early responders" and "late responders" and found no statistically significant difference in the amount of change reported by these two groups. If nonresponders are similar to early or late responders in the amount of change they experience in charitable revenue, the low response rate will not materially affect the estimated rate of change.

2   Bill & Melinda Gates Foundation, Global Health Grants, www.gates.org.

3   "U.S. Invests $9.5 Billion in R&D for Developing Nations," press release, December 20, 2005. www.researchamerica.org.

4   Institute of Medicine of the National Academies, Committee on Prevention of Obesity in Children and Youth, Food and Nutrition Board, Board on Health Promotion and Disease Prevention. (2005) *Preventing Childhood Obesity: Health in the Balance*, Jeffery P. Koplan, Catharyn T. Liverman, Vivica I. Kraak, ed. Washington DC: The National Academies Press.

5   "Kaiser Permanente Announces Over $1 Million in Community Health Grants," *Philanthropy News Digest,* April 30, 2005, http://fdncenter.org.

6   "California Endowment Announces Childhood Obesity Prevention Initiative," *Philanthropy News Digest,* April 4, 2005, http://fdncenter.org.

7   "UPS Foundation Broadens Hunger Initiative to Include Nutrition and Obesity," *Philanthropy News Digest,* January 22, 2005, http://fdncenter.org.

8   "Colorado Trust Launches $13 Million Health Equality Initiative," press release, October 25, 2005, http://fdncenter.org.

9   "New Foundation Awards $16 Million for Physician Education, Patient Safety, and to Improve Health Care Quality," press release, November 7, 2005, www.physiciansfoundations.org.

10   "Robert Wood Johnson Foundation Launches $10 Million Healthcare Quality Initiative," press release, November 15, 2005, www.rwjf.org.

11   Center on Philanthropy Panel Study results are available at www.philanthropy.iupui.edu.

12   Association for Healthcare Philanthropy Released Report on Giving 2004, press release, November 28, 2005, www.ahp.org.

Giving to human services

- Giving to organizations in the human services subsector is estimated to be $25.36 billion in 2005. This is 9.7 percent of total estimated giving.

- In current dollars, giving to human services increased by an estimated 32.3 percent in 2005. Adjusted for inflation, this is growth of 28.0 percent. This is the highest rate of growth on record for this subsector.

- Only some of the growth in human services giving can be attributed to giving for disaster relief. The balance is from other changes. Before the disaster contribution amounts are added, there was growth of 15.0 percent (11.3 percent adjusted for inflation) in contributions reported by the organizations participating in the *Giving USA* survey, reversing a three-year trend of inflation-adjusted declines in giving to organizations in this subsector.

- Survey responses about disaster relief contributions received were supplemented with public records from organizations not returning the survey. Disaster giving reached an estimated $3.31 billion for human services organizations. The largest single recipient was the American Red Cross, with an estimated $2.4 billion received for three disasters: the Indian Ocean tsunami, the hurricanes in the Caribbean that struck the U.S. Gulf Coast, and the earthquake in the mountains of Pakistan. This figure is 72.5 percent of human services giving for crisis relief.

Giving USA findings for benchmarking giving to human services organizations, 2005

Giving to human services organizations includes contributions to organizations formed to strengthen public protection services, provide disaster relief or training to avoid disasters, offer social services, supply basic needs for food or shelter, assist with employment or job training, promote healthy development of youth, or offer recreational opportunities. The American Red Cross, the YMCA, food banks, legal clinics, and Olympic sports are all included in human services. In the National Taxonomy of Exempt Entities (NTEE), human services covers organizations in codes I, J, K, L, M, N, O, and P.

As with all *Giving USA* estimates, the amount estimated in giving to organizations in the human services subsector includes gifts received of cash, cash equivalents (securities), and in-kind gifts (artwork, patents, real estate, and other items of value). *Giving USA* tries to exclude from its estimates the value of deferred or planned gift commitments and new pledges.

Each year, *Giving USA* surveys organizations to develop an estimate of the distribution of charitable giving by subsector. For human services organizations, Table 1 summarizes the average and median amounts raised by organizations providing data about 2004 and 2005, categorized by organizational size.[1] The

Giving to human services

median is the mid-point: half of the organizations responding had higher charitable revenue; the other half had lower charitable revenue.

Table 1
Charitable revenue received by human services organizations in 2004 and 2005, by organizational size

Organizational size	Number of completed surveys	2004 average ($)	2004 median ($)	2005 average ($)	2005 median ($)
Large	19	11,768,430	2,184,113	12,141,103	2,481,929
Medium	50	2,034,654	1,404,440	2,144,330	1,562,307
Small	18	143,238	27,000	172,877	27,000

Large denotes organizations that receive $20 million or more in charitable revenue; medium is used for organizations having revenue between $1 million and $19.99 million, and small is for organizations that have charitable revenue of less than $1 million.

Table 2 summarizes the average and median increases or decreases in charitable revenue reported for 2005 by organizational size. Among human services organizations responding to the *Giving USA* survey, a majority in all size groups reported increasing revenues before receipts for disaster relief. The table below shows amounts reported without including disaster relief contributions.

Table 2
Increases or decreases in charitable revenue of human service organizations, 2005

Organizational size	Number	Percentage of organizations in size group	Average change ($)	Average change (%)	Median change ($)	Median change (%)
Large						
Increase	12	63	956,583	32	623,660	17
Decrease	4	21	-1,121,890	-8	1,115,117	-8
No change	3	16	30,190	<1	0	0
Total	19	100				
All large organizations			372,674	18	201,759	9
Medium						
Increase	32	64	392,329	31	290,868	21
Decrease	10	20	-709,389	-24	-411,906	-17
No change	8	16	3,254	<1	0	0
Total	50	100				
All medium organizations			109,676	15	38,779	8

Giving to human services

Organizational size	Number	Percentage of organizations in size group	Average change ($)	Average change (%)	Median change ($)	Median change (%)
Small						
Increase	10	56	79,622	38	11,161	30
Decrease	3	17	-77,732	-33	-59,000	-27
No change	5	28	0	0	0	0
Total	18	101*				
All small organizations			29,639	16	1,000	13

*Total does not equal 100 due to rounding.

Table 3 shows bequest receipts by organizational size. The average rose among the large organizations reporting bequest receipts, but the median declined. Half the organizations received amounts below the median. The average and the median declined in medium-sized organizations and rose in small organizations.

Table 3
Bequest receipts by organizational size, 2005

Organizational size	Percentage with bequest revenues	2004 average ($)	2004 median ($)	2005 average ($)	2005 median ($)
Large	47	3,029,141	266,805	2,770,594	314,268
Medium	34	279,833	55,000	150,222	44,287
Small*	5	100	100	7,600	7,600

*Only one small human services organization provided bequest information. The result is summarized here but it is not sufficient data to use to generalize to all small human services nonprofits.

Giving for disaster relief was only a fraction of total giving in 2005

The majority of the giving following the tsunami that devastated areas surrounding the Indian Ocean, the trio of American Gulf Coast hurricanes, and the Pakistan earthquake took place during 2005. Although disaster relief giving accounts for a share of the growth in giving in the human services subsector, it is only 3 percent of total U.S. giving during 2005. Table 4 summarizes some of the top recipients of disaster funding in the human services subsector.

Giving to human services

Table 4
Contributions to human services organizations for disaster relief, 2005
Reported by the Center on Philanthropy from data collected from public
records and some organizational self-reports as of December 2005

Organization	Tsunami	Hurricanes Katrina, Rita, Wilma	Pakistan earthquake	Total
American Red Cross	$549,400,000	$1,850,000,000	$12,100,000	$2,416,200,000
America's Second Harvest		27,700,000		27,700,000
Catholic Charities/Catholic Relief Services	4,391,078	132,900,000		137,291,078
Habitat for Humanity International	29,041,489	77,549,676		106,591,165
Salvation Army	26,675,303	295,000,000		321,675,303

Data: The Center on Philanthropy, January 9, 2006, www.philanthropy.iupui.edu.

Gulf Coast hurricane relief gifts address only the beginning of the region's needs
During 2005 organizations in the human services subsector reported hurricane disaster relief donations of an estimated $4.2 billion, according to the Center on Philanthropy at Indiana University, which developed the estimate using household giving data gathered by the Conference Board in its survey of households;[2] an estimate of foundation grantmaking from the Foundation Center;[3] and an estimate of corporate giving (including corporate foundations) from the U.S. Chamber of Commerce.[4]

This amount constitutes the majority of disaster relief giving and includes donations from individuals, corporations, and foundations. In addition to the American Red Cross, the Salvation Army, and Catholic Charities USA, many other organizations received significant donations. Public information sources show contributions to organizations such as Habitat for Humanity, Oxfam America, and many small, local nonprofits that also provided aid in the recovery efforts.

By October 2005 the pace of relief giving had slowed, which caused human services groups to voice concern about funding for long-term recovery needs on the Gulf Coast.[5] Many large gifts during the final months of 2005 focused on rebuilding. The gifts supported the creation of an initiative designed to help position minority entrepreneurs for opportunities in rebuilding Gulf Coast communities,[6] the creation of the New York Regional Association of Grantmakers' task force dedicated to developing long-term funding strategies for recovery and rebuilding, and other activities.

Donor fatigue has little effect on long-term giving
There was widespread discussion in the nonprofit world speculating that the outpouring of donations in response to natural disasters would negatively affect giving to organizations not involved with disaster relief—the concept of "donor

Giving to human services

fatigue." The Center on Philanthropy's study, the Philanthropic Giving Index (PGI), found that there is a striking difference between what fundraising professionals said they experienced at their organizations compared with their perception of the state of nonprofits as a whole. The results of the PGI suggest the same conclusion the Center drew from research it conducted after tracking giving following the attacks of September 11, 2001: some organizations may experience a decrease in donations in the short term, but for the majority of these nonrelief nonprofits, the impact is not expected to be long term.[7]

Federal estate tax returns show human services organizations receive small share of charitable bequests

Among all charities, the highest dollar amount in bequest contributions comes from estates that are required to file federal estate tax returns (gross estate value of $1.5 million or more in 2004 and 2005). From the tax return information, averages can be developed for specific types of charities within a subsector. Table 5 presents seven types of human services charities and summarizes for each the percentage of the number of deductions for charitable bequests claimed on estate tax returns and the average amount per bequest claimed in 2004. The largest percentage of bequests was for religion (24 percent) and the largest average amount claimed was for philanthropy and volunteerism (which includes foundations), with an average of $2.48 million. Human services bequests are a very small percentage of the bequests made and typically average less than $250,000 each.

Table 5
Percentage of bequests claimed and the average amount per bequest for each type of agency
Estate tax returns, 2004

Type of human services charity	Percentage of all bequests on estate tax returns	Average amount per bequest claimed on estate tax returns (in $)
Employment-jobs	<1	64,039
Food, nutrition, agriculture	<1	170,486
Housing-shelter	1	93,672
Public safety/disaster relief, preparedness	<1	100,643
Recreation-leisure-sports, athletics	<1	87,654
Youth development	2	247,374
Human services - other multipurpose	11	230,176

Data: Basic facts about charitable giving, U.S. Department of the Treasury, May 2006.

Million-dollar gifts to human services organizations decrease in number and amount

The Center on Philanthropy's Million Dollar List recorded 56 gifts of $1 million or more from living individuals, foundations, and corporations for human services organizations and for purposes including hurricane or tsunami relief. These gifts totaled $111.9 million. Nearly half of the 2005 large gifts were designated for disaster relief. The majority of the disaster relief gifts (21 of 56) were given to the American Red Cross, with three going to the Salvation Army. Eight of the gifts on the list for 2005 were for $5 million or more. These included contributions to the Hebrew Home of Greater Washington (Maryland), the YMCA of the Fox Cities (Wisconsin), and the Maryland SoccerPlex.[8]

Poverty rose while donations to agencies serving the poor decreased

The U.S. poverty rate rose in 2005 as household incomes failed to increase, despite the consistent GDP growth.[9] This has had a direct effect on the charitable sector. Human services agencies were forced to lay off employees and cut programs and services because of fiscal stress.[10] Compounding the growing poverty rate, donations to human service agencies that serve the poor were down for the third year in a row at the beginning of 2005 and stayed flat (except for disaster giving) during the year.[11] In particular, food banks experienced a dramatic decrease in food donations that was not offset by cash gifts in 2005. Officials reported that in the Chicago area food donations were down 8 percent, in Los Angeles by about 11 percent, and in New York by roughly 2 percent.[12]

Federal budget cuts funding for many charities

Congress passed a $388 billion spending plan for the 2005 fiscal year (beginning in October 2004) that cut federal programs supporting charities. Cuts in the human services sector included:

- A $1.3 billion cut for vocational and technical education;

- A $1.5 billion decrease for Job Corps job training program for youth;

- A $378 million drop in funding for housing programs, including neighborhood planning and development; and

- A $9 million reduction in spending for the Corporation for National and Community Service, which oversees the AmeriCorps national service program.

Some programs experienced an increase in funding, like the Head Start preschool program and the Low-Income Home Energy Assistance Program; however, representatives from these groups did not think the increases would even cover the increase in their costs and inflation.[13]

An article published by Charity Navigator suggests that human services groups lose twice when the government cuts funding. Because government funding is disproportionately higher for human services funding than for other nonprofit subsectors, human services groups have a hard time increasing gifts from other contributors when cuts by the government are made.[14]

Scandals occur but, overall, members of the public continue to support charities

During 2005 the public faced a number of national, highly publicized controversies in human service nonprofits:

- The IRS found that two-thirds of (55 of 82) nonprofit organizations studied because they were suspected of improper political activity during the 2004 presidential election actually violated guidelines, the Associated Press reported.[15]

- The Senate Finance Committee began an inquiry of the American Red Cross following reports of concerns associated with the use of Hurricane Katrina relief funds, governance, and compensation policies.[16]

- Millard Fuller, founder of Habitat for Humanity, was fired after allegations that he had sexually harassed a colleague.[17]

- America's Second Harvest of Wisconsin was under investigation after more than $100,000 "disappeared." Further, the organization was accused of selling food boxes to the poor.[18]

- Boy Scout councils in Alabama and elsewhere were investigated for allegedly creating false reports of the number of members, in an effort to increase contributions by donors and allocations from United Way.[19]

- Workers at two San Diego charities were criminally investigated and charged with multiple counts of grand theft and forgery after they were accused of stealing in-kind donations.[20]

- Focus groups participating in a Public Agenda study reported that they were "well aware" of recent, highly publicized scandals at some charities and that these controversies led the majority of participants to stop giving to those groups. However, Public Agenda concluded that while high-profile scandals can greatly affect the reputations of the small group of involved nonprofits, donors do not project cynicism onto the field as a whole. In fact, study participants—almost all of whom defined the nonprofit sector as charitable, human services organizations—were "enthusiastic and positive" about the recipients of their donations and the sector in general.[21] This work, conducted in focus groups, contradicts earlier surveys in which individuals seemed to have a lower level of trust in charities after the attacks of September 11 and media coverage of management failures in organizations responding to that disaster.[22]

Human services subsector top pick of donors

Ninety percent of the 1,000 Americans surveyed by Freelanthropy reported that they had made a donation to a nonprofit in the past year (almost 25 percent gave less than $100 and 42 percent gave between $100 and $1,000). When asked to specify what subsector they would most likely give to in the coming year, survey participants listed health and human services first followed by education, religious, environment, and arts/culture/humanities organizations. Of all respondents, people between the ages of 18 and 24 and those between the ages of 45 and 64 were most likely to voice a preference for giving to health and human services groups.[23]

Center on Philanthropy Panel Study finds 34 percent of households give for human services; average gift by donors is $459

Using data collected from more than 8,000 households, the Center on Philanthropy at Indiana University analyzed contributions reported for two different types of purposes, both of which are in the human services subsector: to help people meet their basic needs (for housing, food, clothing, etc.) and to help youth and families. Combining these two types of charitable purposes, the Center found that 34 percent of households reported making a donation to at least one of them in 2002. The average total amount contributed for these two purposes was $459.

Considered separately, 29 percent of households reported gifts to help meet people's basic needs, with an average gift of $457, and 11 percent of households made gifts to help youth and families, with an average gift of $198.[24]

Not included in the survey were questions about providing legal services, employment services, or disaster relief services, all of which are also in the human services subsector. More about the panel study findings and methods can be found in the section of this book titled "Overview."

Key findings from annual studies summarized

Table 6 provides three years of findings from annual studies about giving to human services organizations. Web site addresses are provided so readers can access the full reports.

Table 6
Key findings from other studies

$5 million dollar list, gifts from individuals to human services (does not include gifts to foundations) Center on Philanthropy at Indiana University, www.philanthropy.iupui.edu			
	2003	2004	2005
Number of gifts to human services organizations	3	2	8
Largest gift to human services	$11.7 million to create a sports park, estate of Wesley Howard, Medford, Oregon	$1.5 billion to the Salvation Army in a challenge gift, estate of Joan Kroc, widow of the entrepreneur who created McDonald's	$15 million to Hebrew SeniorLife of Boston from Dr. Miriam and Sheldon G. Adelson to support the building of a proposed multigenerational community
Human services dollars given as percentage of all individual gifts on list of $5 million and above	0.2 percent	13.4 percent	1.1 percent

Giving to human services

Foundation Giving Trends: Update on Funding Priorities Grants to human service organizations Foundation Center, www.fdncenter.org			
	2002	2003	2004
Median grant amount	$25,000	$25,000	$25,000
Average grant amount	$70,671	$72,100	$66,464
Human services funding as a percentage of grant dollars (surveyed foundations, including corporate foundations)	14.8 percent	15.6 percent	13.9 percent

IRS tax-exempt organizations in human services Charities and Other Tax-Exempt Organizations, 2000, 2001, and 2002 *Statistics of Income Bulletin*, www.irs.gov			
	2000	2001	2002
Number	88,858	91,131	94,735
Charitable revenue*	$54.36 billion	$59.09 billion	$58.81 billion

*Charitable revenue includes gifts and foundation grants (which is comparable to what *Giving USA* tracks) as well as government grants and allocations from other nonprofit agencies such as United Way and United Jewish Communities (which are not included in *Giving USA* estimates for contributions).

1   *Giving USA* sent surveys to 986 organizations in the human services subsector. Responses were received from 108 organizations (9.2 percent). Not all organizations provided complete information in their survey response. Only 87 surveys could be analyzed. The response rate among large organizations was 26 percent. Just 78 large organizations are estimated to receive approximately 25 percent of all dollars donated to the more than 92,500 human services organizations. The sample was selected based on charitable revenue received circa 2003 (includes some organizations that reported only in 2001 or only in 2002), supplemented with information obtained about human services organizations appearing on the *Chronicle of Philanthropy* list of the 400 charities receiving the most charitable revenue in 2004. Many studies of nonprofit organizations receive a response rate of around 10 percent. *Giving USA* has analyzed the responses of "early responders" and "late responders" and found no statistically significant difference in the amount of change reported by these two groups. If nonresponders are similar to early or late responders in the amount of change they experience in charitable revenue, the low response rate will not materially affect the estimated rate of change.

2   Most Americans gave to hurricane relief and their other charities as well, The Conference Board press release April 17, 2006, www.conference-board.org.

3   S. Lawrence, Snapshot of philanthropy's response to the Gulf Coast hurricanes, Foundation Center, February 2006, http://fdncenter.org.

4   U.S. Chamber of Commerce: Statistics and Research Center, www.uschamber.com.

5   E. Schwinn, Donations to help hurricane victims taper off at some charities, *Chronicle of Philanthropy*, October 6, 2005, http://philanthropy.com.

6   Kauffman Foundation program seeks to assist minority-owned businesses hit by Hurricane Katrina, Ewing Marion Kauffman Foundation press release February 21, 2006, www.kauffman.org.

Giving to human services

7   Nonprofit fundraisers divided on whether hurricane relief giving is hurting nonrelief charities, The
    Center on Philanthropy at Indiana University press release, www.philanthropy.iupui.edu.
8   Center on Philanthropy, www.philanthropy.iupui.edu.
9   D. Leonhardt, U.S. poverty rate was up last year, *New York Times*, August 31, 2005, www.nytimes.com.
10 Thin the soup or shorten the line: Choices facing Washington area nonprofits, Nonprofit Roundtable
    of Greater Washington, March 30, 2004, www.brookings.edu/metro/gwrp/20040330_thinthesoup.htm.
11 Holidays end, need doesn't, Charity Navigator, January 4, 2006, www.charitynavigator.org.
12 Food banks report increase in demand, fewer donations, December 30, 2005. Viewed at
    Philanthropy News Digest, http://fdncenter.org; M. Martinez, Food banks leaner as more in the
    U.S. are hungry, *Chicago Tribune,* December 26, 2005, www.chicagotribune.com.
13 E. Schwinn, Federal budget measure cuts spending on many charity programs, *Chronicle of
    Philanthropy*, December 1, 2004, http://philanthropy.com.
14 E. Navarro, Government funding for charities: When it declines, the charities lose twice, Charity
    Navigator, May 1, 2005, www.charitynavigator.org.
15 IRS: Charities overstepping into politics, *New York Times*, February 24, 2006, www.nytimes.com;
    S. Strom, I.R.S. finds sharp increase in illegal political activity, *New York Times,* February 25, 2006;
    IRS releases new guidance and results of political intervention examinations, Internal Revenue
    Service press release, February 24, 2006, http://www.irs.gov.
16 K. Kreking, Senator seeks records in Red Cross probe, *Associated Press*, 12/30/05. Viewed at
    Philanthropy News Digest, http://fdncenter.org.
17 A. Cooperman, Harassment claims roil Habitat for Humanity; As founder's supporters rally, new
    allegations emerge, *Washington Post*, March 9, 2005.
18 C. Spivak, D. Bice, Food bank thieves took a $300,000 bite, Milwaukee Sentinel Journal, October 6,
    2005, www.jsonline.com.
19 M. Roig-Franzia, Boy Scouts suspected of inflating rolls, *Washington Post*, January 29, 2005,
    cited in the February 2005 issue of *Fundraising and Nonprofit Report*, Copilevitz and Canter,
    www.copilevitz-canter.com.
20 Two charity operators charged with grand theft and forgery, *Associated Press,* September 1, 2005.
    Viewed at the *San Jose Mercury News*, www.mercurynews.com.
21 Public Agenda, *The Charitable Impulse*, 2005, www.publicagenda.org.
22 See *Giving USA 2005*, page 4, for a summary of studies about public trust and charities since
    September 2001.
23 Benchmark Freelanthropy Index tracks state of charitable giving in America, reveals high levels
    by lower income groups, March 16, 2005, http://freelanthropy.com/pr20050316.html.
24 Findings from the Center on Philanthropy Panel Study are available at www.philanthropy.iupui.edu.

Giving to arts, culture, and humanities

- Giving to the arts, culture, and humanities subsector declined in 2005, to $13.51 billion, a drop of 3.4 percent (-6.6 percent adjusted for inflation). This is the first decline before inflation found since 1998.

- Contributions to the arts, culture, and humanities subsector are 5.2 percent of total estimated giving.

- Among organizations responding to the *Giving USA* survey, large arts organizations and small arts organizations reported a decline in charitable gifts received; medium-sized organizations saw growth in giving.

- About 65 large arts organizations receive one-quarter of total contributions in the arts subsector, based on IRS Forms 990 filed in 2003. Changes in the large organizations heavily influence the direction of change for all arts giving.

- Several large donations to arts organizations announced in 2005 were in-kind gifts, including collections given to the Dallas Museum of Art, the Getty Museum, the Detroit Institute of Arts, the de Young Museum, and the Virginia Museum of Fine Arts. The value of in-kind contributions is not sought in the *Giving USA* survey. Donors of collections, however, are allowed by law to claim at least some portion of the value of the gift as a tax deduction. The amount that donors claim is in the estimates of giving by source, but the value of the gift will not appear in the arts subsector. Instead, it forms a part of "unallocated giving."

Giving USA findings for benchmarking giving to arts, culture, and humanities organizations

Giving to arts, culture, and humanities organizations includes contributions to museums; performing arts; historical societies; and other activities involving arts, culture, and humanities. In the National Taxonomy of Exempt Entities (NTEE), arts, culture, and humanities cover organizations in code A.

As with all *Giving USA* estimates, the amount estimated in giving to organizations in the arts, culture, and humanities subsector includes gifts received of cash, cash equivalents (securities), and in-kind gifts (artwork, patents, real estate, and other items of value). *Giving USA* tries to exclude from its estimates the value of deferred or planned gift commitments and new pledges.

Tables 1 through 3 summarize the findings from the 2006 *Giving USA* survey.[1] Table 1 shows the average and median amounts reported in charitable gifts; Table 2 shows the direction of change in giving (increase, decrease, or within 1 percent, which is termed "no change"); and Table 3 shows the percentage of organizations that reported bequest receipts and the average and median amount received from bequests for each organizational size.

Giving to arts, culture, and humanities

Table 1
Charitable revenue received by arts, culture, and humanities organizations in 2004 and 2005, by organizational size

Organizational size	Number of completed surveys	2004 average ($)	2004 median ($)	2005 average ($)	2005 median ($)
Large	15	42,318,170	31,878,179	40,339,755	27,110,915
Medium	59	2,494,757	1,594,648	2,733,357	1,459,761
Small	27	177,109	36,000	159,491	26,936

Large denotes organizations that receive $20 million or more in charitable revenue; *medium* is used for organizations having revenue between $1 million and $19.99 million, and *small* is for organizations that have charitable revenue of less than $1 million.

Table 2
Increases or decreases in charitable revenue of arts, culture, and humanities organizations, 2005

Organizational size	Number	Percentage of organizations in size group	Average change ($)	Average change (%)	Median change ($)	Median change (%)
Large						
Increase	5	33	8,778,434	32	8,123,577	43
Decrease	7	47	-10,531,346	-39	-3,406,469	-43
No change	3	20	50,343	<1	0	0
Total	15	100				
All large organizations			-3,923,485	-8	-447,000	-3
Medium						
Increase	35	59	694,455	34	299,764	20
Decrease	20	34	-511,325	-22	-110,802	-20
No change	4	7	-500	<1	0	0
Total	59	100				
All medium organizations			238,601	13	114,714	5
Small						
Increase	10	37	58,082	97	36,385	24
Decrease	15	56	-70,434	-29	-9,531	-29
No change	2	7	0	0	0	0
Total	27	100				
All small organizations			-17,618	-20	-1,000	-5

Giving to arts, culture, and humanities

Table 3 shows bequest receipts by organizational size. The average and the median declined in large organizations, but rose in medium-sized and small organizations. Nationally overall, bequest revenues are slowing their rate of growth as people live longer and as they draw down their assets (leaving smaller estates).

Table 3
Bequest receipts by organizational size, 2005

Organizational size	Percentage with bequest revenues	2004 average ($)	2004 median ($)	2005 average ($)	2005 median ($)
Large	50	37,564,400	2,220,947	26,950,865	1,550,000
Medium	36	741,653	176,048	1,059,903	114,100
Small*	11	17,460	10,000	97,188	75,000

*For 2005, only a few arts, culture, and humanities organizations provided bequest information. The values are reported here although the number of responses is too low to use in making statistical inferences about all arts, culture, and humanities organizations.

Museums receive significant collections and cash commitments in the hundreds of millions of dollars

The Dallas Museum of Art announced that three couples pledged their collections of modern and contemporary art to the museum, in a gift with a combined reported value of $400 million. The donors were Marguerite and Robert Hoffman, Cindy and Howard Rachofsky, and Deedie and Rusty Rose. The Museum also announced an anonymous $32 million endowment gift made to a foundation that exclusively funds museum acquisitions.[2]

Josephine Ford, a descendent of the carmaker, left artwork valued at $14.7 million and $20 million in cash as a bequest to the Detroit Institute of the Arts.[3] James W. and Frances G. McGlothlin, prominent collectors of American art, pledged a massive donation of artwork and funds to the Virginia Museum of Fine Arts. Their gift is valued at more than $100 million.[4] The de Young Museum in San Francisco received a collection of Oceanic art valued at well over $100 million from John and Marcia Friede.[5]

David Rockefeller, chairman emeritus of the Museum of Modern Art (MOMA), pledged $100 million for its endowment. The museum will receive the gift after Mr. Rockefeller's death. For current operations, Mr. Rockefeller pledged an additional $5 million.[6] The MOMA concluded a multiyear campaign and opened its new facility in late 2004, after raising more than $725 million.[7]

The largest foundation gift to the arts in 2005 was from the Donald W. Reynolds Foundation to the Smithsonian Institution for $45 million.[8]

Performing arts organizations receive major gifts in the tens of millions of dollars
The Donald W. Reynolds Foundation granted $50 million to support the construction of a performing arts center in Las Vegas.[9] Mercedes and Sid Bass contributed $25 million to the Metropolitan Opera, that organization's largest donation on record.[10] The Old Globe Theatre in San Diego received a $10 million gift from Conrad Prebys.[11] Harold and Donna Neubauer gave $10 million to the Philadelphia Orchestra, and Roger and Victoria Sant gave $10 million to the National Symphony Orchestra.[12] Atlanta-area developer John A. Williams contributed $10 million to a performing arts center under construction in Cobb County, northwest of the city center.[13] In a dramatic effort to save the Detroit Jazz Festival, Gretchen Valade pledged $10 million to create an endowment at an organization to be formed to operate and manage the struggling annual event.[14]

Arts receives 14 percent of announced gifts of $5 million or more from individuals
The Center on Philanthropy's Million Dollar List for 2005 shows 23 gifts of $5 million or more from individuals to the arts. The gifts total more than $1 billion, with more than half of that amount from in-kind donations of art collections.[15] If the in-kind donations were received at the organizations (not simply pledged) and included at their reported value as part of the estimate of giving to the arts, donations to the arts, culture, and humanities subsector would be around $14.08 billion. It is difficult to estimate how much more (or less) this amount would be compared with prior years because the prior years' estimates do not include in-kind donations.

The value of the arts donations was 14 percent of all announced gifts from individuals on the list. The Million Dollar List tries to capture publicly announced gifts of $1 million or more, but it is not a complete listing. It can serve as an indicator, but is not proof of a change in giving.

Arts giving to educational institutions counted in education subsector
A number of educational institutions received major gifts for arts programming or for arts facilities. *Giving USA* follows the NTEE in classifying gifts by institutional purpose, not the program supported by the gift. Thus, these contributions are donations to educational institutions. A few of the largest such gifts are summarized here with other arts giving to provide a service for *Giving USA* readers who are interested in the various ways in which donors support the arts.

An anonymous donor committed $100 million to the Yale University School of Music to enable the school to fund graduate students' tuition costs.[16] The Indiana University (IU) School of Music received a $40.6 million donation from Barbara Barrow Jacobs, who graduated from IU in the 1940s and was a member of the IU Foundation board of directors from 1989 until her death in 2005.[17] Alfred University announced a $35 million gift from alumnus Marlin Miller, Jr. The gift includes funds to build a theater and an endowment to support scholarships for students of the arts, professorships, and arts programming.[18] The Julliard School announced a gift of $25 million received from Bruce Kovner.[19] Jerome and Simona Chazen, both alumni of University of Wisconsin-Madison, donated $20 million for a major expansion of the university's museum, now called the Chazen Museum of Art.[20]

Congress proposes cut in federal funding for public broadcasting

The Corporation for Public Broadcasting (CPB) is a Congressionally chartered agency that passes federal money to hundreds of public TV and radio stations. On June 9, 2005, a House subcommittee voted to sharply cut funds for the CPB.[21] As a result of a widespread protest campaign, the House agreed to add back $100 million to the CPB's fiscal 2006 budget and to reverse a committee decision to eliminate all funding for the CPB within two years. However, an additional $102.4 million that had been shorn from separate public broadcasting programs was not restored.[22]

Center on Philanthropy Panel Study shows 8 percent donate to the arts; average gift is $215

In a survey of households representing the U.S. population, the Center on Philanthropy found that 8 percent gave to arts, culture, public broadcasting, or ethnic awareness organizations in 2002. Ethnic awareness organizations include groups such as the Japan Society, National Yiddish Book Center, and Sealaska Heritage Foundation.

Among the households making contributions to the arts, over the course of a year, the average total contributed for arts causes was $215. More than 50 percent of the households supporting the arts gave less than $100 total to all arts organizations they supported. Not surprisingly, the people most likely to support the arts were those living in metropolitan areas, those with a high level of education, those with a high income ($100,000 or more a year), and those in families in which the head of household was 55 or older.[23] The Center on Philanthropy Panel Study reaches more than 8.000 households. More about the panel study findings and methods can be found in the section of this book titled "Overview."

The Foundation Center finds that arts education funding increased between 1999 and 2003

The Foundation Center, in collaboration with Grantmakers in the Arts, provided an analysis of trends in arts education funding from 1999 to 2003.[24] Giving for arts education by funders in the Foundation Center's annual grants set rose 24 percent, from $167.9 million to $208.8 million. The increase for arts education surpassed the growth in arts funding overall. As a result, arts education's share of total arts funding increased slight, to nearly 12 percent. The vast majority of arts education grants were small. In 2003, 46.4 percent of arts education grants were less than $25,000.

Three "spotlight" reports focused on arts education funding in two metropolitan areas and one entire state. In the San Francisco Bay Area, performing arts education programs directed at children and youth accounted for the largest share of arts education giving in 2003.[25] In Ohio, performing arts education grants for programs serving college and graduate students accounted for the largest share of arts education giving.[26] In metropolitan Atlanta, 40 percent of the arts groups expected an increase in foundation grant dollars, yet only 9 percent of the grantmakers expected to increase their giving to the arts in 2005.[27]

Theatre Communications Group finds that the theatre industry rebounded from the financial hardships of the prior year

Based on a study of 1,477 theatres, the total contributions to theatres were estimated to be $715 million in 2004, based on IRS Forms 990 filed and then analyzed by Theatre Communications Group (TCG). In a different approach to studying contributions, TCG surveys a sample of theatres about their finances, including gifts received from individuals, corporations, and foundations, among other (government) funders. The private support for 2004 found among survey respondents was equivalent to 42 percent of the theatres' expenses.[28] The authors of the *Theatre Facts* report wrote, "In 2004, the industry rebounded in many areas, showing that the belt tightening after the hardships of the prior year and vigorous commitment to income generation left the average theatre better off than it was in 2003."[29]

Key data from annual studies summarized

Table 4 presents three years of data from several studies appearing annually about giving to arts, culture, and humanities organizations. Web site addresses are provided so readers can access the full reports.

Table 4
Key findings from other studies

$5 million dollar list, gifts from individuals to the arts (does not include gifts to foundations) Center on Philanthropy at Indiana University, www.philanthropy.iupui.edu			
	2003	2004	2005
Number of gifts to arts, culture, and humanities	17	15	23
Largest gift to arts, culture, and humanities Cash	$200 million, cash or pledge, from the estate of Joan Kroc to National Public Radio	$205 million for the Overture Center for the Arts in Wisconsin from W. Jerome (Jerry) Frautschi	$100 million pledged to the Museum of Modern Art by David Rockefeller
In-kind	$300 million, in-kind gift from Robert and Jane Meyerhoff to the National Gallery of Art	$500 million or more in cash and gifts-in-kind, estate of Caroline Weiss Law to the Houston Museum of Fine Arts	$400 million in art works from Marguerite and Robert Hoffman, Cindy and Howard Rachofsky, and Deedie and Rusty Rose to the Dallas Museum of Art

Giving to arts, culture, and humanities

$5 million dollar list, gifts from individuals to the arts (does not include gifts to foundations) Center on Philanthropy at Indiana University, www.philanthropy.iupui.edu			
	2003	2004	2005
Arts, culture, and humanities giving as percentage of all individual gifts on list of $5 million and above	22 percent	5 percent	14 percent

Foundation Giving Trends: Update on Funding Priorities Grants for the arts Foundation Center, www.fdncenter.org			
	2002	2003	2004
Median grant amount	$25,000	$25,000	$25,000
Average grant amount	$104,198	$100,121	$106,910
Arts funding as percentage of grant dollars (surveyed foundations)	12 percent	13 percent	13 percent

State of North America's Art Museums Survey Association of Art Museum Directors, www.aamd.org			
Survey conducted about significant change in:	2003 N=128	2004 N=114	2005 N=129
Overall Revenue			
Decline	39%	21%	16%
Increase	41%	49%	47%
No change	20%	30%	37%
Individual Gifts			
Decline	10%	8%	7%
Increase	56%	68%	70%
No change	34%	24%	23%
Foundations			
Decline	26%	14%	12%
Increase	39%	40%	50%
No change	35%	46%	38%
Corporations			
Decline	34%	22%	20%
Increase	32%	38%	34%
No change	34%	40%	46%
Earned income			
Decline	32%	25%	16%
Increase	36%	43%	44%
No change	32%	32%	40%

Giving to arts, culture, and humanities

Theatre Facts Theatre Communications Group, www.tcg.org	2002	2003	2004
Average contributions by "Universe Trend" Theatres (n=92) that responded each year over 5 years	$2.95 million	$2.85 million	$3.24 million
Average percentage of contributions in "Trend" Theatres (n=92) from: Individuals Foundations* Corporations Government* Other (in-kind, events, arts funds)	42.8 20.0 10.8 9.4 17.0	34.5 18.8 14.2 13.1 19.4	39.9 16.5 13.6 11.5 18.5
Contributions as a percentage of net income in "Trend" Theatres (n=92)	44.0	42.7	43.7

*Trend skewed by one theatre's exceptional activity.

IRS tax-exempt Organizations in Arts, Culture, and Humanities Charities and Other Tax-exempt Organizations, 2000, 2001, and 2002 Statistics of Income Bulletin, www.irs.gov	2000	2001	2002
Number of organizations	25,307	26,006	27,129
Charitable revenue*	$13.42 billion	$12.93 billion	$12.82 billion

*Charitable revenue includes gifts and foundation grants (which is comparable to what *Giving USA* tracks) as well as government grants and allocations from other nonprofit agencies such as United Way and United Jewish Communities (which are not included in *Giving USA* estimates for contributions).

1   *Giving USA* sent surveys to 1,025 arts organizations, including all organizations that raised $20 million or more in 2003 or 2004 and a random sampling of small and medium-sized organizations. 118 surveys were returned (a response rate of 11.5 percent); 101 could be used for this analysis. Twenty-two percent of the large organizations responded. Less than 10 percent of medium-sized and small organizations replied. The sample was selected based on charitable revenue received circa 2003 (includes some organizations that reported only in 2001 or only in 2002), supplemented with information obtained about environment and animals organizations reporting in 2004 and appearing on the *Chronicle of Philanthropy* list of the 400 charities receiving the most charitable revenue in 2004. Many studies of nonprofit organizations receive a response rate of around 10 percent. *Giving USA* has analyzed the responses of "early responders" and "late responders" and found no statistically significant difference in the amount of change reported by these two groups. If nonresponders are similar to early or late responders in the amount of change they experience in charitable revenue, the low response rate will not materially affect the estimated rate of change.

2   Dallas Museum of Art announces unprecedented gift of 3 private collections encompassing 800 works of art and future acquisitions by collectors, press release, February 16, 2005, www.dallasmuseumofart.org.

3   America's most generous donors: donations in 2005, Chronicle of Philanthropy Gifts and Grants database, http://philanthropy.com/stats/donors/2006/detail.php?ID_Gift=1585.

4   Bequest is 'huge win' for museum; artwork, funds being donated by couple top $100 million in value, Richmond Times Dispatch (Virginia), May 17, 2005. Viewed at www.lexis-nexis.com.

5   City by the bay to get a trove of Oceanic art, New York Times, February 26, 2005. Viewed at www.lexisnexis.com.

6   David Rockefeller gives $100 million to Museum of Modern Art, The Associated Press, April 13, 2005. Viewed at www.lexisnexis.com.

7   The Museum of Modern Art's Capital Campaign Approaches Its Goal with $725 Million Raised, press release, November 15, 2004, www.moma.org.

8   J. Trescott, Smithsonian scores a $45 million gift, Washington Post, October 12, 2005.

9   Foundation pledging $50 million for arts center in Las Vegas, Associated Press, March 18, 2005.

10   Mr. and Mrs. Sid Bass donate $25 million dollars (sic) to the Metropolitan Opera, press release, January 5, 2006, www.metoperafamily.org.

11   $10 million gift is largest in Old Globe's 70-year run, San Diego Union-Tribune, September 21, 2005. Viewed at www.lexisnexis.com.

12   Neubauer Family Foundation announces $10 million challenge grant to Philadelphia Orchestra, Philadelphia Orchestra press release, January 11, 2005. Viewed at Philanthropy News Digest, http://fdncenter.org. J. Trescott, Sants pledge $10 million to the NSO, Washington Post, September 24, 2005.

13   T. Sabulis, Post properties founder donates $10 million to new Cobb Arts Center, Atlanta Journal-Constitution, September 19, 2005. Viewed at Philanthropy News Digest, http://fdncenter.org.

14   M. Stryker, Heiress's offer could secure Detroit Jazz Festival's future, Detroit Free Press, October 26, 2005. Viewed at Philanthropy News Digest, http://fdncenter.org.

15   Million Dollar List data maintained by the Center on Philanthropy, analysis by Giving USA research team.

16   $100M, String attached. Yale music gets a giant gift, Daily News (New York), November 6, 2005. Viewed at www.lexisnexis.com.

17   Former Indians owner, wife give $40 million to music school, The Associated Press, November 17, 2005. Viewed at www.lexisnexis.com.

18   T. Buckham, Alfred U gets $35 million gift, Buffalo News (New York), February 15, 2005. Viewed at www.lexisnexis.com.

19   Gift of the week/perfect pitch, Wall Street Journal, October 7, 2005.

20   UW Art Museum will expand; Elvehjem is renamed for donor couple; $20 million gift, Wisconsin State Journal, May 7, 2005. Viewed at www.lexisnexis.com.

21   Public Broadcasting targeted by House; panel seeks to end CPB's funding within 2 years, The Washington Post, June 10, 2005. Viewed at www.lexisnexis.com.

22   House vote spares Public Broadcasting funds; health, education and labor programs face cuts under major spending bill, The Washington Post, June 24, 2005. Viewed at www.lexisnexis.com.

23   Findings from the Center on Philanthropy Panel Study are available at www.philanthropy.iupui.edu.

24   Foundation funding for arts education, The Foundation Center, http://fdncenter.org; Grantmakers in the Arts, October 2005, www.giarts.org.

25   Spotlight on arts education grantmaking in the San Francisco Bay, The Foundation Center-San Francisco, October 2005, www.fdncenter.org/sanfrancisco/.

26   Spotlight on arts education grantmaking in Ohio, The Foundation Center–Cleveland, October 2005, www.fdncenter.org/cleveland/.

27   Spotlight on arts education grantmaking in metropolitan Atlanta, The Foundation Center-Atlanta, October 2005, www.fdncenter.org/atlanta/.

28   Theatre Facts 2004, Theatre Communications Group, www.tcg.org.

29   Z. Voss and G. Voss, et al., Theatre Facts 2004, p. 1.

Giving to public-society benefit

- Giving to organizations in the public-society benefit subsector is estimated to be $14.03 billion in 2005. This is 5.4 percent of total estimated giving.

- In current dollars, giving to public-society benefit organizations rose by an estimated 8.3 percent in 2005. Adjusted for inflation, this is an increase of 4.7 percent.

- Before disaster relief contributions are included, survey responses showed that giving was up 6.2 percent (2.8 percent adjusted for inflation) for all organizations combined.

- With disaster giving included, large organizations responding to the survey reported an average increase of $344,574 in contributions received. Medium-sized and small organizations in this subsector also reported increased contributions received in 2005.

- United Way of America reported that contributions for hurricane response reached $45 million by October 2005. The Bush-Clinton fund established for response to the tsunami was replicated for the Katrina response. Combined, the two funds raised more than $110 million in 2005. A number of other organizations in the public-society benefit subsector raised funds for disaster response. Not all amounts were available in mid-2006 to add to the estimate for giving to this subsector.

Giving USA findings for benchmarking giving to public-society benefit organizations

Giving to organizations in the public-society benefit subsector includes contributions to nonprofit organizations collecting funds for distribution to a number of other agencies. These organizations include United Ways; Jewish federations and appeals; commercially sponsored donor-advised funds; and combined funds, such as the Combined Federal Campaign, America's Charities, and others. Foundations, both private and community, are treated in a separate section of *Giving USA*. Estimates for giving to foundations appear there.

This subsector includes many other types of nonprofits, including those that work for civil rights or other social action, those dedicated to community improvement and capacity building, and nonmedical research institutes in the sciences and social sciences. In most years, combined fundraising appeals receive the largest share of charitable revenue in this subsector. In the National Taxonomy of Exempt Entities (NTEE), the public-society benefit sector as reported by *Giving USA* includes major category codes R, S, T (except private foundations and community foundations), U, V, and W.

Giving to public-society benefit

As with all *Giving USA* estimates, the amount estimated in giving to public-society benefit organizations includes gifts received of cash, cash equivalents (securities) and in-kind gifts (artwork, patents, real estate, and other items of value). *Giving USA* tries to exclude the value of planned commitments and new pledges from its estimates.

Tables 1 through 3 summarize the findings from the *Giving USA* survey.[1] Table 1 shows the average and median amounts reported in charitable gifts; Table 2 shows the direction of change in giving (increase, decrease, or within 1 percent, which is termed "no change"), and Table 3 shows the percentage of organizations that reported bequest receipts and the average and median amount received from bequests for each organizational size.

Table 1
Charitable revenue received by public-society benefit organizations in 2004 and 2005, by organizational size

Organizational size	Number of completed surveys	2004 average ($)	2004 median ($)	2005 average ($)	2005 median ($)
Large	18	38,649,691	31,514,976	39,021,588	33,147,663
Medium	63	3,108,882	1,604,000	3,224,167	1,660,500
Small	22	46,690	7,500	61,460	9,180

Large denotes organizations that receive $20 million or more in charitable revenue; *medium* is used for organizations having revenue between $1 million and $19.99 million, and *small* is for organizations that have charitable revenue of less than $1 million.

Table 2 summarizes the average and median increases or decreases in charitable revenue reported for 2005 by organizational size. Large and small organizations that responded to the *Giving USA* survey have mixed results, without a majority reporting a change in either direction. In medium-sized organizations, 59 percent reported an increase in the amount of charitable revenue received.

Giving to public-society benefit

Table 2
Increases or decreases in charitable revenue of
public-society benefit organizations, 2005

Organizational size	Number	Percentage of organizations in size group	Average change ($)	Average change (%)	Median change ($)	Median change (%)
Large						
Increase	8	44	3,822,506	11	4,013,531	10
Decrease	5	28	-4,738,456	-30	-3,680,100	-14
No change	5	28	-38,723	<1	0	0
Total	18	100				
All large organizations			344,574	3	35,717	<1
Medium						
Increase	37	59	495,138	28	300,000	13
Decrease	18	29	-613,714	-31	-479,864	-14
No change	8	13	-1,285	<1	0	0
Total	63	101*				
All medium organizations			124,095	8	70,094	4
Small						
Increase	10	45	35,668	82	16,781	47
Decrease	3	14	-10,578	-36	-4,000	-9
No change	9	41	0	0	0	0
Total	22	100				
All small organizations			14,770	32	0	0

*Total does not equal 100 due to rounding.

Table 3 shows bequest receipts by organizational size. The average and the median fell slightly in large organizations but rose in medium-sized organizations. No small organizations responding to the survey reported bequest revenue.

Table 3
Bequest receipts by organizational size, 2005

Organizational size	Percentage with bequest revenues	2004 average ($)	2004 median ($)	2005 average ($)	2005 median ($)
Large	56	1,875,344	932,667	1,840,910	887,502
Medium	29	395,479	78,151	507,224	120,000
Small	–	–	–	–	–

Donations for hurricane relief to public-society benefit organizations exceed $260 million

By mid-October 2005, United Way of America reported gifts of more than $8 million to its hurricane response fund and $16 million donated to local United Ways.[2] By year-end, United Way of America reported donations for hurricane relief totaling $45.8 million. Other organizations in the public-society benefit subsector reporting amount raised just for hurricane disaster relief included the following:

Bush-Clinton Hurricane Relief Fund	$110.0 million
United Jewish Communities, including the federations and their partners	28.5 million
Help America Hear, a business redevelopment program	25.0 million
Knights of Columbus	2.0 million
Associated Black Charities	.6 million
National Association for the Advancement of Colored People	.5 million
Kiwanis International	.5 million
Corporation for National and Community Service	.5 million

There were also a number of corporate donations to disaster relief funds created by employees, such as the Harrah's Employee Recovery Fund, the Ernst & Young Disaster Relief Fund, and others. Funds created by states to receive disaster relief donations—if registered as charities—are in the public-society benefit subsector.

The amounts reported here were collected by the Center on Philanthropy at Indiana University from a variety of sources, including press reports and communications directly with the reporting agencies. Because many organizations did not provide data to the Center, this is only a partial listing. The amounts collected by the Center, supplemented with data about disaster relief giving to organizations in this subsector that was provided in the *Giving USA* survey, total just 1.9 percent of all estimated contributions to the public-society benefit subsector.

Further calls for permitting households to itemize charitable contributions

United Way of America estimated that permitting charitable deductions for households that otherwise do not itemize deductions on tax returns could mean up to $242 million in additional revenue to United Way agencies nationally. Implementing a minimum threshold for the allowed deduction for charitable gifts by those itemizing tax deductions could decrease giving by an estimated $62 million—meaning a combined proposal would result in a net gain of $180 million for United Way alone.[3] The Charity, Recovery, and Empowerment (CARE) Act of 2005 was designed to limit abuses of charities while encouraging increased levels of contributions. Special attention was directed toward provisions for donor-advised funds. The legislation was not finalized in 2005.

One of nation's biggest United Ways toughens eligibility criteria, loses charities

Public attention in Washington, D.C., focused on toughening the eligibility standards applied by the United Way of the National Capital Area. The result was that 150 District of Columbia nonprofits were dropped from eligibility for United Way funds because of errors in their applications. This is especially significant because applications are typically forwarded by the capital area United Way to the Combined Federal Campaign, the annual federated drive for federal workers.[4]

Community redevelopment and affordable home construction initiatives announced

"Access@home" is a $1 billion initiative to develop 15,000 affordable housing units that include built-in Internet access and computing equipment for the residents. The initiative is a partnership of the Local Initiatives Support Corporation, its subsidiary the National Equity Fund, and One Economy Corporation.[5]

The W.K. Kellogg Foundation announced initiatives to support community redevelopment efforts in Detroit and in Battle Creek, Michigan.[6] The combined value of the announced grants was $29.5 million, which is approximately 15.4 percent of all Kellogg Foundation grantmaking ($191,552,690) in 2004.[7] The Ford Foundation announced $7 million in grants to help revitalize Detroit in grants made to the Community Foundation for Southeastern Michigan and the Detroit Riverfront Conservancy.[8]

Center on Philanthropy Panel Study (COPPS) finds combined campaigns account for 10 percent of estimated household giving

Using data collected about giving in 2002, the Center on Philanthropy found that just over one-quarter (27 percent) of households reported giving for a combined purpose, which includes a United Way, a Jewish federation, a donor-advised fund, or a community foundation. After giving to religion (45 percent of households) and giving to help the needy (29 percent of households), giving to combined campaigns is the third-most popular type of charitable contribution in the U.S.

The average gift total among the households that reported a gift to this subsector was $476—the second-highest total (after religion, at an average of $1,703). With gifts averaging $476 from 32 million households (27 percent of an estimated population of 120 million households in 2002), giving for combined campaigns by households is estimated to have been $15.42 billion in 2002. Note that the COPPS estimate includes gifts to community foundations, which are NOT included in this subsector in *Giving USA*. It also includes at least one organization that is not in the public-society benefit subsector. Catholic Charities is listed in the question as an example of a combined fundraising campaign, but it is coded by the National Center for Charitable Statistics as being in the human services subsector. The Center on Philanthropy Panel Study reaches more than 8,000 households. More about the panel study findings and methods can be found in the section of this book titled "Overview."

United Way tops Philanthropy 400 rankings for 2004

According to the annual Philanthropy 400 rankings, United Way of America was the charity that raised the most money in the United States in 2004. The 15th annual survey by *The Chronicle of Philanthropy* of America's biggest charities reported that the nation's 1,350 United Ways raised $23.9 billion in 2004, an increase of 0.4 percent from the previous year.[9]

United Ways and community foundations challenged to coordinate efforts more often

A report examining the growing potential for competition between United Ways and Community Foundations indicates an increasing need to coordinate their efforts as they face increased overlap in board leadership, donor bases, and grantmaking.[10]

Record Combined Federal Campaign for 2005

The Combined Federal Campaign reported raising a record $268.5 million in 2005, up from $256.8 million raised in 2004, an increase of 4.6 percent (1.1 percent after inflation adjustment). More than 300 campaigns worldwide were conducted.[11] In February 2006, the Government Accountability Office launched an investigation to determine whether nonprofit organizations participating in the Combined Federal Campaign have unpaid federal taxes, including payroll taxes.[12] The requirement that a participating nonprofit organization limit overhead expenses to no more than 25 percent of total revenue was lifted for the Make-A-Wish Foundation following a hearing in Phoenix, Arizona after that organization challenged the CFC's overhead expense rules. The CFC proposed in 2006 to lift the limit entirely for all organizations.[13]

United Jewish Communities reports strong results of annual and endowment campaigns as well as online giving

United Jewish Communities (UJC) released an annual report through June 30, 2005, showing that the annual campaigns at participating federations again raised more than $850 million and that more than $1 billion was generated in new endowment funds. They also announced Operation Promise, a $160 million effort to provide new support for the world's poorest Jews. UJC saw results of a concentrated effort to increase e-commerce with online donations surging by 382 percent to $3.67 million.[14]

Commercial donor-advised funds report banner year

Fidelity Charitable Gift fund announced that contributions topped $1 billion in 2005, a level last reached in 2000 before the 2001 recession.[15] At $1 billion or more, this single entity accounted for 7.1 percent of all estimated giving in 2005 to the public-society benefit subsector (including disaster gifts). Distributions from the 34,412 accounts at the Fidelity Charitable Gift Fund were more than $724 million in the fiscal year ending June 30, 2005. That amount was 24 percent of assets at the end of that fiscal year, well beyond the 5 percent payout required for private (independent and corporate) foundations.

Giving to public-society benefit

The *Chronicle of Philanthropy* released results from its survey of commercially sponsored donor-advised funds for 2005, finding that assets rose during the year, buoyed by investment performance and by new gifts.[16] Table 4 summarizes the four largest funds of the 17 that provided information to the *Chronicle*, their assets in 2005, and the amounts distributed to charities. These four funds accounted for approximately $1.147 billion in contributions in the period July 1, 2004 through June 30, 2005.

Table 4
Four largest commercially sponsored donor-advised funds
Assets, distributions, and new gifts received, circa 2005
($ in millions)

	Assets at end of fiscal year	Charitable distributions during year	Percentage of assets distributed	New gifts received
Fidelity Investments Charitable Gift Fund	3,046	736	24	891[1]
Vanguard Charitable Endowment	945	219	23	435[2]
National Philanthropic Trust	502	91	18	113[3]
Schwab Fund for Charitable Giving	480	101	21	266[4]

Data: Assets, Distributions: *Chronicle of Philanthropy*, May 4, 2006.

New gifts: [1]Fidelity Investments Charitable Gift Fund annual report for fiscal year ended June 2005, and www.charitablegiving.org.

[2]IRS Form 990 as of June 2005 available at www.guidestar.org.

[3]IRS Form 990 as of June 2004 available at www.guidestar.org. No more recent information was found at the organization or at Guidestar.

[4]Schwab Fund for Charitable Giving, audited financial statements for the fiscal year ended June 2005, at www.schwabcharitable.org.

Percentage of assets distributed: *Giving USA* divided charitable distributions by assets.

Concern about the relatively unregulated nature of donor-advised funds prompted Congress to attempt more stringent regulatory control. The Tax Relief Act passed by the Senate on November 18, 2005 proposes greater restrictions on these funds, including a minimum 5 percent payout (similar to foundations), stricter controls on administrative expenses, and more specifically defining what constitutes a donor-advised fund. That act did not move to the next step in the legislative process during 2005.

Key findings from other studies summarized

Table 5 presents three years of findings from studies released annually about contributions to public-society benefit organizations. Web site addresses are provided so readers can access the full reports.

Table 5
Key findings from other studies

$5 million dollar list, gifts from individuals to public-society benefit (does not include gifts to foundations) Center on Philanthropy at Indiana University, www.philanthropy.iupui.edu			
	2003	2004	2005
Number of public-society benefit gifts	8	2	None
Largest gift to public-society benefit	$100 million from Paul Allen to the Allen Institute for Brain Science	$12 million from the estate of Werner and Ellen Lange to the Jewish Community Foundation of Los Angeles	
Public-society benefit dollars given as percentage of all individual gifts on list of $5 million and above	5.1 percent	0.2 percent	

Foundation Giving Trends: Update on Funding Priorities Grants to public-society benefit organizations Foundation Center, www.fdncenter.org			
	2002	2003	2004
Median grant amount	$30,000	$30,000	$30,000
Average grant amount	$117,641	$116,483	$125,536
Public-society benefit funding as a percentage of grant dollars (surveyed foundations, including corporate foundations)	11 percent	13 percent	13 percent

Results of United Way campaigns and other fundraising United Way of America, www.unitedway.org			
	2002–2003	2003–2004	2004–2005
Total raised in campaigns	$3.71 billion	$3.59 billion	$3.86 billion
Gifts to specific initiatives	$88 million	$77 million	$83 million
Planned gifts and contingent pledges	$36 million	$58 million*	$62 million*

*2003–2004 and 2004–2005 values are realized bequests, endowment gifts, and other realized planned gifts.

USES OF CONTRIBUTIONS

Giving to public-society benefit

Combined federal campaign Office of Personnel Management, www.opm.gov/cfc			
	2003	2004	2005
Total amount raised	$249.23 million	$256.8 million	$268.5 million
Average gift per donor	$185	$198.52	$214.55
Percentage participation	33.9	32.5	32

IRS tax-exempt organizations in public-society benefit subsector Charities and Other Tax-Exempt Organizations, 2000, 2001, and 2002 *Statistics of Income Bulletin*, www.irs.gov			
	2000	2001	2002
Number	19,854	21,537	21,433
Charitable revenue*	$24.29 billion	$27.36 billion	$25.30 billion

*Charitable revenue includes gifts and foundation grants (which is comparable to what *Giving USA* tracks) as well as government grants and allocations from other nonprofit agencies such as United Way and United Jewish Communities (which are not included in *Giving USA* estimates for contributions).

1 *Giving USA* sent surveys to 1,322 organizations in the public-society benefit subsector in spring 2006. Of the organizations receiving the survey, 130 (10 percent) provided a response to the 10 questions in the study. Not all responses could be used, leaving 103 for analysis (8 percent). The usable response rate from large organizations was higher, at 15.7 percent. All large public-society benefit organizations account for approximately 40 percent of all charitable revenue in the public-society benefit subsector. The sample was selected based on charitable revenue received circa 2003 (includes some organizations that reported only in 2001 or only in 2002), supplemented with information obtained about public-society benefit organizations reporting in 2004 and appearing on the *Chronicle of Philanthropy* list of the 400 charities receiving the most charitable revenue in 2004. Many studies of nonprofit organizations receive a response rate of about 10 percent. *Giving USA* has analyzed the responses of "early responders" and "late responders," and found no statistically significant difference in the amount of change reported by these two groups. If nonresponders are similar to early or late responders in the amount of change they experience in charitable revenue, the low response rate will not materially affect the estimated rate of change.

2 United Way awards over $4 million in grants to Gulf-coast region, United Way of America, press release, October 18, 2005, www.national.unitedway.org.

3 Combined itemizer/non-itemizer deduction to increase charitable giving, United Way, http://national.unitedway.org/files/pdf/UWAStudyofCombinedItemizerNonitemizerDeduction.pdf.

4 J. Salmon, United Way tightens reins on admission, *Washington Post*, December 25, 2005.

5 One Economy announces $1 billion affordable housing, digital divide initiative, *Philanthropy News Digest*, August 15, 2005, http://fdncenter.org.

6 Ford, Kellogg Foundations commit $17 million to Detroit neighborhood, riverfront development, *Philanthropy News Digest*, December 5, 2005, http://fdncenter.org (Detroit for $10 million); Kellogg Foundation builds community to fight economic, racial inequities in Battle Creek, *Philanthropy News Digest*, July 12, 2005, http://fdncenter.org (Battle Creek for 19.5 million).

Giving to public-society benefit

7   W.K. Kellogg Foundation annual report 2004: A legacy of innovation, W.K. Kellogg Foundation, www.wkkf.org.

8   Ford, Kellogg Foundations commit $17 million to Detroit neighborhood, riverfront development, *Philanthropy News Digest*, December 5, 2005, http://fdncenter.org.

9   H. Hall, L. Kerkman, C. Moore, Giving bounces back, *The Chronicle of Philanthropy*, October 27, 2005.

10   CompassPoint Nonprofit Services, Convergence and competition: United Ways & Community Foundations, a national inquiry, August 2005, funded by C.S. Mott Foundation and the Community Foundations Leadership Team of the Council of Foundations, www.compasspoint.org/uwcf.

11   G. Williams, $257-million committed to government charity drive, *The Chronicle of Philanthropy*, June 23, 2005.

12   CFC Memorandum 2006–7 Subject: The Government Accountability Office requests for information, Combined Federal Campaign, February 14, 2006, www.opm.gov/cfc/opmmemos/2006/2006–7.asp.

13   G. Williams, Charities in Combined Federal Campaign face government review, *The Chronicle of Philanthropy*, February 23, 2006.

14   United Jewish Communities: annual report 2005, http://www.ujc.org/.

15   Fidelity Charitable Gift Fund reports 2005 was a record year, press release, February 13, 2006, www.charitablegift.org.

16   L. Kerkman, A soaring year: Assets at donor-advised funds rose by more than 20%, *The Chronicle of Philanthropy*, May 4, 2006, www.philanthropy.com.

Giving to environment and animals

- Giving to organizations in the environment and animals subsector is estimated to be $8.86 billion in 2005. This is 3.4 percent of total estimated giving.

- In current dollars, giving to environment and animals organizations increased by an estimated 16.4 percent in 2005. Adjusted for inflation, this is an increase of 12.6 percent.

- The estimate of giving to this subsector rose in 2005 because 63 percent of organizations reported an increase in charitable revenue from 2004 to 2005. The increases were large, on average 26 percent more than the amount raised in 2004.

- Organizations in all three size groups (large, medium-sized, and small) reported growth in giving. The amount donated to all the large organizations providing data rose by 15 percent; medium-sized organizations received 14 percent more than in 2004; and gifts to small organizations rose by 28 percent.

- Animal rescue efforts in the aftermath of Hurricane Katrina received an estimated $30 million or more in donations, much of which was from online giving.

Giving USA findings for benchmarking giving to environment and animals organizations, 2006

Giving to environment and animals organizations includes contributions to organizations working for land conservation, pollution abatement or control, species preservation, animal rescue, environmental education and outdoor survival, and other activities involving animals or the environment. In the National Taxonomy of Exempt Entities (NTEE), environment and animals covers organizations in codes C and D.

As with all *Giving USA* estimates, the amount estimated in giving to organizations in the environment and animals subsector includes gifts received of cash, cash equivalents (securities), and in-kind gifts (art work, patents, real estate, and other items of value). *Giving USA* tries to exclude from its estimates the value of deferred or planned gift commitments and new pledges.

Tables 1 through 3 summarize the findings from the 2006 *Giving USA* survey.[1] Table 1 shows the average and median amounts reported in charitable gifts; Table 2 shows the direction of change in giving (increase, decrease, or within 1 percent, which is termed "no change"), and Table 3 shows the percentage of organizations that reported bequest receipts and the average and median amount received from bequests for each organizational size.

Giving to environment and animals

Table 1
Charitable revenue received by environment and animals organizations in 2004 and 2005, by organizational size

Organizational size	Number of completed surveys	2004 average ($)	2004 median ($)	2005 average ($)	2005 median ($)
Large	8	39,304,434	34,409,922	45,364,081	39,170,699
Medium	53	2,616,071	1,754,721	2,991,646	1,854,033
Small	28	49,664	27,544	63,601	35,972

Large denotes organizations that receive $20 million or more in charitable revenue; *medium* is used for organizations having revenue between $1 million and $19.99 million, and *small* is for organizations that have charitable revenue of less than $1 million.

Table 2 summarizes the average and median increases or decreases in charitable revenue reported for 2005 by organizational size. In all size groups, a majority of environment and animals organizations responding to the *Giving USA* survey reported growth in charitable revenue.

Table 2
Increases or decreases in charitable revenue of environment and animals organizations, 2005

Organizational size	Number	Percentage of organizations in size group	Average change ($)	Average change (%)	Median change ($)	Median change (%)
Large						
Increase	7	88	6,925,311	17	2,261,000	14
Decrease	0	0	–	–	–	–
No change	1	13	0	0	0	0
Total	8	101*				
All large organizations			6,059,647	15	2,204,441	14
Medium						
Increase	31	58	958,158	46	499,470	38
Decrease	19	36	-499,315	-21	-219,623	-17
No change	3	6	3,134	<1	0	0
Total	53	100				
All medium organizations			375,575	20	250,626	12

*Total does not equal 100 due to rounding.

Giving to environment and animals

Organizational size	Number	Percentage of organizations in size group	Average change ($)	Average change (%)	Median change ($)	Median change (%)
Small						
Increase	18	64	26,518	67	9,738	28
Decrease	3	11	-28,667	-27	-20,000	-20
No change	7	25	-156	<1	0	0
Total	28					
All small organizations			13,937	40	2,691	13

Table 3 shows bequest receipts by organizational size. The average and the median declined in large organizations. The average and the median rose in medium-sized organizations and both rose greatly in small organizations.

Table 3
Bequest receipts by organizational size, 2005

Organizational size	Percentage with bequest revenues	2004 average ($)	2004 median ($)	2005 average ($)	2005 median ($)
Large	75	3,739,692	3,588,575	3,542,759	3,122,989
Medium	64	428,038	179,326	694,375	266,675
Small*	7	5,806	5,806	17,355	20,715

* For 2005, only four small environment and animals organizations provided bequest information. The values are reported here although the number of responses is too low to use in making statistical inferences about small environment and animals organizations.

Gift to Maddie's Fund tops environmental and animals contributions for 2005

Cheryl and David Duffield contributed $93 million to the organization they created called Maddie's Fund (operating within the Duffield Family Foundation). The charity supports animal rescue centers and humane societies that implement procedures to avoid killing animals that are not adopted.

On the list maintained by the Center on Philanthropy of gifts from individuals of $5 million or more, there were 8 contributions for environment or animal-related charities, or 2 percent of the 338 entries. The environment-animals gifts totaled 2 percent of the dollars tallied.

Wal-Mart to donate $35 million for land conservation

Shortly after it came under criticism from environmental, labor, and community organizations, Wal-Mart announced a commitment to donate $35 million over the next 10 years for a conservation effort by the National Fish and Wildlife Foundation. The program, titled "Acres for America," aims to protect hundreds of thousands of acres of land from development. According to a Wal-Mart spokesperson, the program "helps demonstrate that economic growth and development can go hand in hand." The gift was given by the Wal-Mart corporation rather than the foundation. The Wal-Mart Foundation distributed $170 million to charities in 2004.[2]

After Katrina, animal welfare organizations raised record funds online

Support for the pets abandoned as a result of Hurricane Katrina surpassed most expectations. The Humane Society of the United States anticipated raising $1 million after the disaster but ended up raising more than $20 million. Most of the funds, $18 million, were pledged over the Internet. Similarly, 90 percent of the $13 million raised by the American Society for the Prevention of Cruelty to Animals was pledged online. Noah's Wish, a California group dedicated to disaster response for animals, raised $5 million, while the American Humane Association raised $1.6 million. It is estimated that animal welfare organizations cared for 13,000 to 15,000 animals during the six-week rescue operation.[3]

Senate Finance Committee calls for changes after investigating largest environmental charity

Completing a two-year investigation into Arlington, VA-based Nature Conservancy, the Senate Finance Committee issued a report recommending regulatory changes that might affect many nonprofit organizations in the country. The report questioned the Conservancy's compliance with some federal tax laws, the size of tax breaks claimed by donors, and the organization's diligence in monitoring development restrictions on some of the land under its supervision. The report also brought to light the failure of the Conservancy to disclose transactions with officials and corporations whose officers sat on its board. In addition to other recommendations, the report called for conservation groups to develop a system of accreditation and to set limits on tax deductions for easements.[4] If adopted, the report's recommendations will affect the entire nonprofit sector, especially with regard to greater public disclosure of charitable organizations' activities.[5]

Environmental organizations across the country were concerned that enactment of Congressional recommendations regarding easements and donations of land could virtually stop private donations of land to conservation organizations. The Land Trust Alliance, which represents more than 1,500 land trusts around the country, developed a training and accreditation program for land conservation organizations that receive private donations.[6]

Polls consistently show strong support for environmental movement

Nearly three-quarters of the 1,217 adults surveyed in an October 2005 Harris Interactive telephone poll agreed that "protecting the environment is so important that requirements and standards cannot be too high, and continuing environmental improvements must be made regardless of cost." The top priority among respondents was water pollution, followed by air pollution. Other concerns included global warming, ozone depletion, and the loss of forest lands.[7]

Grantmakers encourage environmental conflict resolution (ECR) as tool for environmental advocates

The William and Flora Hewlett Foundation published "Environmental Conflict Resolution" as a guide to environmental grantmakers who are striving to strengthen their power to address pressing environmental challenges. The primer outlines the advantages of ECR over traditional legislative, administrative, and legal procedures, explains ECR processes, including examples of ECR in action, and suggests ways of measuring outcomes. The guide also contains an extensive list of resources, including people, organizations, web sites, and publications.[8]

Major gifts support environmental solutions through multi-disciplinary collaboration at universities

Funds for environmental research encourage innovative and multidisciplinary approaches to conservation. A $30 million commitment by Stanford University trustee Ward W. Woods and his wife Priscilla will fund collaborative research at the Stanford Institute for the Environment.[9] The Yale Environment Management Center received a $1.5 million grant from the Moore Foundation to support a joint master's degree program at the Yale School of Management and the Yale School of Forestry and Environmental Studies.[10]

Center on Philanthropy Panel Study finds 8 percent of households give for environment or animal-related causes; average gift is $157 per donor household

Using data collected in 2003 about giving in 2002 (and released late in 2004), the Center on Philanthropy found that 8 percent of households reported charitable gifts made to organizations working for the environment or on animal-related causes. Among the households giving for these purposes, the average gift for environment charities or for animal organizations was $157. Environmental donors number about the same as arts donors, and the average gift amount for the environment is slightly less than giving to help youths (which was $198, on average) and slightly more than gifts for neighborhood or community ($139, on average). The Center on Philanthropy Panel Study reaches more than 8,000 households. More about the panel study findings and methods can be found in the section of this book titled "Overview."

Key findings from annual studies summarized

Table 4 presents three years of findings from studies released annually about contributions to environmental or animal-related organizations. Web site addresses are provided to help readers get access to the full report.

Table 4
Key findings from other studies

$5 million dollar list, gifts from individuals to environment and animals (does not include gifts to foundations) Center on Philanthropy at Indiana University, www.philanthropy.iupui.edu			
	2003	2004	2005
Number of gifts to organizations in the environment and animals subsector	4	3	8
Largest gift to an organization in the environment and animals subsector	$28.6 million to the Nature Conservancy from the estate of Priscilla Bullitt Collins	$180 million (value) in the form of 146,000 acres of Missouri forest to the L-A-D Foundation, an operating foundation, from Leo and Kay Drey	$93 million from Dave and Cheryl Duffield to Maddie's Fund, to support humane, no-kill treatment of stray and abandoned animals
Environment and animals dollars given as percentage of all individual gifts on list of $5 million and above	2.2 percent	2.3 percent	2.0 percent

Foundation Giving Trends: Update on Funding Priorities Grants to environment and animals Foundation Center, www.fdncenter.org			
	2002	2003	2004
Median grant amount	$30,000	$30,000	$30,000
Average grant amount	$120,452	$120,698	$110,296
Environment and animals funding as a percentage of grant dollars (surveyed foundations, including corporate foundations)	5.9 percent	6.2 percent	5.3 percent

IRS tax-exempt organizations in environment and animals category Charities and other tax-exempt organizations, 2000, 2001, 2002 *Statistics of Income Bulletin*, www.irs.gov			
	2000	2001	2002
Number	7,859	8,697	9,413
Charitable revenue*	$4.97 billion	$5.38 billion	$5.98 billion

*Charitable revenue includes gifts and foundation grants (which is comparable to what *Giving USA* tracks) as well as government grants and allocations from other nonprofit agencies, such as United Way and United Jewish Communities (which are not included in *Giving USA* estimates for contributions).

Giving to environment and animals

1   *Giving USA* sent surveys to 815 organizations in the environment and animals subsector. Responses were received from 94 organizations (12 percent); 89 could be analyzed. The response rate among large organizations was 27 percent. Just 30 large organizations are estimated to receive approximately 20 percent of all dollars donated to the more than 10,500 environment and animals organizations. The sample was selected based on charitable revenue received circa 2003 (includes some organizations that reported only in 2001 or only in 2002), supplemented with information obtained about environment and animals organizations reporting in 2004 and appearing on the *Chronicle of Philanthropy* list of the 400 charities receiving the most charitable revenue in 2004.

2   Stephanie Strom, Wal-Mart Donates $35 Million for Conservation and Will Be Partner With Wildlife Group. *New York Times*, April 13, 2005. http://web.lexis-nexis.com.proxy.ulib.iupui.edu/universe/document.

3   *Philanthropy News Digest*, November 17, 2005, http://fdncenter.org/pnd/news/story.

4   *Philanthropy News Digest*, June 9, 2005, The Foundation Center, http://fdncenter.org/pnd/news/story.

5   Mary Dalrymple, Senate panel examines nonprofit world through land conservation. Associated Press, June 7, 2005. http://web.lexis-nexis.com.proxy.ulib.iupui.edu/universe/document.

6   See the accreditation information at http://www.lta.org/accreditation/.

7   Nearly Half of Americans Cite "Too Little" Environment Regulation. *Wall Street Journal Online*, 13 October 2005, http://online.wsj.com/public/article_print.

8   William and Flora Hewlett Foundation, http://www.hewlett.org/Publications/ecr.htm.

9   $30 Million Gift Jump-Starts Environmental Effort at Stanford. *Business Wire*, 14 February 2006, http://web.lexis-nexis.com.proxy.ulib.iupui.edu/universe/document.

10 $1.5 Million Moore Foundation Grant to Build Environmental Leadership in Amazon. Ascribe Newswire, 12 September 2005, http://web.lexis-nexis.com.prox.ulib.iupui.edu/universe/document.

Giving to international affairs

- Cash and in-kind giving to organizations in the international affairs subsector is estimated to be $6.39 billion in 2005, which includes at least $1.14 billion in gifts for relief work after the tsunami in December 2004 and after the October 2005 earthquake in Pakistan.

- International affairs giving is 2.5 percent of total estimated giving.

- In current dollars, giving to international affairs grew by an estimated 19.4 percent in 2005. Adjusted for inflation, this is a change of 15.6 percent.

- The estimated $1.14 billion for tsunami relief and earthquake relief that went to organizations in the international affairs subsector is 17.8 percent of total estimated international affairs contributions in 2005.

- Calculated without the disaster giving, gifts to the international affairs subsector fell by 1.9 percent (to an estimated $5.25 billion in 2005). This would be an inflation-adjusted drop of 5.1 percent.

Giving USA findings for benchmarking giving to international affairs, 2004

Giving to the international affairs subsector includes contributions to organizations formed for purposes of providing international relief and development aid, promoting international understanding or exchange, engaging in policy issues related to national and international security, or advancing human rights internationally. Organizations in this subsector are classified in the National Taxonomy of Exempt Entities (NTEE) as being in Major Category Q.

As with all *Giving USA* estimates, the amount estimated in giving to organizations in the international subsector includes gifts received of cash, cash equivalents (securities), and in-kind gifts (artwork, patents, real estate, and other items of value). *Giving USA* tries to exclude from its estimates the value of deferred or planned gift commitments and new pledges.

Table 1 summarizes the average and median amounts raised by international affairs organizations in 2004 and 2005 based on organizational size.[1] The median is the mid-point. One-half of the organizations responding had higher charitable revenue; the other one-half had lower. The survey asked organizations to report disaster giving separately. These figures are calculated without disaster relief giving included.

Table 2 summarizes the average and median increases or decreases in charitable revenue reported for 2005 by organizational size. On average, large and small organizations in this subsector saw increases in gifts received. For medium-sized organizations, the average dollar change was a decline.

Giving to international affairs

Table 1
Charitable revenue received by international affairs organizations in 2004 and 2005 by organizational size (changes calculated before addition of disaster giving)

Organizational size	Number of completed surveys	2004 average ($)	2004 median ($)	2005 average ($)	2005 median ($)
Large	16	84,741,231	30,173,680	111,833,742	37,867,443
Medium	44	5,432,140	2,951,355	5,818,907	3,508,828
Small	13	192,132	250,000	220,269	300,000

Large denotes organizations that receive $20 million or more in charitable revenue; *medium* is used for organizations having revenue between $1 million and $19.99 million, and *small* is for organizations that have charitable revenue of less than $1 million.

Table 2
Increases or decreases in charitable revenue of international affairs organizations, 2005 (changes calculated before addition of disaster giving)

Organizational size	Number	Percentage of organizations in size group	Average change ($)	Average change (%)	Median change ($)	Median change (%)
Large						
Increase	14	88	32,041,790	65	14,146,669	34
Decrease	2	13	-7,552,438	-14	7,552,438	-14
No change	0	–	–	–	–	–
Total	16	101*				
All large organizations			13,829,665	-3	2,760,854	23
Medium						
Increase	25	57	1,471,979	46	711,641	24
Decrease	17	39	-1,163,633	-14	-329,000	-12
No change	2	5	0	0	0	0
Total	44	101*				
All medium organizations			-66,216	-11	55,720	2
Small						
Increase	6	46	73,896	32	70,053	23
Decrease	4	31	-19,398	-15	-7,860	-16
No change	3	23	0	0	0	0
Total	13	100				
All small organizations			28,137	10	0	0

*Total does not equal 100 due to rounding.

Table 3 shows bequest receipts by organizational size. The average and the median amounts increased in large and medium-sized organizations. Only one small organization reported bequest revenue, not enough to track a direction of change.

Organizational size	Percentage with bequest revenues	2004 average ($)	2004 median ($)	2005 average ($)	2005 median ($)
Large	69	2,187,548	1,646,062	2,787,743	1,868,394
Medium	30	90,582	66,718	198,872	93,381
Small*	8	12,000	12,000	10,000	10,000

*Only one small international organization provided bequest information. The value is reported here, although the response is too low to use in making statistical inferences about small international organizations.

International funding is not always in the international subsector

Many organizations in other subsectors conduct international activities, funding for which is not recorded in this section. These organizations include universities, health care organizations, arts and cultural institutions, youth development programs, religious entities, and many more. In addition, some donors, including individuals and corporations, direct financial support to charitable purposes in other nations. These transfers are not tracked in the U.S. tax system as charitable gifts because they are made to organizations not recognized as eligible, tax-exempt charities in the United States. Foundation grantmaking to organizations in other countries is included in *Giving USA* as part of the total amount contributed by foundations.

Study of international activity finds donations of $24 billion, including foundation grants, corporate donations, and charitable expenditures abroad

In early 2006, the Hudson Institute released its inaugural Index of Global Philanthropy.[2] This report presents estimates of international private giving in the United States and from people in other countries. For 2004, according to this study, donors in the United States directed $71 billion to other countries, which includes at least $47 billion in *remittances* (transfers of money that are sent to family members or others in one's country of origin). Of the estimated philanthropic giving as *Giving USA* measures it, the Hudson Institute finds $24.2 billion is directed to activities in other countries. Table 4 summarizes the Hudson Institute's findings about private assistance from the United States to other nations.

Major gifts for international affairs announced

The Center on Philanthropy's Million Dollar List included five major gifts of more than $5 million from an individual donor to U.S.-registered organizations in the international affairs subsector. They include a payment of $53 million from Robert Edward (Ted) Turner, an Atlanta businessman, to the United Nations Foundation.

Table 4
**Private assistance going from organizations or donors in the United States
to support activities in other countries
($ in billions)**

Source of aid	Amount
Foundations	3.4
Corporations	4.9
Private and voluntary organizations*	9.7
Universities and colleges	1.7
Religious organizations	4.5
Total	24.2

Source: *Index of Global Philanthropy*, Hudson Institute, April 2006, page 15.

*The estimate for private and voluntary organizations is based on data from 503 organizations registered with the U.S. Agency for International Development, which were integrated into a complex set of formulas and assumptions. It will not match the *Giving USA* estimate for cash donations to organizations in the international affairs subsector, which looks at different organizations and focuses on cash donations only.

Giving to international affairs or relief organizations for tsunami relief

Major international relief organizations dedicated funds from their reserves immediately upon learning about the December 26, 2004, tsunami that devastated coastal areas around the Indian Ocean, but especially on the island of Sumatra. By June 2005, at least $2 billion had been contributed to agencies in the United States. The exceptionally high level of giving by Americans can be explained by extensive media coverage of the waves, by the fact that the news arrived in the holiday season, or by other factors. A survey of households conducted as part of the Center on Philanthropy Panel Study in conjunction with the University of Michigan's Panel Study of Income Dynamics found that 30 percent of families reported making a donation for tsunami relief. The average donation was $125, but most donations were smaller, with half the donations reported as being $50 or less.

Corporations responded quickly with in-kind gifts and with cash contributions. The U.S. Chamber of Commerce established a clearinghouse for corporations wanting to identify unmet needs, to collaborate with other funders, and to learn about government efforts. With a disaster that affected dozens of nations, the logistics of organizing a relief effort were at times overwhelming.[3]

The scale of the disaster and the relief effort led to many attempts to learn from events and prepare better for the future. They ranged from installing better warning systems to evaluating the delivery of aid by the Fritz Institute, which polled survivors in India and Sri Lanka. Among the top-line findings of the Fritz Institute survey were that in-kind donations, especially of used clothing, were often inappropriate and too numerous to be managed.[4] Another important finding was that local organizations played a more prominent role than did the international nongovernmental organizations. The Fritz Institute concluded that local capacities for response and collaboration are essential for effective relief work. An example provided in the report cites one survivor as saying, "All were thinking of material like food, water, and clothes, but what was necessary was sanitation (p. 5)."

African famine overwhelms relief efforts

More than 9 million people faced severe food shortages in 2005 across West Africa's Sahel region because of poor harvests following years of drought and a locust plague in 2004. Donations began to flow for relief in Niger after media coverage intensified in July 2005, reportedly beginning in the United Kingdom.[5] The World Food Programme received more pledges in 10 days after that broadcast than it had in the previous 8 months.[6]

In April 2006, the World Food Programme announced it had received just 32 percent of the amount it projected would be needed to provide food in Sudan, another African nation with a famine. John Ambler of Oxfam America said that a permanent fund that can be accessed early when famine first threatens can feed a child for $1; but to raise money after the crisis starts and rely on a complex chain of supply can increase that cost to $80 per child.[7]

Israel withdraws from West Bank and Gaza Strip; donations flow for Jews relocated and for Palestinians remaining

In mid-2005, Israel mandated the departure of Jewish settlers from the West Bank and on the Gaza Strip—two territories Israel gained after the 1967 War.[8] Various humanitarian and religious organizations reported raising funds to assist the settlers leaving the areas and to provide support for Palestinians.[9]

World prepares to deal with possibility of H5N1 epidemic

With the influenza virus dubbed "bird flu" (and officially termed H5N1) appearing in people in Asian nations, Turkey, and parts of Europe, world health officials began serious efforts to prepare for a potential pandemic. The strain of the virus active in 2005 was not transmitted from person to person, only from a bird to a person who handled the living animal. Knowing that the virus mutates quickly and can develop into a form that does pass among humans through contact or through air or water, a major conference occurred in November 2005 that was jointly sponsored by the World Health Organization (WHO), the Federation of African Nations, the World Bank, and OIE (the World Organization for Animal Health).[10] Nations pledged $1.9 billion in resources to study the virus, develop vaccines, and create social methods (hand washing, limiting contact, etc.) to combat H5N1 influenza. Households, charities, businesses, and governments were encouraged to plan ahead and prepare for the time when a flu pandemic, widely regarded by health experts as inevitable,[11] will erupt.

Center on Philanthropy Panel Study finds 4 percent of households give for international relations, international aid, or peace and security causes; average gift is $293 per donor household

Using data about giving in 2002, the Center on Philanthropy at Indiana University found that 4 percent of households reported contributions made to organizations in the international affairs subsector. Among the households giving for these purposes, the average gift was $293. The Center on Philanthropy Panel Study reaches more than 8,000 households. More about the panel study findings and methods can be found in the section of this book titled "Overview."

Key findings from annual studies summarized

Table 5 summarizes key findings from studies released annually with information about giving to organizations in the international affairs subsector or about foundation giving for international purposes. Web site addresses are provided so readers can access the full reports.

Table 5
Key findings from other studies

$5 million dollar list, gifts from individuals to international affairs (does not include gifts to foundations) Center on Philanthropy at Indiana University, www.philanthropy.iupui.edu			
	2003	2004	2005
Number of international affairs gifts	2	1	5
Largest gift to international affairs	$28.6 million from the estate of Priscilla Bullitt Collins for CARE	$15 million from Herbert and Marion Sandler to Human Rights Watch	$53 million from Robert Edward (Ted) Turner to the United Nations Foundation
International affairs dollars given as percentage of all individual gifts on list of $5 million and above	1.4 percent	0.2 percent	1.1 percent

Foundation Giving Trends: Update on Funding Priorities Grants in the major subject category of international affairs, development, and peace Foundation Center, www.fdncenter.org			
	2002	2003	2004
Median grant amount	$45,000	$50,000	$50,000
Average grant amount	$136,668	$140,828	$150,202
International subsector funding as a percentage of grant dollars (surveyed foundations, including corporate foundations)	2.6 percent	2.5 percent	2.76 percent

Giving to international affairs

IRS tax-exempt organizations in international affairs Charities and Other Tax-Exempt Organizations, 2000, 2001, and 2002 *Statistics of Income Bulletin*, www.irs.gov			
	2000	2001	2002
Number filing IRS Form 990	2,970	3,360	3,505
Charitable revenue reported*	$8.13 billion	$9.33 billion	$11.40 billion

*Charitable revenue includes gifts and foundation grants (which is comparable to what *Giving USA* tracks) as well as government grants and allocations from other nonprofit agencies such as United Way and United Jewish Communities (which are not included in Giving USA estimates for contributions).

1   *Giving USA* sent surveys to 538 organizations in the international affairs subsector. Responses were received from 88 organizations (14 percent); 73 could be used for this analysis. The response rate from large organizations was 49 percent. About 35 large organizations account for approximately three-quarters of the total charitable revenue in this subsector of an estimated 2,500 organizations. The sample was selected based on charitable revenue received circa 2003 (includes some organizations that reported only in 2001 or only in 2002), supplemented with information obtained about international organizations reporting in 2004 and appearing on the *Chronicle of Philanthropy* list of the 400 charities receiving the most charitable revenue in 2004. Many studies of nonprofit organizations receive a response rate of around 10 percent. *Giving USA* has analyzed the responses of "early responders" and "late responders," and found no statistically significant difference in the amount of change reported by these two groups. If nonresponders are similar to early or late responders in the amount of change they experience in charitable revenue, the low response rate will not materially affect the estimated rate of change.

2   *The Index of Global Philanthropy*, Hudson Institute, April 2006, www.global-prosperity.org.
3   E. Girardet, When the world forgets who comes to help, *National Geographic*, December 2005.
4   Lessons from the tsunami: Top line findings, The Fritz Institute, September 2005, www.fritzinstitute.org.
5   Food shortages ease slightly in Niger, *The Economist,* August 18, 2005, www.economist.com.
6   M. Fleshman, A famine foretold, *Africa Renewal*, October 2005. Viewed at www.un.org.
7   John Ambler, quoted on Online Newshour, an interview transcript from August 23, 2005 at www.pbs.org.
8   West Bank pullout ends, Cox News Service, August 24, 2005. Viewed at lexis-nexis.com.
9   Evangelical Christians donate $40,000 to Gaza evacuees, Associated Press, October 17, 2005. Viewed at www.monabaker.com; H. Morris, Wolfenson breaks Gaza deadlock with personal donation of $500,000, *Financial Times*, August 13, 2005; How old friends of Israel gave $14 million to help the Palestinians, *New York Times,* August 18, 2005; Palestinian women farmers receive MCC [Mennonite Central Committee] financial aid, *Canadian Mennonite*, August 22, 2005. Viewed at www.lexisnexis.com.
10   Avian influenza and human pandemic influenza meeting presentations, World Health Organization, www.who.int.
11   J. Adler, Could this bird kill you? Avian flu threatens to be the next big epidemic, *Herald News*, December 20, 2005. Viewed at www.lexis-nexis.com.

Legal and legislative issues

This chapter presents an overview of legal and regulatory developments that may affect fundraising and the nonprofit sector. The first part of the chapter is organized by level of government: federal and then state. Within each governmental section are discussions of legislative activity, judicial decisions, and regulatory actions. The chapter concludes with a discussion of several steps that nonprofit organizations are taking to set their own standards and create structures that promote greater accountability.

Federal-level activity

This section discusses Congressional, judicial and administrative action related to nonprofit organizations at the federal level. Congress considered legislation to extend a tax deduction for charitable gifts to tax filers who otherwise do not itemize deductions, but action taken after Hurricane Katrina to provide tax relief took precedence. The Senate Finance Committee investigated several nonprofits and issued statements about vehicle donations and other possible abuses of the spirit of regulations about charitable deductions.

Legislation from House and Senate

During 2005 Congress focused considerable attention on nonprofit reform and tax relief. Both the House and the Senate introduced acts that would provide some additional tax benefits for some donors. None were passed except for the Katrina Emergency Tax Relief Act of 2005 (KETRA), signed into law on September 23, 2005. For updates about introduced legislation, see the "Bill Tracker" service for federal legislation at INDEPENDENT SECTOR's web site.[1]

KETRA includes a number of provisions for those directly affected by the destruction of Hurricane Katrina and for individuals and businesses that provide charitable gifts, whether for hurricane aid or other purposes. These provisions, which expired on December 31, 2005, include:

- Deductions for those providing shelter to victims
- Special rules for victims deducting losses
- No tax on debt forgiveness
- Low-interest mortgages
- Penalty-free retirement fund withdrawals for victims
- Extension of tax deadlines for those directly affected by the hurricane
- Tax deductions for vehicle use in aiding victims
- Special tax incentives for businesses to donate books and food
- Tax incentives for employing victims
- Small business tax credits
- Other incentives for charitable gifts

Of special note is the temporary suspension of limits or adjustments to charitable deductions claimed by individuals and corporations. In the case of the corporations, the 10 percent of taxable income limit is waived for contributions to organizations that provided relief to those affected by Hurricane Katrina. For individuals, KETRA suspended the tax law provision that usually applies for households with income above a specified amount. Under the usual provision, some claimed deductions (including charitable donations) are reduced by three percent of all adjusted gross income above the income limit, which was $149,950 for a married couple filing jointly in 2005. That reduction did not apply for charitable gifts in cash made to public charities between August 28 and December 31, 2005.[2] Further, itemized deductions for cash gifts to qualified charities were allowed up to 100 percent of adjusted gross income (for gifts made between August 28 and December 31) instead of the usual 50 percent.[3] The gifts could not be made to private foundations or to other types of funds where the money is not available for use immediately by the charity (e.g., trusts, donor-advised funds, and supporting organizations that raise funds for another entity).

Congressional Committees

Congressional committees were actively involved in investigating possible abuse and reforms within the nonprofit sector. The Senate Finance Committee concluded two long-running investigations. The House Ways and Means Committee reviewed the disaster response to Hurricane Katrina and called for better coordination among responding agencies, including charities, government, and others.

Senate Finance Committee concludes long-running investigations of charities
The Senate Finance Committee released a report in early summer 2005 concluding its two-year review of some of the financial transactions of the Nature Conservancy. The report focused on issues around the value of conservation easements; the practice known as "conservation buying"; ventures between for-profit entities and nonprofit entities, which complicate reporting and tax law compliance (and enforcement); and inadequacies in the financial reporting structure required by the Internal Revenue Service. The report concluded that the Nature Conservancy had already redressed many of the concerns revealed in media coverage of the organization in 2003 and included several other recommendations or remaining areas of concern.[4]

In a separate investigation, the committee found nothing "alarming" in the financial records of nearly two dozen Muslim groups the committee reviewed searching for terrorist connections.[5] The committee sought the records of the Muslim groups in December 2003, and almost two years later U.S. Senator Charles Grassley said in a statement, "We did not find anything alarming enough that required additional follow-up beyond what law enforcement is already doing."

House Ways and Means Subcommittee hearing on charities' response to Hurricane Katrina
At a December 13, 2005, hearing of the Oversight Subcommittee of the House Ways and Means Committee, participants praised charities' and volunteers' efforts to respond to Hurricane Katrina, while also highlighting shortcomings and lessons for future disasters.[6] Witnesses included Congressman Jim McCrery (R-LA) and representatives from the American Red Cross, the Salvation Army of America, the Baton Rouge Area Foundation, and from the disabled community. Congressman McCrery and other witnesses emphasized the importance of better coordination among charities, reaching out to minority and disabled communities, and ensuring that charitable dollars are not lost to fraud. Congressman McCrery noted that the American Red Cross has primary responsibility for mass care after a disaster and questioned whether one organization should shoulder such a large responsibility. He suggested that Congress reexamine its charter with the Red Cross, which it formally authorized to provide a national system of disaster response. Joseph Becker, Senior Vice President for Preparedness and Response at the American Red Cross, acknowledged challenges and assured subcommittee members that the organization had learned important lessons about how to improve its response to future disasters.

Senate Finance Committee Questions American Red Cross
In a December 29, 2005, letter to the American Red Cross, Senate Finance Committee Chair Charles Grassley (R-IA) questioned the organization's effectiveness and governance in the wake of Hurricane Katrina and asked for more details regarding the recent resignation of its president and CEO, Marsha Evans. Senator Grassley also questioned the charity's compensation practices and requested copies of Internal Revenue Service filings. In a December 29, 2005, statement, the American Red Cross promised to respond by January 30, 2006, as requested by Senator Grassley.[7]

Senate Finance Committee chair urges regulator changes for car donations
Senate Finance Committee Chair Grassley sent a December 19, 2005, letter to the IRS urging the agency to curtail abuses by some charities reselling donated cars to low-income consumers and requesting clarification about when charitable organizations must sell vehicles donated to the groups to comply with new IRS vehicle donation rules.

The IRS issued an announcement on December 22, 2005, clarifying regulations about timing of the vehicle sales and the need for written acknowledgment.[8] The IRS will not recognize certain deductions claimed by taxpayers for donated vehicles later sold at auction.[9] Although in most cases tax deductions of more than $500 for charitable vehicle donations are limited to the sale price obtained by a nonprofit, donors may claim a fair market value deduction if the vehicle was given or sold to a needy individual at a price significantly below fair market value. The IRS announced that it had become aware of charities that sold donated vehicles at auction and then claimed the sales were to needy individuals at prices below fair market value. The

IRS will, therefore, no longer consider vehicles sold at auction as qualifying for the fair market value deduction.

Court cases and rulings

There were 46 cases in U.S. federal court during 2005 that involved nonprofit organizations. Nonprofit advocacy organizations, in particular, were extremely active at the federal appellate level. Two interesting cases related to fundraising in 2005 were:

- A federal appeals court ruled that North Dakota's telemarketing law that permits volunteers to call people on the state's "do not call list" but prohibits paid fundraisers from making the calls doesn't violate the free-speech rights of nonprofits that use professional fundraisers. The 2-1 decision by the 8th U.S. Circuit Court of Appeals reversed an October 2003 decision by U.S. District Judge Ralph R. Erickson, who ruled that the law was unfair to charities. North Dakota Attorney General Wayne Stenehjem, who appealed the decision, called it a "victory for North Dakota's citizens and their right to privacy."[10]

- A nonprofit religious organization sued the City of Los Angeles, challenging definitions used in that city's law requiring an application in advance from organizations seeking to fundraise. The Court of Appeals found that the city's ordinance was not unconstitutionally vague and that the ordinance's definitions of "charitable" and "solicitation" were not unconstitutional.[11]

Federal agencies

Issues involving federal agencies include IRS inquiries into political activities of several churches during the 2004 presidential campaign; proposed new IRS regulations on imposing excise taxes and revoking charitable status; lawsuits filed against the Federal Bureau of Investigation by charities for alleged spying on citizens and domestic organizations; and the postal rate increase that will directly impact mailing costs for fundraising.

Internal Revenue Service investigates churches for political activity

The IRS sent a letter in June 2005 to begin investigation of a California Episcopal church, where a retired pastor preached a November 2004 sermon that included remarks criticizing the war in Iraq.[12] The IRS argued that the comments were a type of campaign intervention, which is prohibited to nonprofits, including churches. The church denied the allegations. An investigation was also opened about a Florida church, at which Senator John Kerry participated in services during the 2004 election. That case was concluded in early 2006 when the IRS found that there was no partisan political activity.[13] Churches can address social issues, public policy concerns, and even support specific legislation, but like other charities, they are prohibited from endorsing specific candidates.

Intermediate sanctions rules proposed

In early 2005, the IRS issued proposed new regulations outlining the facts and circumstances that would justify the imposition of intermediate sanctions pursuant to section 4958 which calls for excise taxes and potential revocation of charitable status.[14] The factors listed include the size and scope of the regular ongoing activity that further the exempt purposes of the organization; the size and scope of the excess benefit transaction or transactions in relation to the size of the organization; whether the organization has been involved in repeated incidents; whether the organization has established safeguards; and whether the excess benefit transaction has been corrected and the organization has acted in good faith to seek correction from the disqualified person or persons.

Federal Bureau of Investigation charged with domestic spying on charities
A number of nonprofit organizations that work on environmental issues, animal rights issues, and civil rights issues joined together to sue the FBI, according to news stories appearing in December 2005.[15] The American Civil Liberties Union represented the plaintiffs, which included People for the Ethical Treatment of Animals, Greenpeace, the American-Arab Anti-Discrimination Committee and the ACLU itself. The ACLU's suit claims that "FBI and government Joint Terrorism Task Forces across the country have expanded the definition of domestic terrorism to people who engage in mainstream political activity, including nonviolent protest and civil disobedience." The *Washington Post* article cited FBI officials as saying that the agency does not investigate groups for terrorism as a means of suppressing domestic dissent. The FBI said that it must investigate if a group or its members have ties to others who are guilty or suspected of violence or illegal conduct.

U.S. Post Office raises rates again, with more increases in sight for 2007
Late in 2005, the U.S. Postal Rate Commission recommended postal increases that would affect the mailing costs for charities. The rate increases vary by the type of mail and the types of services, with an increase of 12 percent for the nonprofit Enhanced Carrier Route rate.[16]

State-level activity
Eighteen states settled with a marketing firm that promoted "charity sweepstakes." In other news, states increasingly regulated charitable fundraising activities, with registration requirements and restrictions on the use of some kinds of contact with prospective donors (e.g., some types of mail and fax). In the state courts, a Michigan court ruled that a gift agreement did not state explicitly enough that a building would be named in consideration for the gift, making the gift agreement unenforceable.

States settle with firm that created deceptive sweepstakes as a fundraiser
Massachusetts-based Newport Creative Communications reached a settlement with a number of states over deceptive sweepstakes claims the company made in charity solicitations.[17] Newport Creative Communications is a fundraising consultant for charities. The states alleged that some of Newport's promotions were illegal and misleading, guaranteeing prizes or claiming that recipients had already won a sweepstakes prize. Under the terms of the agreement, Newport's direct-mail

solicitations will no longer claim that the recipient has already won a prize or will be guaranteed a prize by responding to the charitable solicitation. Newport will also cease creating mailings unless there is a prize ultimately awarded by the charity. In addition to changing their charity pitches, Newport also will pay $400,000, which will be dispersed among participating states to defray the costs of investigation. The states involved in the agreement are Arkansas, California, Kentucky, Massachusetts, Michigan, Minnesota, Montana, Nevada, New Jersey, North Carolina, Ohio, Oregon, Pennsylvania, South Carolina, Tennessee, Texas, Virginia, Washington and Wisconsin.

Legislative efforts to curb fundraising practices

States continue to be concerned about nonprofit organization fundraising practices. Thirty-two states were attempting to pass 69 bills or resolutions in 2005.[18] Of these, 14 states were successful in adopting 18 different bills or resolutions affecting nonprofit organizations. The major focus of the adopted bills was to limit bulk mail or fax solicitation. As a result of new legislation, nonprofits face greater restrictions on bulk mail and fax solicitations in Arkansas, California, Colorado, and New Jersey.[19]

States also were concerned with the use of "professional fundraisers," resulting in four states passing legislation that affects fundraising professionals. The laws in Colorado, Connecticut, Indiana and Virginia range from requiring greater disclosure when dealing with professional fundraisers to allowing professional fundraisers to file their registrations online.[20]

The state of Louisiana enacted legislation granting the legislative auditor authority to examine and audit books of Louisiana nonprofit organizations created for the purpose of disaster relief.[21] The Louisiana legislature also passed a concurrent resolution encouraging the state attorney general and state treasurer to ask charitable organizations for records related to the receipt and disbursement of donations for hurricane relief.

The state of Illinois passed a resolution urging federal agencies to develop a list of charitable organizations, including Muslim organizations, which are safe for all Americans to support without fear of prosecution and with assurance that their contributions will be used for the intended purposes.[22]

West Virginia passed legislation that would require organizations formed under Section 527 of the Internal Revenue Code to register with that state's Secretary of State prior to soliciting or accepting contributions. The law also prohibits these organizations, which played a prominent role in the 2004 presidential election, from accepting contributions in excess of $1,000.[23]

State courts

A state court decision in Michigan has a direct bearing on how gift agreements are worded in that state and may be applicable elsewhere. A family charitable foundation, which entered into an endowment agreement with a cancer center, brought action against the cancer center and the center's law firm after the center was not renamed pursuant to a provision included in the endowment agreement. [24] The family foundation claimed that the center had breached the agreement with the donor. The Court of Appeals held that the naming provision of the endowment agreement was unenforceable. The agreement did not specify that the gift was in consideration for the naming. Instead, the naming was in recognition for current and past support received.

Nonprofit advocacy

Charitable organizations belong to larger groups that represent the interests of charitable entities in a number of ways. INDEPENDENT SECTOR, one such membership organization, convened a Panel on the Nonprofit Sector in 2004 at the invitation of the Senate Finance Committee. That Panel concluded its work and released a report in 2005. In another initiative, a group of Muslim charities formed a new association to draw up financial and governance standards appropriate for their work.

The Panel on the Nonprofit Sector issues final report

The Panel on the Nonprofit Sector convened by INDEPENDENT SECTOR issued a final report in June 2005.[25] The Panel recommended more than 120 actions to be taken by charitable organizations, by Congress, and by the Internal Revenue Service, which together would strengthen the sector's transparency, governance, and accountability. Representing the collective expertise of hundreds of nonprofit leaders, these recommendations, if implemented, would constitute the most sweeping changes to the governance, operations, and regulation of charities and foundations in three decades.

Among the proposals:

- **To strengthen governance**, the Panel recommends that charitable organizations adopt, implement, and publicize audit procedures and policies on travel expenses, conflicts of interest, and whistleblower protection.

- **To make financial information** more reliable, the Panel recommends that Congress require audits by charitable organizations with annual revenues of $1 million or greater and an independent accountant's review for organizations with annual revenues between $250,000 and $1 million. The Panel also calls for Congress to require mandatory electronic filing of charitable organizations' annual information returns, the Forms 990; the IRS to improve the design of and instructions for Forms 990; and charitable organizations to have their CEOs or CFOs certify the accuracy of their information returns.

- **To prevent abuse of charitable entities**, the Panel recommends that Congress establish clearer legal guidelines for donor-advised funds, Type III supporting organizations (charities operated exclusively for the benefit of other public charities), and participation by tax-exempt entities in potentially abusive tax shelters. It also urges Congress to tighten up rules and strengthen penalties to help prevent transactions that benefit donors, rather than the public.

- **To ensure that non-cash contributions support charitable causes**, rather than provide improper tax deductions for donors, the Panel recommends that Congress establish clearer rules for valuing donated property and mandate stricter guidelines for appraisals of land and other appreciated property.

- **To address instances of excessive executive compensation**, the Panel recommends that Congress strengthen the penalties on board members who approve and executives who receive excessive compensation, that the IRS revise the Forms 990 to make the total compensation of executives clearer to the public and regulators, and that charitable organization boards approve executive compensation each year.

A copy of the Panel on the Nonprofit Sector report and other details are available at www.NonprofitPanel.org.

New membership group will set standards for Islamic charities

To help promote charitable giving by Muslim Americans and other donors, a group of nonprofit organizations formed a membership association that will set financial and governance standards for Islamic charities.[26] During a conference in Chicago in March 2005, a group of about 20 Muslim international-aid groups, advocacy organizations, and other charities announced plans to establish the National Council of American Muslim Nonprofits. The meeting was organized by the Islamic Society of North America, located in Plainfield, IN, and the Muslim Public Affairs Council, in Los Angeles. The new organization will be known as the National Council of American Muslim Non-Profits.

---

1   Independent Sector Bill Tracker, Key Legislation in the 109th Congress, www.independentsector.org.
2   Extraordinary tax benefits for cash gifts made to public charities before December 31, 2005, I.P. Hunt Foundation, www.iphuntfoundation.org.
3   The Sharpe Group, October 12, 2005, Memorandum to Development Executives
4   See www.senate.gov/~finance/hearings/other/tnccontents.pdf for the Senate Finance Committee Report and www.nature.org/pressroom/press/press1954.html for the organization's news release about the study and about its work to address concerns raised.
5   R. King, Indiana-based Islamic Society of North America cleared in Senate investigation, November 15, 2005, www.indystar.com or www.isna.net.
6   Independent Sector, Ways and Means Subcommittee hearing on charities' response to Hurricane Katrina, www.independentsector.org.
7   Senator Grassley letter to the American Red Cross, http://finance.senate.gov.
8   Senator Grassley letter to the IRS, www.senate.gov.
9   www.irs.gov/charities/index.html.
10 Fraternal Order of Police, ND State Lodge v. Stenehjem. 431 F.3d 591. CA8 (ND) 2005. Text available at www.ca8.uscourts.gov/opndir/05/12/033848P.pdf.
11 Gospel Missions of America, a religious corporation v. City of Los Angeles, 419 F.3d 1042 United States Court of Appeals (Ninth Circuit).

12   P. Ward Biederman and J. Felch, Antiwar sermon brings IRS warning, *Los Angeles Times*, November 7, 2005, www.latimes.com.

13   Florida church is subject to IRS inquiry for political activities, April 4, 2005, and IRS clears Florida church of political activity, January 11, 2006, both at www.Ombwatch.org in the area on nonprofit advocacy.

14   Fundraising and Non-Profit Report, electronic newsletter from Copilevitz and Canter, January 2005, www.copilevitz-canter.com.

15   S. Hsu, FBI papers show terror inquiries into PETA; other groups tracked, *Washington Post*, December 20, 2005, www.washingtonpost.com.

16   Nonprofit postal rates to increase, Association of Fundraising Professionals, November 7, 2005, www.afpnet.org.

17   www.consumeraffairs.com.

18   Independent Sector 2005 Nonprofit Reform – State Legislative Tracker, www.independentsector.org.

19   Ibid.

20   Ibid.

21   Ibid.

22   Ibid.

23   Ibid.

24   Prentis Family Foundation v. Barbara Ann Karmanos Cancer Institute, 266 Mich.App. 39, 698 N.W.2d 900, Mich. App.

25   Independent Sector Press Release. www.independentsector.org.

26   Muslim Public Affairs Council web site: www.mpac.org.

Gifts of $5 million or more in 2005

The Center on Philanthropy at Indiana University issues a quarterly list of announced gifts of $1 million or more. From this list, *Giving USA* has compiled gifts or pledges of $5 million or more made by individuals (not corporations or foundations) and announced in 2005. The amounts reported here are those that appear in newspapers. They have not been verified with the recipient institution.

This is not a complete listing of all gifts in the United States of $5 million or more because many such gifts are not reported in the press. It also does not represent actual transfers made to institutions in 2005. Many of the gifts are pledges or estate gifts that will be paid over time. Gifts in kind are reported at values announced in the media.

Gifts are organized in descending order by size and then alphabetically by donor's last name. The size categories are $250 million to $499.99 million, $100 million to $249.99 million, $50 million to $99.99 million, $25 million to $49.99 million, $10 million to $24.99 million, and $5 million to $9.99 million.

Gifts of $250 million to $499.99 million

Amount ($)	Donor	Recipient
400,000,000	Cordelia Scaife May (estate)	Colcom Foundation
400,000,000	Marguerite and Robert Hoffman, Cindy and Howard Rachofsky, and Debbie and Rusty Rose	Dallas Museum of Art
320,000,000	Bill and Melinda Gates	Bill & Melinda Gates Foundation

Gifts of $100 million to $249.99 million

Amount ($)	Donor	Recipient
205,900,000	George Soros	Central European University
165,000,000	T. Boone Pickens	Oklahoma State University
150,000,000	Eli and Edythe L. Broad	Broad Foundations
147,000,000	Josephine F. Ford (estate)	Detroit Institute of the Arts (in-kind gift of artwork)
115,000,000	Lawrence J. Ellison	Harvard University
105,000,000	Jan T. Vilcek	New York University School of Medicine
100,000,000	Anonymous	Yale University
100,000,000	Eli and Edythe Broad	Harvard University
100,000,000	Ira J. and Mary Lou Fulton	Arizona State University
100,000,000	Sir Thomas Hunter	Unnamed organizations that will help the poorest of the poor out of poverty in Africa
100,000,000	James Martin	Oxford University
100,000,000	James W. and Frances G. McGlothlin	Virginia Museum of Fine Arts

Gifts of $50 million to $99.99 million

Amount ($)	Donor	Recipient
93,000,000	Dave and Cheryl Duffield	Maddie's Fund
70,000,000	Anonymous	Indiana University
70,000,000	Sydell L. Miller	The Cleveland Clinic
53,000,000	Robert Edward (Ted) Turner	United Nations Foundation and the Better World Fund

Gifts of $5 million or more in 2005

Gifts of $50 million to $99.99 million (cont'd)

Amount ($)	Donor	Recipient
52,000,000	John Ellis (estate)	Arizona Community Foundation
51,000,000	Business partners Bradford Freeman and Ronald Spogli	Stanford University for International Studies
50,000,000	James Barksdale	Reading Institute
50,000,000	James Barksdale	Mississippi Public School System
50,000,000	Marion and Henry W. Bloch with Don and Adele Hall and Morton and Estelle Sosland	Nelson-Atkins Museum of Art
50,000,000	Edward R. Broida	Museum of Modern Art
50,000,000	Josephine F. Ford (estate)	College for Creative Studies
50,000,000	Bill and Louise Meiklejohn	Saddleback Memorial Medical Center
50,000,000	Annette and Harold C. Simmons	University of Texas Southwestern Medical Center

Gifts of $25 million to $49.99 million

Amount ($)	Donor	Recipient
40,600,000	Barbara Barrow Jacobs (estate) and other family members	Indiana University
40,600,000	Donald and Barbara Jonas	Jewish Communal Fund through the sale of a portion of the Jonas's art collection
40,000,000	Anonymous	Community of Christ Church, formerly known as the Reorganized Church of Jesus Christ of Latter Day Saints
40,000,000	John W. Jordan III	University of Notre Dame
40,000,000	Li Ka-shing	University of California at Berkeley
38,000,000	Lawrence J. Ellison	Ellison Medical Foundation
36,000,000	Oprah Winfrey	Oprah Winfrey Foundation
35,000,000	Marlin Miller, Jr. and Regina Miller	Alfred University
35,000,000	Cynthia and George Mitchell	Texas A&M University
34,000,000	Alfred Taubman and Richard Manoogian	Detroit Institute of Arts
32,500,000	Alice and William H. Goodwin, Jr.	Virginia Commonwealth University
30,000,000	Anne T. and Robert M. Bass	Stanford University
30,000,000	A. James Clark	University of Maryland, College Park
30,000,000	Richard and Joyce Farmer	Farmer Family Foundation for a gift directed to Miami University of Ohio
30,000,000	Robert Fischell	University of Maryland, College Park
30,000,000	Edyth and Carl Lindner	University of Cincinnati
30,000,000	Paul Merage	University of California-Irvine Graduate School of Management
30,000,000	Red and Charline McCombs	University of Texas M.D. Anderson Cancer Center
30,000,000	Oscar M. Ruebhausen (estate)	Yale University
30,000,000	Robert H. Smith	University of Maryland, College Park
29,300,000	K. Raymond Clark (estate)	Coe College
28,500,000	Oscar Boonshoft	Wright State University School of Medicine
28,400,000	Theodore (Ted) and Vada Stanley	Stanley Medical Research Institute
28,000,000	J. William and Mark K. Diederich	Marquette University
27,000,000	Helen Snell Cheel (estate)	Clarkson University
27,000,000	Leonie Faroll (estate)	Wellesley College
26,000,000	Andrew S. Grove	City University of New York
26,000,000	Edward Warner	Colorado State University
25,000,000	Anonymous	University of California Berkeley Haas School of Business
25,000,000	Anonymous	Phillips Exeter Academy
25,000,000	Bill Greehey	St. Mary's University

Gifts of $5 million or more in 2005

Gifts of $25 million to $49.99 million (cont'd)

Amount ($)	Donor	Recipient
25,000,000	Bruce Kovner	Julliard School
25,000,000	David and Phyllis Komansky	New York-Presbyterian Hospital
25,000,000	DeVoe Moore and Family	Florida State University at Tallahassee
25,000,000	Dorrance H. Hamilton	Thomas Jefferson University
25,000,000	Helen and Peter Bing	Stanford University
25,000,000	Madeleine Thomas Schneider (estate)	Findlay-Hancock Community Foundation
25,000,000	Ruth and Raymond Perelman	University of Pennsylvania
25,000,000	William J. Godfrey	Indiana University
25,000,000	William S. Boyd	University of Nevada at Las Vegas Law School

Gifts of $10 million to $24.99 million

Amount ($)	Donor	Recipient
24,200,000	George Soros	Central European University
23,500,000	William H. and Sue Gross	Duke University
22,600,000	Larry and Gail Miller	Salt Lake Community College
22,500,000	Arthur E. Benning (estate)	University of Utah School of Medicine
22,000,000	Sidney Kimmel	Sidney Kimmel Foundation
21,700,000	Pamela and Pierre M. Omidyar	Omidyar Network (nonprofit arm)
21,000,000	Peter B. Lewis	Princeton University
21,000,000	Frank E. Eck	University of Notre Dame
21,000,000	Lois Bates Acheson (estate)	Oregon State University
20,000,000	Albert Willner	American Committee for the Weizmann Institute of Science
20,000,000	Anonymous	Detroit Institute of the Arts
20,000,000	Anonymous	Rice University
20,000,000	Anonymous Brown trustee	Brown University
20,000,000	C. Michael Armstrong	The Johns Hopkins University
20,000,000	Michael Bloomberg	Carnegie Corporation
20,000,000	John M. and Mary Jo Boler	Rush University Medical Center
20,000,000	Simona and Jerome A. Chazen	University of Wisconsin-Madison
20,000,000	Shelby and Gale Davis	Middlebury College
20,000,000	Ira J. and Mary Lou Fulton	Brigham Young University
20,000,000	William H. and Sue Gross	Hoag Memorial Hospital
20,000,000	Joan and William Hank	Loyola University Chicago
20,000,000	Martin Kelley	Oregon State University School of Electrical Engineering and Computer Science
20,000,000	Christine E. Lynn	Boca Raton Community Hospital
20,000,000	Peggy and Lowry Mays	University of Texas
20,000,000	Harvey and Phyllis Sandler	Boca Raton Community Hospital
20,000,000	T. Denny Sanford	Sioux Valley Hospital
20,000,000	T. Denny Sanford	University of South Dakota
20,000,000	Prince Alwaleed Bin Talal	Louvre Museum
20,000,000	Prince Alwaleed Bin Talal	Harvard University
20,000,000	Prince Alwaleed Bin Talal	Georgetown University
20,000,000	Robert and Jan Weissman	Babson College
19,000,000	Rita and Gustave Hauser	New York University School of Law
18,500,000	Kiran and Pallavi Patel	University of South Florida
18,000,000	Fred Anderson	Sutter Medical Center Foundation
17,500,000	Dr. Min H. Kao	University of Tennessee Knoxville College of Engineering
16,500,000	Paul Allen	Allen Institute for Brain Science
16,500,000	Jack Blais	Dana-Farber Cancer Institute

Gifts of $5 million or more in 2005

Gifts of $10 million to $24.99 million (cont'd)

Amount ($)	Donor	Recipient
16,500,000	Helen Snell Cheel (estate)	Emma Willard School
16,000,000	Charles T. Travers	University of California at Berkeley
15,000,000	Dr. Miriam and Sheldon G. Adelson	Hebrew SeniorLife of Boston
15,000,000	Anonymous	Wesleyan College
15,000,000	Anonymous	University of Oregon
15,000,000	Marcia and Eugene Applebaum	Mayo Clinic
15,000,000	Robert M. Arnold	Fred Hutchinson Cancer Research Center
15,000,000	Frances and J. Paul Breitbach	Loras College
15,000,000	Jesse Cox	Indiana University
15,000,000	Jan and Bob Davidson	University of Nevada, Reno
15,000,000	Mary and Ed Firstenburg	Southwest Washington Medical Center
15,000,000	William and Carol Foley	U.S. Military Academy
15,000,000	Susan Phifer and George Dean Johnson, Jr.	Converse College
15,000,000	Nick J. Labedz	Wayne State University
15,000,000	Henrietta C. Lee	USC/Norris Comprehensive Cancer Center
15,000,000	Dr. Richard Mazurek (estate)	Wayne State University
15,000,000	Sharmin and Bijan Mossavar-Rahmani	Harvard University John F. Kennedy School of Government
15,000,000	Patricia and David Nierenberg	Southwest Washington Medical Center
15,000,000	Herbert and Marion Sandler	Human Rights Watch
15,000,000	T. Denny Sanford	Mayo Clinic
15,000,000	Ivan G. Seidenberg	Pace University
15,000,000	Arthur Zankel (estate)	Skidmore College
14,000,000	Robert Thompson	Skillman Foundation
14,000,000	George Weiss	University of Pennsylvania
13,000,000	Leanne B. Roberts (estate)	San Francisco Society for the Prevention of Cruelty to Animals (SPCA)
12,600,000	Theodora Peigh (estate)	University of California, Davis
12,500,000	David "Duddie" Massad	University of Massachusetts Memorial Medical Center
12,400,000	Robert Edward (Ted) Turner	Turner Foundation
12,000,000	Clarice and Robert H. Smith and Arlene and Robert Kogod	Hebrew Home of Greater Washington
12,000,000	Gerry Lenfest	Columbia University
12,000,000	Thomas J. Petters	Rollins College
12,000,000	Michael and Judy Steinhardt	Brandeis University
11,000,000	Oprah Winfrey	Oprah Winfrey Operating Foundation
10,500,000	Gordon Inman	Belmont University
10,000,000	Judy and Paul Andrews	Baylor All Saints Medical Center
10,000,000	Anonymous	University of Pennsylvania
10,000,000	Anonymous	University of Cincinnati College of Pharmacy
10,000,000	Anonymous	University of Arkansas at Fayetteville
10,000,000	Jim Ayers	Vanderbilt-Ingram Cancer Center
10,000,000	Geoffrey Beene (estate)	American Society for the Prevention of Cruelty to Animals (ASPCA)
10,000,000	Geoffrey Beene (estate)	Animal Medical Center
10,000,000	Leon D. Black	Mount Sinai School of Medicine
10,000,000	Neil G. Bluhm	Northwestern Cardiovascular Institute at Northwestern Memorial Hospital
10,000,000	Marjorie and Lawrence Bradley (estate)	Polk County Community Foundation
10,000,000	Victor Clarke	Baptist Hospital of Miami
10,000,000	Roy and Patricia Disney	Providence St. Joseph Medical Center
10,000,000	Fred and Barbara Erb	University of Michigan

Gifts of $5 million or more in 2005

Gifts of $10 million to $24.99 million (cont'd)

Amount ($)	Donor	Recipient
10,000,000	Doris and Don Fisher	Teach for America
10,000,000	Edward P. Fitts	North Carolina State University
10,000,000	Jay Furman	New York University School of Law
10,000,000	Larry and Lucienne Glaubinger	Indiana University
10,000,000	Dorothy and Lacy Harber	Abilene Christian University
10,000,000	Shirley and Vernon Hill	University of Pennsylvania
10,000,000	Roger C. Hobbs	Chapman University
10,000,000	Lillian Lincoln Howell	Pomona College
10,000,000	Janice Bryant Howroyd	University of Southern California
10,000,000	Thomas C. Jones	University of Michigan Stephen M. Ross School of Business
10,000,000	Tom Kivisto	University of Kansas
10,000,000	Charles Lakin Family	City of Council Bluffs
10,000,000	Dan and Patricia McDonnell Jorndt	Drake University
10,000,000	James J. Maguire	St. Joseph's University
10,000,000	Bernadette and Timothy Marquez	Colorado School of Mines
10,000,000	Manny and Neda Mashouf	San Francisco State University
10,000,000	Linda and Doug Mills	Carle Foundation Hospital
10,000,000	Arthur and Pat Modell	The Johns Hopkins Heart Institute
10,000,000	John Morgridge	Cisco's Wireless Initiative for Mississippi schools damaged by Hurricane Katrina
10,000,000	Joseph Neubauer and his wife	Philadelphia Orchestra
10,000,000	Herald and Donna Nokes	University of Idaho
10,000,000	T. Boone Pickens	Ronald Reagan Presidential Library Endowment
10,000,000	Conrad Prebys	The Old Globe Theatre
10,000,000	Dr. Robert and Dorothy Rector (estate)	Dickinson College
10,000,000	Col. John Harvey Robinson (estate)	University of North Carolina at Chapel Hill
10,000,000	James E. Rogers	University of Southern California Law School
10,000,000	Roger and Victoria Sant	Smithsonian Institution
10,000,000	Victoria and Roger Sant	National Symphony Orchestra
10,000,000	Mignon C. Smith	J. Craig and Page T. Smith Scholarship Foundation
10,000,000	George Soros	Open Society Institute
10,000,000	Althea Stroum	University of Washington
10,000,000	Richard and Maria Sulpizio	University of California, San Diego
10,000,000	Jack Taylor	Donald Danforth Plant Science Center
10,000,000	Preston Robert Tisch Family	Duke University
10,000,000	Gretchen Valade	Detroit International Jazz Festival
10,000,000	Sara and Ernst Volgenau	George Mason University
10,000,000	Anthony Welters	New York University School of Law
10,000,000	Leonard Wiff	New York University School of Law
10,000,000	John Williams	Cobb Energy Performing Arts Center
10,000,000	Oprah Winfrey	Angel Network

Gifts of $5 million to $9.99 million

Amount ($)	Donor	Recipient
9,600,000	Charlotte G. Gragnani (estate)	Lombardi Comprehensive Cancer Center
9,000,000	Artie McFerrin	Texas A&M University
9,000,000	Yousif Ghafari	Wayne State University
9,000,000	B. Thomas Golisano	Rochester General Hospital
9,000,000	Bill Greehey	Greehey Family Foundation
9,000,000	Paggy and Walter Helmerich	Oklahoma State University
8,735,000	Helen Guinn Adams (estate)	University of Arkansas for Medical Sciences

Gifts of $5 million or more in 2005

Gifts of $5 million to $9.99 million (cont'd)

Amount ($)	Donor	Recipient
8,700,000	Margaret and Matthew Faithe (estate)	University of South Dakota
8,500,000	Mary Celestia Fisher (estate)	Children's Medical Center Dallas
8,500,000	W. Frank Barton (estate)	Wichita State University
8,500,000	Dolph C. Simons, Jr.	University of Kansas
8,500,000	William and Nancy Thompson	University of Missouri-Columbia
8,300,000	Charles Kasych, Jr.	Lehigh Valley Hospital
8,100,000	T. Boone Pickens	Texas Scottish Rite Hospital for Children
8,000,000	Daniel Slane	Ohio State University
8,000,000	George and Kathy Irwin	University of Illinois at Chicago
8,000,000	Sidney Knafel	Wellesley College
8,000,000	Gerald A. and Karen A. Kolschowsky	Iowa State University
8,000,000	Enid and Mel Zuckerman	Community Foundation of Southern Arizona
7,600,000	Bruce and Barbara Purdy	The YMCA of the Fox Cities
7,600,000	Tyson Family	University of Arkansas at Fayetteville
7,500,000	David Morris (estate)	Michigan State University
7,300,000	Mary and Jack Bayramian (estate)	California State University at Northridge
7,000,000	Spencer and Cleone Eccles	University of Utah
7,000,000	Mitzi and Warren Isenberg and Susan and Leonard Feinstein	New Museum of Contemporary Art
7,000,000	James and Miriam Mulva	St. Norbert College
7,000,000	T. Boone Pickens	American Red Cross
6,920,000	Joe Kimmel	Western Carolina University
6,900,000	Joe Weston	Weston Public Foundation Charitable Trust
6,500,000	Lorry Lokey	University of Oregon
6,500,000	Paul Allen	Experience Music Project and the Science Fiction Museum
6,250,000	Bob and Kari Grimm	Concordia University
6,000,000	George and Roberta Berry; John and Shirley Berry; Charles Berry	Dartmouth College
6,000,000	Allen and Joan Bildner	Dartmouth College
6,000,000	John and Dorothy Byrne	Dartmouth College
6,000,000	James C. Curvey	Villanova University
6,000,000	Emily and Joseph Fisher	Christian Academy
6,000,000	Thomas Golisano	SUNY Upstate Medical University
6,000,000	Maureen and John Hendricks	Maryland SoccerPlex
6,000,000	Kathleen and Aubrey McClendon	Duke University
6,000,000	Colin B. McKay (estate)	University of New Brunswick
6,000,000	David Craig Purcell (estate)	Presbyterian Home of High Point
6,000,000	Bertie Deming Smith and her late husband, John Deming	Tulane University
6,000,000	Bertie Murphy Deming Smith	Mary Baldwin College
6,000,000	Stephen and Roberta Weiner	Beth Israel Deaconess Medical Center
5,800,000	Anonymous	High Point University
5,800,000	Penelope Perkins Wilson	Bennington College
5,700,000	Anonymous	High Point University
5,700,000	Helen Snell Cheel (estate)	Canton-Potsdam Hospital
5,500,000	Katharine Graham (estate)	University of Chicago
5,500,000	Bruce R. Lauritzen	Princeton University
5,500,000	Hilda Niess (estate)	Washington University School of Medicine in St. Louis
5,400,000	Emily Rauh Pulitzer	Contemporary Art Museum of St. Louis
5,400,000	E. V. Williams (estate)	Old Dominion University Business School
5,400,000	E. V. Williams (estate)	Physicians for Peace

Gifts of $5 million or more in 2005

Gifts of $5 million to $9.99 million (cont'd)

Amount ($)	Donor	Recipient
5,300,000	Mary and Wayne Hockmeyer	Purdue University
5,250,000	Tagliatela Family	University of New Haven School of Engineering and Applied Science
5,100,000	Alicia McEvoy (estate)	Dominican University of California
5,000,000	Susan Allen	Longmont Humane Society
5,000,000	Anonymous	Archer School for Girls
5,000,000	Anonymous	Doane College
5,000,000	Anonymous	Jewish Theological Seminary
5,000,000	Anonymous	John Brown University
5,000,000	Anonymous	The University of Texas Health Science Center
5,000,000	Anonymous	University of Richmond
5,000,000	Anonymous	University of South Dakota
5,000,000	Anonymous	University of Texas Southwestern Medical Center
5,000,000	Anonymous couple	Burr and Burton Academy
5,000,000	George and Julia Argyros	Horatio Alger Association of Distinguished Americans
5,000,000	Jim Ayers	Jackson-Madison County General Hospital
5,000,000	James Barksdale	National D-Day Museum
5,000,000	Myron Blank	Des Moines' Blank Park Zoo
5,000,000	Johnny Carson (estate)	Faith Regional Health Services
5,000,000	Johnny Carson (estate)	University of Nebraska at Lincoln
5,000,000	Lawrence J. DeGeorge	Scripps Florida
5,000,000	Barbara and Eric Dobkin	Jewish Women's Archive
5,000,000	Ray and Dagmar Dolby	California Institute for Regenerative Medicine
5,000,000	Sidney Frank	Brown University
5,000,000	Sidney Frank	New York Medical College
5,000,000	Jerry Frautschi	Madison Children's Museum
5,000,000	Susan and Richard Friedman	Brown University
5,000,000	Mildred and Shirley L. Garrison	Texas Tech University Health Sciences Center
5,000,000	Jack and Carol Gilbert	California Lutheran University
5,000,000	Paul F. Glenn	Harvard Medical School
5,000,000	Renee and John Grisham	Rebuild the Coast Fund
5,000,000	Willard Hackerman	The Johns Hopkins University
5,000,000	Lacy and Dorothy Harber	Texoma Medical Center Foundation (from the donors' eventual estate)
5,000,000	Lacy and Dorothy Harber	Wilson N. Jones Medical Center Foundation
5,000,000	Leona Helmsley	American Red Cross of Greater New York
5,000,000	Roger Hertog	Birthright Israel Foundation
5,000,000	Jackie Lee and Jim Houston	McCallum Theatre
5,000,000	J. B. and Johnelle Hunt	University of Arkansas at Fayetteville
5,000,000	Loring C. Jensen (estate)	Western Railway Museum
5,000,000	Barry Kaye	Florida Atlantic University
5,000,000	Donna and Stewart Kohl	Oberlin College
5,000,000	Ronya Kozmetsky and the family of her children, Greg Kozmetsky and Nadya Scott	Dell Children's Medical Center of Central Texas
5,000,000	Nancy S. and W. A. Krause	University of Iowa Foundation
5,000,000	L. W. (Bill) Lane Jr.	Stanford University
5,000,000	Larry Lee	Indiana University-Purdue University at Fort Wayne
5,000,000	Raymond L. and Beverly Lutgert	Florida Gulf Coast University
5,000,000	Elizabeth and Doug Manchester	San Diego State University

Gifts of $5 million or more in 2005

Gifts of $5 million to $9.99 million (cont'd)

Amount ($)	Donor	Recipient
5,000,000	Elizabeth and Doug Manchester	Wake Forest University
5,000,000	John and Mari Ann Martin and Mick and Susie McMurry	University of Wyoming
5,000,000	Ralph E. Martin	University of Arkansas
5,000,000	Mark Mazzarino	Mayo Clinic at Scottsdale
5,000,000	Janet McKinley and George Miller	Grameen Foundation USA
5,000,000	Janet McKinley and George Miller	Oxfam America
5,000,000	Bernard Newcomb	Peninsula Community Foundation
5,000,000	James and Nancy O'Neal	The Johns Hopkins University
5,000,000	Christa Anderson Overcash	Levine Children's Hospital
5,000,000	Donnie Pendergraft	University of Arkansas-Fort Smith Health Sciences Center
5,000,000	Roxelyn and Richard Pepper	Northwestern University
5,000,000	Lois Pope	Disabled Veterans Life Memorial Foundation
5,000,000	Alexis and Jim Pugh	University of Florida
5,000,000	David Rockefeller	Museum of Modern Art
5,000,000	David Rockefeller	Rockefeller University
5,000,000	Sandra Priest Rose	Cooper Union
5,000,000	Michael and Iris Smith	National Jewish Medical and Research Center
5,000,000	Norman Snyder, Jr.	SUNY at Albany
5,000,000	Theodore (Ted) and Vada Stanley	Cold Spring Harbor Laboratory
5,000,000	Theodore (Ted) and Vada Stanley	NARSAD, The Mental Health Research Association
5,000,000	Martha Stewart	Mount Sinai Hospital
5,000,000	Chris Sullivan and Family	University Community Hospital
5,000,000	Jack C. Taylor	Forest Park Forever
5,000,000	Henry B. Tippie	University of Iowa Foundation
5,000,000	Sheila and Walter Umphrey	Lamar University
5,000,000	Marcus and Carole Weinstein	University of Richmond
5,000,000	Dorothy Wenberg (estate)	Charleston (SC) Association for the Blind
5,000,000	Helene and Grant Wilson	Pace University
5,000,000	Rosemary Willson	Julliard School
5,000,000	Helen Zell	University of Michigan

For more information about these and other gifts, see the web site of the Center on Philanthropy, www.philanthropy.iupui.edu.

Sources used for the Million Dollar List maintained by the Center on Philanthropy include the *Chronicle of Philanthropy*, the *Chronicle of Higher Education*, *Philanthropy News Digest*, and newspaper articles, tracked for the Center by FundraisingINFO.com.

Giving by source, 1965–2005
(In billions of current dollars)

	Total	Percent change	Corpora-tions	Percent change	Founda-tions	Percent change	Bequests	Percent change	Individuals	Percent change
1965	14.71	8.2	0.74	17.5	1.13	36.1	1.02	7.4	11.82	5.6
1966	15.79	7.3	0.79	6.8	1.25	10.6	1.31	28.4	12.44	5.2
1967	17.03	7.9	0.82	3.8	1.40	12.0	1.40	6.9	13.41	7.8
1968	18.85	10.7	0.90	9.8	1.60	14.3	1.60	14.3	14.75	10.0
1969	20.66	9.6	0.93	3.3	1.80	12.5	2.00	25.0	15.93	8.0
1970	21.04	1.8	0.82	-11.8	1.90	5.6	2.13	6.5	16.19	1.6
1971	23.44	11.4	0.85	4.2	1.95	2.6	3.00	40.8	17.64	9.0
1972	24.44	4.3	0.97	14.1	2.00	2.6	2.10	-30.0	19.37	9.8
1973	25.59	4.7	1.06	9.3	2.00	0.0	2.00	-4.8	20.53	6.0
1974	26.88	5.0	1.10	3.8	2.11	5.5	2.07	3.5	21.60	5.2
1975	28.56	6.3	1.15	4.5	1.65	-21.8	2.23	7.7	23.53	8.9
1976	31.85	11.5	1.33	15.7	1.90	15.2	2.30	3.1	26.32	11.9
1977	35.21	10.5	1.54	15.8	2.00	5.3	2.12	-7.8	29.55	12.3
1978	38.57	9.5	1.70	10.4	2.17	8.5	2.60	22.6	32.10	8.6
1979	43.11	11.8	2.05	20.6	2.24	3.2	2.23	-14.2	36.59	14.0
1980	48.63	12.8	2.25	9.8	2.81	25.4	2.86	28.3	40.71	11.3
1981	55.28	13.7	2.64	17.3	3.07	9.3	3.58	25.2	45.99	13.0
1982	59.11	6.9	3.11	17.8	3.16	2.9	5.21	45.5	47.63	3.6
1983	63.21	6.9	3.67	18.0	3.60	13.9	3.88	-25.5	52.06	9.3
1984	68.58	8.5	4.13	12.5	3.95	9.7	4.04	4.1	56.46	8.5
1985	71.69	4.5	4.63	12.1	4.90	24.1	4.77	18.1	57.39	1.6
1986	83.25	16.1	5.03	8.6	5.43	10.8	5.70	19.5	67.09	16.9
1987	82.20	-1.3	5.21	3.6	5.88	8.3	6.58	15.4	64.53	-3.8
1988	88.04	7.1	5.34	2.5	6.15	4.6	6.57	-0.2	69.98	8.4
1989	98.30	11.7	5.46	2.2	6.55	6.5	6.84	4.1	79.45	13.5
1990	100.52	2.3	5.46	0.0	7.23	10.4	6.79	-0.7	81.04	2.0
1991	104.92	4.4	5.25	-3.8	7.72	6.8	7.68	13.1	84.27	4.0
1992	111.79	6.5	5.91	12.6	8.64	11.9	9.54	24.2	87.70	4.1
1993	116.86	4.5	6.47	9.5	9.53	10.3	8.86	-7.1	92.00	4.9
1994	120.29	2.9	6.98	7.9	9.66	1.4	11.13	25.6	92.52	0.6
1995	123.68	2.8	7.35	5.3	10.56	9.3	10.41	-6.5	95.36	3.1
1996	139.10	12.5	7.51	2.2	12.00	13.6	12.03	15.6	107.56	12.8
1997	162.99	17.2	8.62	14.8	13.92	16.0	16.25	35.1	124.20	15.5
1998	176.80	8.5	8.46	-1.9	17.01	22.2	12.98	-20.1	138.35	11.4
1999	202.74	14.7	10.23	20.9	20.51	20.6	17.37	33.8	154.63	11.8
2000	229.71	13.3	10.74	5.0	24.58	19.8	19.88	14.5	174.51	12.9
2001	231.08	0.6	11.66	8.6	27.22	10.7	19.80	-0.4	172.40	-1.2
2002	231.54	0.2	10.79	-7.5	26.98	-0.9	20.90	5.6	172.87	0.3
2003	236.28	2.0	11.06	2.5	26.84	-0.5	18.19	-13.0	180.19	4.2
2004	245.22	3.8	11.24	1.6	28.41	5.8	18.46	1.5	187.11	3.8
2005	260.28	6.1	13.77	22.5	30.00	5.6	17.44	-5.5	199.07	6.4

Source for foundation giving: The Foundation Center
Note: All figures are rounded. *Giving USA* changed its rounding procedure from the 2003 edition forward. All estimates are rounded to two places then operations performed. In the past, the operations were performed first and the results were rounded.

Giving by source, 1965–2005
(In billions of inflation-adjusted dollars)

	Total	Percent change	Corpora-tions	Percent change	Founda-tions	Percent change	Bequests	Percent change	Individuals	Percent change
1965	91.20	6.4	4.59	15.6	7.01	34.0	6.32	5.5	73.28	3.93
1966	95.17	4.4	4.76	3.7	7.53	7.4	7.90	25.0	74.98	2.32
1967	99.60	4.7	4.80	0.8	8.19	8.8	8.19	3.67	78.42	4.59
1968	105.78	6.2	5.05	5.2	8.98	9.6	8.98	9.6	82.77	5.5
1969	109.95	3.9	4.95	-2.0	9.58	6.7	10.64	18.5	84.78	2.4
1970	105.89	-3.7	4.13	-16.6	9.56	-0.2	10.72	0.8	81.48	-3.9
1971	113.01	6.7	4.10	-0.7	9.40	-1.7	14.46	34.9	85.05	4.4
1972	114.20	1.1	4.53	10.5	9.35	-0.5	9.81	-32.2	90.51	6.4
1973	112.58	-1.4	4.66	2.9	8.80	-5.9	8.80	-10.3	90.32	-0.2
1974	106.50	-5.4	4.36	-6.4	8.36	-5.0	8.20	-6.8	85.58	-5.2
1975	103.66	-2.7	4.17	-4.4	5.99	-28.3	8.09	-1.3	85.41	-0.2
1976	109.34	5.5	4.57	9.6	6.52	8.8	7.90	-2.3	90.35	5.8
1977	113.47	3.8	4.96	8.5	6.45	-1.1	6.83	-13.5	95.23	5.4
1978	115.55	1.8	5.09	2.6	6.50	0.8	7.79	14.1	96.17	1.0
1979	115.92	0.3	5.51	8.3	6.02	-7.4	6.00	-23.0	98.39	2.3
1980	115.26	-0.6	5.33	-3.3	6.66	10.6	6.78	13.0	96.49	-1.9
1981	118.78	3.1	5.67	6.4	6.60	-0.9	7.69	13.4	98.82	2.4
1982	119.63	0.7	6.29	10.9	6.40	-3.0	10.54	37.1	96.40	-2.4
1983	123.95	3.6	7.20	14.5	7.06	10.3	7.61	-27.8	102.08	5.9
1984	128.90	4.0	7.76	7.8	7.42	5.1	7.59	-0.3	106.13	4.0
1985	130.12	0.9	8.40	8.2	8.89	19.8	8.66	14.1	104.17	-1.8
1986	148.35	14.0	8.96	6.7	9.68	8.9	10.16	17.3	119.55	14.8
1987	141.31	-4.7	8.96	0.0	10.11	4.4	11.31	11.3	110.93	-7.2
1988	145.36	2.9	8.82	-1.6	10.15	0.4	10.85	-4.1	115.54	4.2
1989	154.83	6.5	8.60	-2.5	10.32	1.7	10.77	-0.7	125.14	8.3
1990	150.21	-3.0	8.16	-5.1	10.80	4.7	10.15	-5.8	121.10	-3.2
1991	150.44	0.2	7.53	-7.7	11.07	2.5	11.01	8.5	120.83	-0.2
1992	155.62	3.4	8.23	9.3	12.03	8.7	13.28	20.6	122.08	1.0
1993	157.93	1.5	8.74	6.2	12.88	7.1	11.97	-9.9	124.34	1.9
1994	158.53	0.4	9.20	5.3	12.73	-1.2	14.67	22.6	121.93	-1.9
1995	158.50	0.0	9.42	2.4	13.53	6.3	13.34	-9.1	122.21	0.2
1996	173.14	9.2	9.35	-0.7	14.94	10.4	14.97	12.2	133.88	9.5
1997	198.33	14.5	10.49	12.2	16.94	13.4	19.77	32.1	151.13	12.9
1998	211.84	6.8	10.14	-3.3	20.38	20.3	15.55	-21.3	165.77	9.7
1999	237.67	12.2	11.99	18.2	24.04	18.0	20.36	30.9	181.28	9.4
2000	260.53	9.6	12.18	1.6	27.88	16.0	22.55	10.8	197.92	9.2
2001	254.84	-2.2	12.86	5.6	30.02	7.7	21.84	-3.1	190.12	-3.9
2002	251.37	-1.4	11.71	-8.9	29.29	-2.4	22.69	3.9	187.68	-1.3
2003	250.80	-0.2	11.74	0.3	28.49	-2.7	19.31	-14.9	191.26	1.9
2004	253.54	1.1	11.62	-1.0	29.37	3.1	19.09	-1.1	193.46	1.2
2005	260.28	2.7	13.77	18.5	30.00	2.1	17.44	-8.6	199.07	2.9

Source for foundation giving: The Foundation Center
Note: *Giving USA* uses the Consumer Price Index to adjust for inflation. All figures are rounded. *Giving USA* changed its rounding procedure from the 2003 edition forward. All estimates are rounded to two places then operations performed. In the past, the operations were performed first and the results were rounded.

Contributions by type of recipient organization, 1965–2005
(In billions of current dollars)

	Total	Percent change	Religion	Percent change	Edu-cation	Percent change	Health	Percent change	Human services	Percent change
1965	14.71	8.2	6.72	9.4	2.01	8.6	1.60	3.2	2.07	7.8
1966	15.79	7.3	7.22	7.4	2.06	2.5	1.69	5.6	2.01	-2.9
1967	17.03	7.9	7.58	5.0	2.13	3.4	1.91	13.0	2.07	3.0
1968	18.85	10.7	8.42	11.1	2.38	11.7	2.08	8.9	2.31	11.6
1969	20.66	9.6	9.02	7.1	2.54	6.7	2.31	11.1	2.71	17.3
1970	21.04	1.8	9.34	3.5	2.60	2.4	2.40	3.9	2.92	7.7
1971	23.44	11.4	10.07	7.8	2.75	5.8	2.61	8.8	3.01	3.1
1972	24.44	4.3	10.10	0.3	2.98	8.4	2.80	7.3	3.16	5.0
1973	25.59	4.7	10.53	4.3	3.10	4.0	3.10	10.7	3.07	-2.8
1974	26.88	5.0	11.84	12.4	3.05	-1.6	3.37	8.7	3.02	-1.6
1975	28.56	6.3	12.81	8.2	2.83	-7.2	3.61	7.1	2.94	-2.6
1976	31.85	11.5	14.18	10.7	3.28	15.9	3.92	8.6	3.02	2.7
1977	35.21	10.5	16.98	19.7	3.62	10.4	4.09	4.3	3.57	18.2
1978	38.57	9.5	18.35	8.1	4.11	13.5	4.52	10.5	3.87	8.4
1979	43.11	11.8	20.17	9.9	4.54	10.5	4.94	9.3	4.48	15.8
1980	48.63	12.8	22.23	10.2	4.96	9.3	5.34	8.1	4.91	9.6
1981	55.28	13.7	25.05	12.7	5.77	16.3	5.79	8.4	5.62	14.5
1982	59.11	6.9	28.06	12.0	6.00	4.0	6.15	6.2	6.33	12.6
1983	63.21	6.9	31.84	13.5	6.65	10.8	6.68	8.6	7.16	13.1
1984	68.58	8.5	35.55	11.7	7.29	9.6	6.84	2.4	7.88	10.1
1985	71.69	4.5	38.21	7.5	8.17	12.1	7.72	12.9	8.50	7.9
1986	83.25	16.1	41.68	9.1	9.39	14.9	8.44	9.3	9.13	7.4
1987	82.20	-1.3	43.51	4.4	9.84	4.8	9.22	9.2	9.84	7.8
1988	88.04	7.1	45.15	3.8	10.23	4.0	9.58	3.9	10.49	6.6
1989	98.30	11.7	47.77	5.8	10.95	7.0	9.93	3.7	11.39	8.6
1990	100.52	2.3	49.79	4.2	12.41	13.3	9.90	-0.3	11.82	3.8
1991	104.92	4.4	50.00	0.4	13.45	8.4	9.68	-2.2	11.11	-6.0
1992	111.79	6.5	50.95	1.9	14.29	6.2	10.24	5.8	11.57	4.1
1993	116.86	4.5	52.89	3.8	15.40	7.8	10.83	5.8	12.47	7.8
1994	120.29	2.9	56.43	6.7	16.61	7.9	11.53	6.5	11.71	-6.1
1995	123.68	2.8	58.07	2.9	17.61	6.0	12.59	9.2	11.70	-0.1
1996	139.10	12.5	61.90	6.6	19.16	8.8	13.90	10.4	12.17	4.0
1997	162.99	17.2	64.69	4.5	22.00	14.8	14.04	1.0	12.67	4.1
1998	176.80	8.5	68.25	5.5	25.32	15.1	16.89	20.3	16.08	26.9
1999	202.74	14.7	71.25	4.4	27.46	8.5	17.95	6.3	17.36	8.0
2000	229.71	13.3	76.95	8.0	31.67	15.3	18.82	4.8	17.99	3.6
2001	231.08	0.6	79.87	3.8	31.98	1.0	19.31	2.6	20.71	15.1
2002	231.54	0.2	82.91	3.8	31.83	-0.5	18.87	-2.3	18.65	-9.9
2003	236.28	2.0	84.57	2.0	32.11	0.9	20.89	10.7	18.89	1.3
2004	245.22	3.8	87.95	4.0	34.10	6.2	21.95	5.1	19.17	1.5
2005	260.28	6.1	93.18	5.9	38.56	13.1	22.54	2.7	25.36	32.3

Giving USA changed its rounding procedure from the 2003 edition forward. All estimates are rounded to two places then operations performed. In the past, the operations were performed first and the results were rounded.

	Arts, culture, humanities	Percent change	Public-society benefit	Percent Change	Environment/ animals	Percent Change	International affairs	Percent Change	Gifts to foundations	Percent change	Unallocated
1965	0.44	0.0	0.38	-2.6							1.49
1966	0.54	22.7	0.39	2.6							1.88
1967	0.56	3.7	0.41	5.1							2.37
1968	0.60	7.1	0.43	4.9							2.63
1969	0.72	20.0	0.56	30.2							2.80
1970	0.66	-8.3	0.46	-17.9							2.66
1971	1.01	53.0	0.68	47.8							3.31
1972	1.10	8.9	0.820	20.6							3.48
1973	1.26	14.5	0.620	-24.4							3.91
1974	1.15	-8.7	0.670	8.1							3.78
1975	1.24	7.8	0.790	17.9							4.34
1976	1.38	11.3	1.03	30.4							5.04
1977	2.32	68.1	1.22	18.4							3.41
1978	2.40	3.4	1.08	-11.5					1.61		2.63
1979	2.73	13.8	1.23	13.9					2.21	37.3	2.81
1980	3.15	15.4	1.46	18.7					1.98	-10.4	4.60
1981	3.66	16.2	1.79	22.6					2.39	20.7	5.21
1982	4.96	35.5	1.68	-6.1					4.00	67.4	1.93
1983	4.21	-15.1	1.89	12.5					2.71	-32.3	2.07
1984	4.50	6.9	1.94	2.6					3.36	24.0	1.22
1985	5.08	12.9	2.22	14.4					4.73	40.8	-2.94
1986	5.83	14.8	2.45	10.4					4.96	4.9	1.37
1987	6.31	8.2	2.87	17.1	1.99		0.78		5.16	4.0	-7.32
1988	6.79	7.6	3.21	11.8	2.22	11.4	0.86	10.3	3.93	-23.8	-4.42
1989	7.50	10.5	3.84	19.6	1.91	-14.0	1.01	17.4	4.41	12.2	-0.41
1990	7.89	5.2	4.92	28.1	2.50	30.9	1.31	29.7	3.83	-13.2	-3.85
1991	8.81	11.7	4.93	0.2	2.77	10.7	1.86	42.0	4.46	16.4	-2.15
1992	9.32	5.8	5.05	2.4	2.95	6.5	2.23	19.9	5.01	12.3	0.18
1993	9.57	2.7	5.44	7.7	3.01	2.2	2.18	-2.2	6.26	25.0	-1.19
1994	9.68	1.1	6.05	11.2	3.34	11.0	2.38	9.2	6.33	1.1	-3.77
1995	9.96	2.9	7.10	17.4	3.76	12.5	2.93	23.1	8.46	33.6	-8.50
1996	10.92	9.6	7.57	6.6	3.82	1.6	2.75	-6.1	12.63	49.3	-5.72
1997	10.61	-2.8	8.39	10.8	4.10	7.4	2.63	-4.4	13.96	10.5	9.90
1998	10.53	-0.8	10.86	29.4	5.25	28.0	2.89	9.9	19.92	42.7	0.81
1999	11.07	5.1	10.95	0.8	5.83	11.0	3.57	23.5	28.76	44.4	8.54
2000	11.50	3.9	11.59	5.8	6.16	5.7	3.66	2.5	24.71	-14.1	26.66
2001	12.14	5.6	11.82	2.0	6.41	4.0	4.14	13.0	25.67	3.9	19.03
2002	12.22	0.7	11.60	-1.9	6.59	2.8	4.62	11.6	19.16	-25.4	25.09
2003	13.11	7.3	12.13	4.6	7.11	7.9	5.30	14.7	21.62	12.8	20.55
2004	13.99	6.7	12.96	6.8	7.61	7.0	5.35	0.9	20.32	-6.0	21.82
2005	13.51	-3.4	14.03	8.3	8.86	16.4	6.39	19.4	21.70	6.8	16.15

Note: Gifts to foundations for 1992–2004 represent total gifts reported to the Foundation Center minus gifts to corporate foundations. The Foundation Center also provided data on the assets transferred to health care foundations for the years 1992–1999. These are not charitable gifts, but transfers resulting from conversions of hospitals and other health care institutions from nonprofit to for-profit status. These were subtracted from the Foundation Center's report of gifts to foundations. Gifts to foundations for 2005 are estimated here by the Foundation Center, which will release the final figure in early 2007. Funds given to nonprofits not reported by an organization in a subsector are included in "Unallocated Gifts." See "The Numbers" section of this book for a definition of Unallocated.

Contributions by type of recipient organization, 1965–2005
(In billions of inflation-adjusted dollars)

	Total	Percent Change	Religion	Percent Change	Edu-cation	Percent Change	Health	Percent Change	Human services	Percent Change
1965	91.20	6.4	41.66	7.7	12.46	6.9	9.92	1.5	12.83	6.0
1966	95.18	4.4	43.52	4.5	12.42	-0.3	10.19	2.7	12.12	-5.5
1967	99.59	4.6	44.33	1.9	12.46	0.3	11.17	9.6	12.11	-0.1
1968	105.78	6.2	47.25	6.6	13.36	7.2	11.67	4.5	12.96	7.0
1969	109.95	3.9	48.00	1.6	13.52	1.2	12.29	5.3	14.42	11.3
1970	105.90	-3.7	47.01	-2.1	13.09	-3.2	12.08	-1.7	14.70	1.9
1971	113.02	6.7	48.55	3.3	13.26	1.3	12.58	4.1	14.51	-1.3
1972	114.21	1.1	47.20	-2.8	13.93	5.1	13.08	4.0	14.77	1.8
1973	112.58	-1.4	46.33	-1.8	13.64	-2.1	13.64	4.3	13.51	-8.5
1974	106.50	-5.4	46.91	1.3	12.08	-11.4	13.35	-2.1	11.97	-11.4
1975	103.67	-2.7	46.50	-0.9	10.27	-15.0	13.10	-1.9	10.67	-10.9
1976	109.34	5.5	48.68	4.7	11.26	9.6	13.46	2.7	10.37	-2.8
1977	113.47	3.8	54.72	12.4	11.67	3.6	13.18	-2.1	11.50	10.9
1978	115.55	1.8	54.97	0.5	12.31	5.5	13.54	2.7	11.59	0.8
1979	115.98	0.4	54.26	-1.3	12.21	-0.8	13.29	-1.8	12.05	4.0
1980	115.26	-0.6	52.69	-2.9	11.76	-3.7	12.66	-4.7	11.64	-3.4
1981	118.78	3.1	53.82	2.1	12.40	5.4	12.44	-1.7	12.08	3.8
1982	119.63	0.7	56.79	5.5	12.14	-2.1	12.45	0.1	12.81	6.0
1983	123.94	3.6	62.43	9.9	13.04	7.4	13.10	5.2	14.04	9.6
1984	128.91	4.0	66.82	7.0	13.70	5.1	12.86	-1.8	14.81	5.5
1985	130.13	0.9	69.36	3.8	14.83	8.2	14.01	8.9	15.43	4.2
1986	148.34	14.0	74.27	7.1	16.73	12.8	15.04	7.4	16.27	5.4
1987	141.31	-4.7	74.80	0.7	16.92	1.1	15.85	5.4	16.92	4.0
1988	145.35	2.9	74.54	-0.3	16.89	-0.2	15.82	-0.2	17.32	2.4
1989	154.83	6.5	75.24	0.9	17.25	2.1	15.64	-1.1	17.94	3.6
1990	150.21	-3.0	74.40	-1.1	18.54	7.5	14.79	-5.4	17.66	-1.6
1991	150.44	0.2	71.69	-3.6	19.29	4.0	13.88	-6.2	15.93	-9.8
1992	155.61	3.4	70.92	-1.1	19.89	3.1	14.25	2.7	16.11	1.1
1993	157.94	1.5	71.48	0.8	20.81	4.6	14.64	2.7	16.85	4.6
1994	158.53	0.4	74.37	4.0	21.89	5.2	15.20	3.8	15.43	-8.4
1995	158.50	0.0	74.42	0.1	22.57	3.1	16.13	6.1	14.99	-2.9
1996	173.14	9.2	77.05	3.5	23.85	5.7	17.30	7.3	15.15	1.1
1997	198.33	14.5	78.72	2.2	26.77	12.2	17.08	-1.3	15.42	1.8
1998	211.84	6.8	81.78	3.9	30.34	13.3	20.24	18.5	19.27	25.0
1999	237.68	12.2	83.53	2.1	32.19	6.1	21.04	4.0	20.35	5.6
2000	260.53	9.6	87.27	4.5	35.92	11.6	21.35	1.5	20.40	0.2
2001	254.83	-2.2	88.08	0.9	35.27	-1.8	21.29	-0.3	22.84	12.0
2002	251.37	-1.4	90.01	2.2	34.56	-2.0	20.49	-3.8	20.25	-11.3
2003	250.80	-0.2	89.77	-0.3	34.08	-1.4	22.17	8.2	20.05	-1.0
2004	253.54	1.1	90.93	1.3	35.26	3.5	22.69	2.3	19.82	-1.1
2005	260.28	2.7	93.18	2.5	38.56	9.4	22.54	-0.7	25.36	28.0

Giving USA uses the Consumer Price Index to adjust for inflation.
Giving USA changed its rounding procedure from the 2003 edition forward. All estimates are rounded to two places then operations performed. In the past, the operations were performed first and the results were rounded.

	Arts, culture, humanities	Percent Change	Public-society benefit	Percent Change	Environ-ment/ animals	Percent Change	Inter-national affairs	Percent Change	Gifts to foun-dations	Percent change	Unallo-cated
1965	2.73	-1.4	2.36	-4.1							9.24
1966	3.25	19.0	2.35	-0.4							11.33
1967	3.27	0.6	2.40	2.1							13.86
1968	3.37	3.1	2.41	0.4							14.76
1969	3.83	13.6	2.98	23.7							14.90
1970	3.32	-13.3	2.32	-22.1							13.39
1971	4.87	46.7	3.28	41.4							15.96
1972	5.14	5.5	3.83	16.8							16.26
1973	5.54	7.8	2.73	-28.7							17.20
1974	4.56	-17.7	2.65	-2.9							14.98
1975	4.50	-1.3	2.87	8.3							15.75
1976	4.74	5.3	3.54	23.3							17.30
1977	7.48	57.8	3.93	11.0							10.99
1978	7.19	-3.9	3.24	-17.6					4.82		7.88
1979	7.34	2.1	3.31	2.2					5.95	23.4	7.56
1980	7.47	1.8	3.46	4.5					4.69	-21.2	10.90
1981	7.86	5.2	3.85	11.3					5.14	9.6	11.19
1982	10.04	27.7	3.40	-11.7					8.10	57.6	3.91
1983	8.25	-17.8	3.71	9.1					5.31	-34.4	4.06
1984	8.46	2.5	3.65	-1.6					6.32	19.0	2.29
1985	9.22	9.0	4.03	10.4					8.59	35.9	-5.34
1986	10.39	12.7	4.37	8.4					8.84	2.9	2.44
1987	10.85	4.4	4.93	12.8	3.42		1.34		8.87	0.3	-12.58
1988	11.21	3.3	5.30	7.5	3.67	7.3	1.42	6.0	6.49	-26.8	-7.30
1989	11.81	5.4	6.05	14.2	3.01	-18.0	1.59	12.0	6.95	7.1	-0.65
1990	11.79	-0.2	7.35	21.5	3.74	24.3	1.96	23.3	5.72	-17.7	-5.75
1991	12.63	7.1	7.07	-3.8	3.97	6.1	2.67	36.2	6.40	11.9	-3.08
1992	12.97	2.7	7.03	-0.6	4.11	3.5	3.10	16.1	6.97	8.9	0.25
1993	12.93	-0.3	7.35	4.6	4.07	-1.0	2.95	-4.8	8.46	21.4	-1.61
1994	12.76	-1.3	7.97	8.4	4.40	8.1	3.14	6.4	8.34	-1.4	-4.97
1995	12.76	0.0	9.10	14.2	4.82	9.5	3.75	19.4	10.84	30.0	-10.89
1996	13.59	6.5	9.42	3.5	4.75	-1.5	3.42	-8.8	15.72	45.0	-7.12
1997	12.91	-5.0	10.21	8.4	4.99	5.1	3.20	-6.4	16.99	8.1	12.05
1998	12.62	-2.2	13.01	27.4	6.29	26.1	3.46	8.1	23.87	40.5	0.97
1999	12.98	2.9	12.84	-1.3	6.83	8.6	4.19	21.1	33.72	41.3	10.01
2000	13.04	0.5	13.15	2.4	6.99	2.3	4.15	-1.0	28.03	-16.9	30.24
2001	13.39	2.7	13.03	-0.9	7.07	1.1	4.57	10.1	28.31	1.0	20.99
2002	13.27	-0.9	12.59	-3.4	7.15	1.1	5.02	9.8	20.80	-26.5	27.24
2003	13.92	4.9	12.88	2.3	7.55	5.6	5.63	12.2	22.95	10.3	21.81
2004	14.46	3.9	13.40	4.0	7.87	4.2	5.53	-1.8	21.01	-8.5	22.56
2005	13.51	-6.6	14.03	4.7	8.86	12.6	6.39	15.6	21.70	3.3	16.15

Note: Gifts to foundations for 1992-2004 represent total gifts reported to the Foundation Center, minus gifts to corporate foundations. The Foundation Center also provided data for 1992-1999 about the value of assets transferred to health care foundations. These are not charitable gifts but transfers resulting from conversions of hospitals and other health care institutions from nonprofit to for-profit status. These were subtracted in those years. Funds given to nonprofits but not reported by an organization coded in a subsector are in the category "Unallocated Gifts." The amount for gifts to foundations in 2005 is estimated by the Foundation Center, which will release the final figure in early 2007.

Giving as a percentage of gross domestic product (GDP), 1965–2005

(In billions of inflation-adjusted dollars)

Year	Total giving	GDP	Giving as a percentage of GDP
1965	91.20	4,458.15	2.0
1966	95.17	4,748.64	2.0
1967	99.60	4,869.01	2.0
1968	105.78	5,106.62	2.1
1969	109.95	5,240.02	2.1
1970	105.89	5,226.47	2.0
1971	113.01	5,434.43	2.1
1972	114.20	5,786.45	2.0
1973	112.58	6,083.15	1.9
1974	106.50	5,942.95	1.8
1975	103.66	5,946.64	1.7
1976	109.34	6,266.05	1.7
1977	113.47	6,544.96	1.7
1978	115.55	6,874.48	1.7
1979	115.92	6,892.44	1.7
1980	115.26	6,611.76	1.7
1981	118.78	6,721.96	1.8
1982	119.63	6,587.74	1.8
1983	123.95	6,934.71	1.8
1984	128.90	7,393.23	1.7
1985	130.12	7,660.74	1.7
1986	148.35	7,952.25	1.9
1987	141.31	8,147.67	1.7
1988	145.36	8,426.28	1.7
1989	154.83	8,638.21	1.8
1990	150.21	8,671.70	1.7
1991	150.44	8,597.51	1.7
1992	155.62	8,821.97	1.8
1993	157.93	8,997.70	1.8
1994	158.53	9,320.24	1.7
1995	158.50	9,480.58	1.7
1996	173.14	9,729.77	1.8
1997	198.33	10,105.01	2.0
1998	211.84	10,480.47	2.0
1999	237.67	10,865.65	2.2
2000	260.53	11,134.17	2.3
2001	254.84	11,168.95	2.3
2002	251.37	11,366.41	2.2
2003	250.80	11,645.47	2.2
2004	253.50	12,132.24	2.1
2005	260.28	12,487.10	2.1

Note: Percentages include computer rounding.
Giving USA 2006 uses the data for Gross Domestic Product available from the Bureau of Economic Analysis, release of March 30, 2006. Adjustment for inflation is done with the Consumer Price Index values found for 1964-2005 at www.bls.gov, for $100 in 2005.

Individual giving as a percentage of personal income and disposable personal income, 1965–2005

(In billions of inflation-adjusted dollars)

Year	Personal income	Disposable personal income	Individual giving	Giving as a a percentage of personal income	Giving as a percentage of disposable personal income
1965	3,445.13	3,088.03	73.28	2.1	2.4
1966	3,640.14	3,239.90	74.98	2.1	2.3
1967	3,791.23	3,364.33	78.42	2.1	2.3
1968	3,995.51	3,507.30	82.77	2.1	2.4
1969	4,143.16	3,587.01	84.78	2.0	2.4
1970	4,221.44	3,702.57	81.48	1.9	2.2
1971	4,356.32	3,865.96	85.05	2.0	2.2
1972	4,638.79	4,061.21	90.51	2.0	2.2
1973	4,886.49	4,304.00	90.32	1.8	2.1
1974	4,843.90	4,245.64	85.58	1.8	2.0
1975	4,845.74	4,309.98	85.41	1.8	2.0
1976	5,062.82	4,471.34	90.35	1.8	2.0
1977	5,263.29	4,626.81	95.23	1.8	2.1
1978	5,505.39	4,818.15	96.17	1.7	2.0
1979	5,545.04	4,822.53	98.39	1.8	2.0
1980	5,470.25	4,761.79	96.49	1.8	2.0
1981	5,567.90	4,826.17	98.82	1.8	2.0
1982	5,616.88	4,900.22	96.40	1.7	2.0
1983	5,805.29	5,114.51	102.08	1.8	2.0
1984	6,183.27	5,473.68	106.13	1.7	1.9
1985	6,401.71	5,644.04	104.17	1.6	1.8
1986	6,632.93	5,853.71	119.55	1.8	2.0
1987	6,785.97	5,945.16	110.93	1.6	1.9
1988	7,022.78	6,189.04	115.54	1.6	1.9
1989	7,226.02	6,334.38	125.14	1.7	2.0
1990	7,290.20	6,404.36	121.10	1.7	1.9
1991	7,242.62	6,401.35	120.83	1.7	1.9
1992	7,463.81	6,613.86	122.08	1.6	1.8
1993	7,512.50	6,638.60	124.34	1.7	1.9
1994	7,699.66	6,789.40	121.93	1.6	1.8
1995	7,884.53	6,930.92	122.21	1.5	1.8
1996	8,116.26	7,080.53	133.88	1.6	1.9
1997	8,414.58	7,287.42	151.13	1.8	2.1
1998	8,894.08	7,663.43	165.77	1.9	2.2
1999	9,147.01	7,848.77	181.28	2.0	2.3
2000	9,560.73	8,159.24	197.92	2.1	2.4
2001	9,620.75	8,256.29	190.12	2.0	2.3
2002	9,642.71	8,500.81	187.68	1.9	2.2
2003	9,732.62	8,671.27	191.26	2.0	2.2
2004	10,042.70	8,958.02	193.46	1.9	2.2
2005	10,248.30	9038.60	199.07	1.9	2.2

Note: Percentages include computer rounding.
Giving USA 2006 uses the data for personal income and disposable personal income from the Bureau of Economic Analysis, National Income and Product Accounts, Table 2.1, lines 1 and 26, March 30, 2006. Inflation adjustment uses the Consumer Price Index calculator available at www.bls.gov for values in prior years when 2005 = $100.

Individual giving as a percentage of personal consumption expenditures without energy and food, 1965–2005

(In billions of inflation-adjusted dollars)

Year	Personal consumption expenditures	Personal consumption expenditures excluding food and energy	Individual giving	Giving as a a percentage of personal consumption expenditures	Giving as a percentage of personal consumption expenditures excluding food and energy
1965	2,751.39	1,940.48	73.28	2.7	3.8
1966	2,898.73	2,045.21	74.98	2.6	3.7
1967	2,969.59	2,112.28	78.42	2.6	3.7
1968	3,131.31	2,241.86	82.77	2.6	3.7
1969	3,220.86	2,312.93	84.78	2.6	3.7
1970	3,263.71	2,330.15	81.48	2.5	3.5
1971	3,384.28	2,447.44	85.05	2.5	3.5
1972	3,600.93	2,621.50	90.51	2.5	3.5
1973	3,750.11	2,718.87	90.32	2.4	3.3
1974	3,698.10	2,629.16	85.58	2.3	3.3
1975	3,754.63	2,663.88	85.41	2.3	3.2
1976	3,954.34	2,825.27	90.35	2.3	3.2
1977	4,120.53	2,963.26	95.23	2.3	3.2
1978	4,279.51	3,098.56	96.17	2.2	3.1
1979	4,281.26	3,063.19	98.39	2.3	3.2
1980	4,164.73	2,942.64	96.49	2.3	3.3
1981	4,170.82	2,963.04	98.82	2.4	3.3
1982	4,204.21	3,018.01	96.40	2.3	3.2
1983	4,491.37	3,289.61	102.08	2.3	3.1
1984	4,705.45	3,498.12	106.13	2.3	3.0
1985	4,937.92	3,723.36	104.17	2.1	2.8
1986	5,166.96	3,968.46	119.55	2.3	3.0
1987	5,329.55	4,121.71	110.93	2.1	2.7
1988	5,536.73	4,298.99	115.54	2.1	2.7
1989	5,667.82	4,402.90	125.14	2.2	2.8
1990	5,738.05	4,450.24	121.10	2.1	2.7
1991	5,715.66	4,445.51	120.83	2.1	2.7
1992	5,895.46	4,638.64	122.08	2.1	2.6
1993	6,052.03	4,786.19	124.34	2.1	2.6
1994	6,251.05	4,972.32	121.93	2.0	2.5
1995	6,376.78	5,099.83	122.21	1.9	2.4
1996	6,543.19	5,245.21	133.88	2.0	2.6
1997	6,750.30	5,441.83	151.13	2.2	2.8
1998	7,044.69	5,734.48	165.77	2.4	2.9
1999	7,365.18	6,012.78	181.28	2.5	3.0
2000	7,643.64	6,214.59	197.92	2.6	3.2
2001	7,780.11	6,333.70	190.12	2.4	3.0
2002	7,980.35	6,533.06	187.68	2.4	2.9
2003	8,183.74	6,671.37	191.26	2.3	2.9
2004	8,492.87	6,879.45	193.46	2.3	2.8
2005	8,745.70	7,014.80	199.07	2.3	2.8

Note: Percentages include computer rounding.
Giving USA 2006 uses the data for personal income expenditures with and without food and energy from the Bureau of Economic Analysis, National Income and Product Accounts, Table 2.3.5, lines 1 and 23, March 30, 2006. Inflation adjustment uses the Consumer Price Index calculator available at www.bls.gov for values in prior years when 2005 = $100.

Corporate giving as a percentage of pretax corporate profits, 1965–2005

(In billions of inflation-adjusted dollars)

Year	Corporate giving	Corporate pretax profits	Giving as a percentage of pretax profits
1965	4.59	496.90	0.9
1966	4.76	522.60	0.9
1967	4.80	488.58	1.0
1968	5.05	518.74	1.0
1969	4.95	486.27	1.0
1970	4.13	407.61	1.0
1971	4.10	447.75	0.9
1972	4.53	503.79	0.9
1973	4.66	593.26	0.8
1974	4.36	585.42	0.7
1975	4.17	528.28	0.8
1976	4.57	616.90	0.7
1977	4.96	678.10	0.7
1978	5.09	737.38	0.7
1979	5.51	731.17	0.8
1980	5.33	600.84	0.9
1981	5.67	523.73	1.1
1982	6.29	401.83	1.6
1983	7.20	458.62	1.6
1984	7.76	504.90	1.5
1985	8.40	467.30	1.8
1986	8.96	438.28	2.0
1987	8.96	545.99	1.6
1988	8.82	637.40	1.4
1989	8.60	604.42	1.4
1990	8.16	611.96	1.3
1991	7.53	606.53	1.2
1992	8.23	641.81	1.3
1993	8.74	698.88	1.3
1994	9.20	760.49	1.2
1995	9.42	864.15	1.1
1996	9.35	912.42	1.0
1997	10.49	971.23	1.1
1998	10.14	860.62	1.2
1999	11.99	909.58	1.3
2000	12.18	877.17	1.4
2001	12.86	780.67	1.6
2002	11.71	834.25	1.4
2003	11.74	994.75	1.2
2004	11.62	1,095.26	1.1
2005	13.77	1,438.30	1.0

Note: Percentages include computer rounding.
Giving USA 2006 uses the data for corporate pretax profits from the Bureau of Economic Analysis, National Income and Product Accounts, Table 6.17, line 1, March 30, 2006 for values 1965 to 2004. For 2005, the value is from the BEA press release dated March 30, 2006. Inflation adjustment uses the Consumer Price Index calculator available at www.bls.gov for values in prior years when 2005 = $100.

Brief summary of methods used

Overview of methodology for 2005 estimates

Giving USA presents estimates for the four primary sources of giving and for nine principal types of recipients of contributions. These are preliminary estimates for 2005, which use the best information available in March and April 2006. They will be revised in 2006 and in 2007 as more data are available. Revisions of *Giving USA*'s estimates for 2004 and earlier are reflected in the data tables in this volume.

The *Giving USA* estimates apply methods developed by scholars of giving and are reviewed and approved by the members of the *Giving USA* Advisory Council on Methodology. Members of that group include research directors from a number of other organizations involved in studying the nonprofit sector and are listed in this volume.

The rest of this chapter provides an overview of the methods used to develop the estimates for 2005, organized to present the sources of giving first, followed by the types of recipients. An expanded discussion of methodologies used for the 2005 estimates and a thorough review of revisions made to earlier years' estimates are in the *Giving USA* methodology papers available at www.givinginstitute.org and at www.philanthropy.iupui.edu. Separate methodology papers are available for estimating giving by individuals, corporations, and bequest; and for estimating giving to religion. Another methodology paper discusses the *Giving USA* survey that is used to estimate amounts received by the types of recipient organizations.

Estimate of giving by individuals

For giving in 2005, we used the final IRS data about itemized deductions for charitable contributions claimed on individual income tax returns for 2003. To this total are added estimated changes in itemized charitable contributions for 2004 and 2005, plus estimates of giving by households that do not itemize. The nonitemizer household estimate is based on the Center on Philanthropy Panel Study (COPPS), which asks more than 7,800 households about their charitable giving. The Boston College Center on Wealth and Philanthropy (CWP) did the analysis of COPPS data to develop an estimate of giving by nonitemizing households. The Center on Philanthropy used survey results from the COPPS data for 2005 and from the April 2006 release from the Conference Board to estimate contributions made for disaster relief in 2005.

Table 1 shows the components of the estimates of individual giving for 2003, 2004, and 2005.

Brief summary of methods used

Table 1
Components of the estimate of individual giving, 2003 through 2005
($ in billions)

2003

Itemized deductions for charitable contributions, IRS	145.702
Estimated giving by nonitemizers, CWP using COPPS	34.488
Total estimated individual giving	180.190

2004

2003 itemized deductions for charitable contributions, IRS	145.702
Estimated change in giving by itemizers, 2004, *GUSA*	5.940
Estimated giving by nonitemizers, CWP using COPPS	35.465
Total estimated individual giving	187.107

2005

2003 itemized deductions for charitable contributions, IRS	145.702
Estimated change in giving, 2004 itemizers, *GUSA*	5.940
Estimated change in giving, 2005 itemizers, *GUSA*	4.680
Estimated giving by nonitemizers, CWP using COPPS	36.919
Total estimated individual giving before disaster relief aid	193.241
Disaster relief giving by individuals in 2005, COP	5.830
	199.071

Data sources: IRS=Internal Revenue Service; *GUSA=Giving USA*; CWP=Center on Wealth and Philanthropy, Boston College; COPPS=Center on Philanthropy Panel Study; COP=Center on Philanthropy, using data from COPPS for tsunami giving and from the Conference Board for giving after hurricanes Katrina, Rita, and Wilma.

The estimated change in individual giving before the inclusion of disaster relief giving is developed using government data about changes in personal income, tax rates, and the change in the Standard & Poor's 500 Index. The amount of estimated change is based on the long-term historical relationship between these economic variables and changes in itemized deductions for charitable contributions. This method was developed and tested by economists Partha Deb, Mark Wilhelm, and Patrick Rooney.[1] Among many methods studied, this estimating procedure was found to be the most accurate over time for predicting changes in individual itemized charitable deductions.

Estimate of giving by bequest
The method of estimating contributions by bequest follows procedures introduced in *Giving USA 2005*. The new procedure uses data collected by the Council for Aid to Education about bequests received. Over the period 1987 through 2002, the CAE bequest figure averaged 15.1 percent of the total amount claimed on estate tax returns. The consistency of educational charitable bequests as a percentage of all claimed charitable bequests is the basis for the current estimate.

Brief summary of methods used

For charitable bequests in 2005, the estimate of giving by bequest relies on total bequest gifts received at institutions of higher education surveyed by the Council for Aid to Education (CAE). To estimate bequest giving for 2005, *Giving USA* took the CAE result for 2004–2005 and divided it by 15.1 percent (the 15-year average from 1987 through 2002).

Giving USA also estimates giving by estates below the federal estate tax filing threshold. This estimate considers the number of deaths of adults aged 55 and above; the average net worth of adults in that age group; and, based on estate tax returns, the average percentage of net estate value left to charity by adults in that age group.

Table 2 shows components of the bequest estimate for 2005.

Table 2
Bequest estimate, 2005
($ in billions)

Council for Aid to Education (CAE) findings, bequest receipts, higher educational institutions, 2004–2005	2.086
CAE result divided by 0.151 to yield estimate of all giving by estates that file estate tax returns, *GUSA*	13.810
Estimate, giving by estates below $1.5 million, 2005, *GUSA*	+ 3.627
Total estimated giving by bequest	17.437

Data sources: CAE = Council for Aid to Education; *GUSA* = *Giving USA*.

A more detailed explanation of both elements of the bequest estimate—the relationship between the CAE survey and overall itemized charitable gifts from estates and the estimate of giving by estates below the federal estate tax filing threshold—appears in a methodology paper about estimating giving by bequest, released in summer 2006, at www.givinginstitute.org, at www.philanthropy.iupui.edu, and at www.bc.edu/~cwp.

Estimate of giving by foundations
The estimate of giving by foundations uses the figures released by the Foundation Center for giving by independent, community, and operating foundations in 2005.[2] The Foundation Center also estimates giving by corporate foundations. That component is moved from the Foundation Center's estimate of giving by all types of foundations and put in the *Giving USA* estimate of giving by corporations.

Estimate of giving by corporations
The estimate of giving by corporations is based on the most recent final data available for itemized contributions claimed on federal tax returns, which is modified to

1) Add changes in corporate giving found in an estimating procedure used by *Giving USA*;

Brief summary of methods used

2) Deduct corporate contributions to corporate foundations, as estimated by *Giving USA* for the most recent year based on findings about the prior year released by the Foundation Center;

3) Add the Foundation Center's estimate of giving by corporate foundations; and

4) For 2005 only, add corporate giving for disaster relief tallied by the U.S. Chamber of Commerce after removing corporate foundation giving, which is in the estimate from the Foundation Center.

For giving in 2005, the final IRS data about deductible contributions itemized by corporations are available for 2003. Table 3 illustrates components of the estimate of corporate giving for 2003, 2004, and 2005.

Table 3
Corporate giving estimate, 2003–2005
($ in billions)

2003

Corporate itemized deductions for contributions, IRS	10.823
Minus corporate contributions to corporate foundations, FC	– 3.234
Subtotal: Corporate giving net of gifts to corporate foundations	7.589
Plus corporate foundation giving, FC	+ 3.466
Total corporate giving	11.055

2004

2003 corporate itemized contributions, IRS	10.823
Plus estimated change in corporate giving, 2004, *GUSA*	+ 0.657
Subtotal: estimated itemized contributions	11.480
Minus corporate giving to corporate foundations, FC	– 3.667
Subtotal: estimated itemized deductions net of gifts to corporate foundations	7.813
Plus corporate foundation giving, FC	+ 3.430
Total estimated corporate giving	11.243

2005

2003 corporate itemized contributions, IRS	10.823
Plus estimated change in corporate giving, 2004, *GUSA*	+ 0.657
Plus estimated change in corporate giving 2005, *GUSA*	+ 0.794
Subtotal: estimated itemized contributions	12.274
Less estimated giving to corporate foundations, FC	– 3.400
Subtotal: estimated itemized deductions net of gifts to corporate foundations	8.874
Estimated corporate foundation grantmaking, FC	+ 3.600
Total estimated corporate giving before disaster relief gifts	12.474
Disaster relief giving in 2005, USCC	1.380
Corporate foundation disaster giving, USCC	– 0.084
	13.770

Data sources: IRS=Internal Revenue Service; *GUSA*=*Giving USA*; FC=Foundation Center; USCC=U.S. Chamber of Commerce, figures adjusted to remove gifts in 2004 for tsunami relief.

Brief summary of methods used

A more technical explanation of the *Giving USA* estimating procedure for corporate giving appears in a paper written in 2004 by W. Chin, M. Brown, and P. Rooney that is available at www.aafrc.org and at www.philanthropy.iupui.edu.

Estimates of giving to types of recipient organizations

Giving USA relies on data provided by other research organizations for some components of the estimates of giving by type of recipient. *Giving USA* also conducts a survey of some subsectors to gather data about changes in charitable gifts. The following sections describe briefly the data sources and methods used in developing estimates for each subsector.

Estimate of giving to religion

- A baseline estimate from 1986 of $50 billion in giving to religion that was developed separately by three different organizations.[3]
- A percentage change in giving to religion developed when summing contributions data released by the National Council of Churches of Christ of the USA, as compiled by Joseph Claude Harris for the Roman Catholic Church, and (new for 2006) as reported by selected members of the Evangelical Council for Financial Accountability.

Because the denominational contributions data are typically released a year or more after *Giving USA* releases its initial estimates for giving by subsector, the current year's estimate of giving to religion is a *Giving USA* estimate based on the past 10 years of changes. *Giving USA* averaged the inflation-adjusted percentage changes found in giving to religion from 1995 through 2004, excluding an exceptionally high value in 2000. Adjusted for inflation, the multiple-year average is 2.0 percent. Converted to remove the inflation adjustment, that is an estimated 3.5 percent change in giving to religion in 2005, before adding amounts given to religious organizations for disaster relief. Table 4 delineates the steps used in estimating giving to religion.

Table 4
Components of the estimate of giving to religion, 2005
($ in billions)

Inflation-adjusted estimate for 2004, to equivalent of 2005 dollars *GUSA* + change from NCCC, ECFA, JCH		90.93
Estimated percentage change, 2005, *GUSA**	2.0%	
Dollar change, 2004 using rate of previous change (inflation-adjusted dollars)		1.82
Subtotal, 2005 in 2005 dollars		92.75
Disaster relief receipts reported by denominations		+ 0.43
Total, 2005 estimate		93.18

*Inflation-adjusted rate, averaged 1995–2004 excluding 2000, was 2.0 percent change. With inflation in 2005 at 3.5 percent, this equates to a 5.5 percent change in current dollars (without inflation adjustment).

Data sources: NCCC = National Council of Churches of Christ; ECFA = Evangelical Council for Financial Accountability; JCH = Joseph Claude Harris, who studies giving to the Roman Catholic Church; *GUSA* = *Giving USA*.

Brief summary of methods used

Estimate of giving to education

The estimate of giving to educational organizations relies on data from three sources:

1) An estimate of giving to higher education for the prior fiscal year (July 1, 2004 through June 30, 2005) based on a survey by the Council for Aid to Education.

2) A survey conducted by *Giving USA* from which is estimated
   a) a rate of change in giving to higher education for the balance
      of the calendar year (July 1, 2005 through December 31, 2005)
   b) estimated giving to other educational organizations

3) Data collected by the Center on Philanthropy in its Million Dollar List.

Table 5 summarizes the components of the estimate of giving to education for 2005.

Table 5
Estimate of giving to education
($ in billions)

One-half of estimate of CAE 2004–2005 estimate of giving to higher education to yield estimate of giving for first half of year.		12.800
Rate of change found in *Giving USA* survey.	13.2 %	
Applied to CAE estimate to get estimate for 2005–2006 to yield estimate of giving to higher education in second half of 2005.		14.490
Subtotal estimated giving to higher education.		27.290
Estimate of giving to other educational organizations not in CAE estimate and surveyed by *Giving USA*.		10.323
Announced gifts of $100 million or more reportedly received at institutions in the fourth quarter of 2005. These institutions were not in the data collected by the *Giving USA* survey. Source of gift information: Million Dollar List.		0.669
Announced grants and gifts to public schools, all of $1 million or more. Public schools are not included in the *Giving USA* survey, but are receiving an increasing amount of funding from foundations and private donors.		0.164
Announced gifts and grants to private schools, all of $1 million or more and not in *Giving USA* survey.		0.086
Announced gifts of $1 million or more going to religious elementary and secondary schools that were not included in *Giving USA* surveys, $1 million list.		0.013
Disaster relief gifts.		0.010
Estimated total giving to education.		38.555

Estimate of giving to foundations
The Foundation Center estimates contributions to foundations of $21.70 billion for 2005. Approximately 30 percent of giving to foundations in any one year is from estates that file income tax returns, based on *Giving USA*'s comparison of estate tax return information about charitable bequests and the Foundation Center's reports of giving to foundations. Typically, major estate gifts to foundations arrive at the foundations over time as the estate is settled.

Giving USA 2006 *survey for estimating giving to other subsectors*
The estimates of giving to health, human services, arts, public-society benefit, environment, and international affairs rely on data from two sources:

- An earlier estimate of giving to the subsector.

- A rate of change developed from the *Giving USA* survey of organizations in the subsector. The rate of change is multiplied by the prior year's estimate to generate a dollar amount of change. That dollar change is added to the prior year's estimate to yield this year's estimate.

The *Giving USA 2006* survey was sent to a sample of 7,262 unduplicated organizations. A total of 804 returned the survey, for an overall response rate of 11.1 percent. When surveys that could not be delivered are removed from the sample, there were 6,624 unduplicated organizations, and the response rate was 12.1 percent. Not all surveys are completed, and some have such unusual results that they are outliers (exceptionally large rates of change, either up or down). Usable surveys numbered 688.

The sample includes every large organization that can be identified as having received charitable contributions of $20 million or more in a year between 2002 and 2004 and random samples of medium-sized and small organizations. Medium-sized organizations are those that raised between $1 million and $20 million in charitable contributions. Small organizations raised less than $1 million.

The survey included nonprofit organizations in the following subsectors:

Arts

Education

Environment

Health

Human services

International affairs

Public-society benefit (including selected community foundations)

Religion (selected religious organizations on the *Chronicle of Philanthropy*'s list of the 400 nonprofits that raised the most money in 2004)

Brief summary of methods used

The survey asked organizations to report total charitable revenue for 2004 and total charitable revenue for 2005. For each subsector, all the usable responses for organizations in that subsector were tallied to estimate total giving to that subsector for 2004 and total giving for that subsector in 2005. Then, the difference between the two years was calculated to get the percentage rate of change. The percentage rate of change is applied to the estimated total published in *Giving USA* for the prior year.

The total giving estimate uses weighting techniques to take into account how many nonprofits in that size group are in the subsector and how many were in the sample. For information about how many organizations of each size group were in the study for each subsector, and for an explanation of the method for estimating total charitable revenue in a given year using survey results, please see the longer methodology paper at www.givinginstitute.org, which is accessible with the user name and password printed on the first page of this volume.

Giving USA's estimates of giving to each subsector are based on data collected in a survey of nonprofit organizations of all sizes that was conducted in the early 1970s by the Commission on Private Philanthropy and Public Needs (also known as the Filer Commission—after the chairman, John Filer). In recent years, only nonprofits that file an IRS Form 990 are surveyed annually to gauge the rate of change in giving.

Estimates before and after disaster giving is added
Based on the survey responses and the weighted estimates of the rates of change in giving for 2005, *Giving USA* developed two sets of estimates for giving: one before disaster giving was included and the published values in this book that do include disaster giving. Table 6 shows the estimates before and after inclusion of disaster giving as reported by recipient organizations.

Why *Giving USA* makes revisions
Because *Giving USA*'s results are a series of estimates, they are subject to revision as additional information becomes available. A discussion of the revisions made to prior years' estimates is available at www.givinginstitute.org for purchasers of this volume, with the user name and password appearing on the first page.

Brief summary of methods used

Table 6
Estimated giving before and after adding disaster relief
($ in billions)

Surveyed subsectors	2004 estimate	Rate of change	Dollar change	2005 estimate before disaster relief	Disaster relief	Total 2005 estimate with disaster relief
Education	34.10	13.05%	4.45	38.55	0.01	38.56
Health	21.95	2.65%	0.58	22.53	0.01	22.54
Human services	19.17	15.00%	2.88	22.05	3.31	25.36
Arts	13.99	-3.70%	-0.52	13.47	0.04	13.51
Public-society benefit	12.96	6.23%	0.81	13.77	0.26	14.03
Environment and animals	7.61	16.00%	1.22	8.83	0.03	8.86
International affairs	5.35	-1.90%	-0.10	5.25	1.14	6.39

Not in survey, estimated in other ways

Religion	87.95	5.5%	4.80	92.75	0.43	93.18
Foundations	20.32	6.5%	1.33	21.65	0.05	21.70

1   Deb, P., M. Wilhelm, M. Rooney, and M. Brown, Estimating charitable giving, *Nonprofit and Voluntary Sector Quarterly*, December 2004.
2   L. Renz, S. Lawrence, and J. Atienza, *Foundation Growth and Giving Estimates: 2006 Preview*, The Foundation Center, 2006, www.fdncenter.org.
3   An examination of *Giving USA*'s estimate of giving to religion, compared with estimates developed using two other methods, appears in the paper "Reconciling estimates of religious giving," written in 2005 by J. C. Harris, M. Brown, and P. Rooney. The three methods yield estimates within 5 percent of one another, offering some reassurance that using 1986 findings as a baseline is at least as good as some other approaches.

Glossary

Certain terms used throughout this volume are defined here. Some of the definitions are provided by the National Center for Charitable Statistics at its web site: http://nccs.urban.org/glossary.htm.

Average: In statistics, the *mean*. This figure is calculated by summing the values from each respondent or reporting organization and then dividing by the number of respondents. An average can be a good representation of a trend if the organizations in the group report amounts that are relatively close together. It can misrepresent a trend if the difference between the highest amount reported and the lowest amount reported is very large. In that instance, a median might be a better point of comparison. *See also* **Median**.

Charitable revenue: Philanthropic gifts received by a charity organization. *Giving USA* asks organizations that participate in its survey to report cash received or the cash value of in-kind gifts. Where possible, we ask that unpaid pledges be excluded from the total reported charitable revenue.

Charity or charitable organization: In this book, charitable organization denotes a religious organization or an entity recognized as tax-exempt under section 501(c)(3) of the Internal Revenue Code. Charitable organizations are exempt from federal income taxes because of their religious, educational, scientific, and public purposes. They are eligible to receive tax-deductible gifts. *See also* **Public charity**, **Private foundation**.

Direct public support: As used on IRS Form 990, direct public support appears on line 1a and represents charitable revenue (gifts and grants).

Gift: Transfer of cash or other asset with cash value by an individual, corporation, or from an estate (or in the form of a bequest); grants from foundations. Gifts do not include government grants or contracts or allocations from nonprofit organizations, such as United Ways or communal funds. Gifts also do not include distributions from donor-advised funds.

Indirect public support: As used on IRS Form 990, indirect public support appears on line 1b and includes transfers from one nonprofit organization to another. This includes allocations from federated campaigns, distributions from donor-advised funds, and contributions from a religious organization to another nonprofit, among other transfers.

Glossary

IRS Form 990: An annual return filed with the Internal Revenue Service by nonprofit, tax-exempt organizations (even those that are not charities) with gross receipts for the year of $25,000 or more. May be submitted on a 990-EZ (when receipts are from $25,000 to $100,000 and assets are less than $250,000). Private foundations use a variation of the form, the Form 990-PF, with additional information required about investments, grantmaking, and assets.

Large organization: *Giving USA* defines large organizations as those that had charitable revenue of $20 million or more.

Mean: *See* **Average**.

Median: In a summary of data, the median is the middle response. When the responses are organized sequentially, one-half of the responses given are lower than the median, and one-half are higher. Typically, when the amounts reported in a survey are close together, the median and the mean (average) will be close together. If the answers are very different from one another, the average and the median can be very different. Median values are less sensitive to the effects of outliers than are mean values. *See also* **Average**.

Medium-sized organization: *Giving USA* defines medium-sized organizations as those with total charitable revenue between $1 million and $19.99 million.

National Taxonomy of Exempt Entities: A definitive classification system for nonprofit organizations that are recognized as tax-exempt under section 501(c)(3) of the Internal Revenue Code. See pages 216 to 217 for a listing of the 26 major groups (named by letters of the alphabet) and examples of organizations within each group. Major groups have been clustered into 10 subsectors as follows. *See also* **Subsector**.

Subsector	Major Groups Included
Arts, culture, and humanities	A
Education	B
Environment/animals	C, D
Health	E, F, G, H
Human services	I, J, K, L, M, N, O, P
International affairs	Q
Public-society benefit	R, S, T, U, V, W
Religion related	X
Mutual/membership benefit*	Y
Unknown, unclassified	Z

*This subsector is not tracked by *Giving USA*.

Glossary

Nonprofit organization: An organization whose net revenue is not distributed to individuals or other stakeholders, but is used to further the organization's mission. The organization is not owned by but is governed by a board of trustees. Not all nonprofit organizations are charities.

Nonprofit sector: A sector of the economy, apart from the government, for which profit is not a motive. Organizations in the nonprofit sector in some cases may be exempt from various federal, state, and local taxes. Includes houses of worship; charitable organizations formed under section 501(c) (3) of the Internal Revenue Code; and organizations formed under other sections of the Code, such as advocacy organizations, membership organizations, and others.

NTEE: *See* **National Taxonomy of Exempt Entities**.

Planned gift: The Association of Fundraising Professionals says a planned gift is structured and integrates personal, financial, and estate-planning goals with the donor's lifetime or testamentary (will) giving. A planned gift can be transmitted through a legal instrument, such as a will or a trust. A planned gift can transfer assets to a charitable organization immediately, or the transfer can be deferred. Many planned gift vehicles are used, including bequests, charitable trusts, and charitable annuities.

Private foundation: Private foundation status is granted to an organization formed for a charitable purpose under section 501(c)(3) of the Internal Revenue Code that does not receive one-third or more of its support from public donations. Most, but not all, private foundations give grants to public charities. *See also* **Charity or charitable organization**, **Public charity**.

Public charity: An organizations that qualifies for status as a public charity under Section 509 (a) of the Internal Revenue Code. A public charity includes tax-exempt organizations formed for certain purposes (a church; an educational organization, including public schools; a hospital or medical research facility; or an endowment operated for the benefit of a higher education institution). An organization formed for other purposes can also be a public charity if it has a broad base of public support, receiving a substantial part of its support from the general public. Support from a governmental unit is considered public support by proxy via taxes. Complete information about public charities can be found in IRS Publication 557. Note that some, but not all, charitable organizations formed under section 501(c)(3) of the Internal Revenue Code can be public charities. *See also* **Charity or charitable organization**, **Private foundation**.

Public support: As used by the Internal Revenue Service on IRS Form 990, line 1d, public support is the sum of line 1a or "direct public support," generally charitable gifts or grants; line 1b or "indirect public support," generally transfers from other nonprofits; and line 1c or government grants.

Glossary

Reporting organization: A charitable organization that files an IRS Form 990.

Sector: The portion of the national economy that fits certain criteria for ownership and distribution of surplus. Examples include the business sector, the government sector, and the nonprofit sector. *See also* **Subsector.**

Small organization: *Giving USA* identifies small organizations as those with less than $1 million in charitable revenue.

Subsector: Within the nonprofit sector, there are several subsectors defined by the National Taxonomy of Exempt Entities. *See also* **National Taxonomy of Exempt Entities, Sector.**

Tax-deductible: A contribution to an organization is deductible for income tax purposes if the organization is a church or is registered with and recognized by the IRS as a tax-exempt, nonprofit charity.

Tax-exempt: An organization may be exempt because it is a church or because of registration within a state or with the Internal Revenue Service. State exemptions may cover sales tax, property tax, and/or state income tax. Approved registration with the IRS will exempt an organization from federal income tax. Organizations that have more than $5,000 in gross revenues annually are legally responsible for registering with the IRS.

Not all tax-exempt, nonprofit organizations are charities eligible to receive tax-deductible contributions. Examples of tax-exempt nonprofits that are not charities include advocacy organizations organized under section 501(c)(4) of the Internal Revenue Code, credit unions, farmers' cooperatives, business leagues, and professional membership associations.

Summary of the National Taxonomy of Exempt Entities

A-Arts, culture, humanities activities
- arts & culture (multipurpose activities)
- media & communications
- visual arts
- museums
- performing arts
- humanities
- historical societies & related historical activities

B-Educational institutions & related activities
- elementary & secondary education (preschool-grade 12)
- vocational/technical schools
- higher education
- graduate/professional schools
- adult/continuing education
- libraries
- student services & organizations

C-Environment quality, protection
- pollution abatement & control
- natural resources conservation & protection
- botanic/horticulture activities
- environmental beautification & open spaces
- environmental education & outdoor survival

D-Animal-related activities
- animal protection & welfare
- humane society
- wildlife preservation & protection
- veterinary services
- zoos & aquariums
- specialty animals & other services

E-Health-general & rehabilitative
- hospitals, nursing homes & primary medical care
- health treatment, primarily outpatient
- reproductive health care
- rehabilitative medical services
- health support services
- emergency medical services
- public health & wellness education
- health care financing/insurance programs

F-Mental health, crisis intervention
- addiction prevention & treatment
- mental health treatment & services
- crisis intervention
- psychiatric/mental health-primary care
- half-way houses (mental health)/transitional care

G-Disease/disorder/medical disciplines (multipurpose)
- birth defects & genetic diseases
- cancer
- diseases of specific organs
- nerve, muscle & bone diseases
- allergy-related diseases
- specific named diseases
- medical disciplines/specialties

H-Medical research
- identical hierarchy to diseases/disorders/medical disciplines in major field "G"
- example: G30 represents American Cancer Society; H30 represents cancer research

I-Public protection: crime/courts/legal services
- police & law enforcement agencies
- correctional facilities & prisoner services
- crime prevention
- rehabilitation of offenders
- administration of justice/courts
- protection against/prevention of neglect, abuse, exploitation
- legal services

J-Employment/jobs
- vocational guidance & training (such as on-the-job programs)
- employment procurement assistance
- vocational rehabilitation
- employment assistance for the handicapped
- labor union/organizations
- labor-management relations

K-Food, nutrition, agriculture
- agricultural services aimed at food procurement
- food service/free food distribution
- nutrition promotion
- farmland preservation

L-Housing/shelter
- housing development/construction
- housing search assistance
- low-cost temporary shelters such as youth hostels
- homeless, temporary shelter
- housing owners/renters organizations
- housing support services

Summary of the National Taxonomy of Exempt Entities

M-Public safety/disaster preparedness & relief
- disaster prevention, such as flood control
- disaster relief (US domestic)
- safety education
- civil defense & preparedness programs

N-Recreation, leisure, sports, athletics
- camps
- physical fitness & community recreation
- sports training
- recreation/pleasure or social clubs
- amateur sports
- Olympics & Special Olympics

O-Youth Development
- youth centers (such as boys/girls clubs)
- scouting
- big brothers/sisters
- agricultural development (such as 4-H)
- business development, Junior Achievement
- citizenship programs
- religious leadership development

P-Human service-other/multipurpose
- multipurpose service organizations
- children & youth services
- family services
- personal social services
- emergency assistance (food, clothing)
- residential/custodial care
- centers promoting independence of specific groups, such as senior or women's centers

Q-International
- exchange programs
- international development
- international relief services (foreign disaster relief)
- peace & security
- foreign policy research & analyses (U.S. domestic)
- international human rights

R-Civil rights/civil liberties
- equal opportunity & access
- voter education/registration
- civil liberties

S-Community improvement/development
- community/neighborhood development
- community coalitions
- economic development, urban and rural
- business services
- community service clubs (such as Junior League)

T-Philanthropy & voluntarism
- philanthropy association/society
- private foundations, funds (e.g. women's funds), and community foundations
- community funds and federated giving
- voluntarism promotion

U-Science
- scientific research & promotion
- physical/earth sciences
- engineering/technology
- biological sciences

V-Social sciences
- social science research/studies
- interdisciplinary studies, such as black studies, women's studies, urban studies, etc.

W-Public affairs/society benefit
- public policy research, general
- government & public administration
- transportation systems
- public utilities
- consumer rights/education

X-Religion/spiritual development
- Christian churches, missionary societies and related religious bodies
- Jewish synagogues
- other specific religions

Y-Mutual membership benefit organizations
- insurance providers & services (other than health)
- pension/retirement funds
- fraternal beneficiary funds
- cemeteries & burial services

Z99-unknown, unclassifiable

Source: *The Foundation Grants Index,* The Foundation Center
Note: In 1994, community funds and federated giving programs were moved from letter **S** to letter **T**. They are still in the same broad category, called "public-society benefit."

Member firms

A.L. Brourman Associates, Inc.
Alexander Haas Martin & Partners, Inc.
The Alford Group Inc.
American City Bureau, Inc.
Arnoult & Associates, Inc.
Blackburn Associates, Inc.
Campbell & Company
Carlton & Company
The Clements Group, LC
The Collins Group, Inc.
Compton International Fundraising
The Covenant Group
DataFund Services, Inc.
Durkin Associates
The EHL Consulting Group, Inc.
eTapestry
Ferguson Development Group
Fund Inc.®
Grenzebach Glier & Associates, Inc.
Hodge, Cramer & Associates, Inc.
IDC
Jeffrey Byrne & Associates, Inc.
The Kellogg Organization, Inc.
Marts & Lundy, Inc.
Miller Group Worldwide, LLC
National Community Development Services, Inc.
The Oram Group, Inc.
Raising More Money
Raybin Associates, Inc.
Ruotolo Associates Inc.
Semple Bixel Associates, Inc.
The Sharpe Group
Smith Beers Yunker & Company, Inc.
StaleyRobeson®
Viscern/Ketchum/RSI
Whitney Jones, Inc.
Woodburn, Kyle & Company

Committees

Editorial Review Board

James D. Yunker, Ed.D., *Chair*
Smith Beers Yunker & Company, Inc.

Leo P. Arnoult, CFRE
Arnoult & Associates, Inc.

Alan Axelrod
Raising More Money

David W. Blackburn
Blackburn Associates, Inc.

Gary Cardaronella
Cardaronella Stirling Associates

Edith H. Falk, CFRE
Campbell & Company

Henry (Hank) Goldstein, CFRE
The Oram Group, Inc.

David R. Luckes
Greater St. Louis Community Foundation

Benjamin G. Middleton, CFRE
The Rhode Island Foundation

Leonard J. Moisan, Ph.D.
The Covenant Group

Nancy L. Raybin
Raybin Associates, Inc.

Donna Wiley, Ph.D.
Grenzebach Glier & Associates, Inc.

Cover Photograph Contest Committee

Del Martin, CFRE, *Chair*
Alexander Haas Martin & Partners, Inc.

Stephen Bollinger, ACS
LOMA

Sharon Bond
AMC

Barry E. Dodd
Alexander Haas Martin & Partners, Inc.

John Lawrence
Lamar Dodd Art Center, LaGrange College

David Lester
Lester & Associates

Leslie Biggins Mollsen
American City Bureau, Inc.

J.D. Scott
J.D. Scott Photography

Richard S. Belous, Ph.D.
Vice President, Research,
United Way—National Headquarters

Freddie Cross
Director of Research and Information,
Council for Advancement and Support
of Education

Daniel Feenberg, Ph.D.
Research Associate, National Bureau
of Economic Research

Kirsten Grønbjerg, Ph.D.
Efroymson Chair in Philanthropy and
Professor of Public and Environmental
Affairs, Indiana University, The Center on
Philanthropy at Indiana University

Theodore R. Hart, CFRE
President and CEO,
ePhilanthropyFoundation.Org

John J. Havens, Ph.D.
Senior Research Associate, Center on
Wealth and Philanthropy, Boston College

Nadine T. Jalandoni
Director, Research Services,
INDEPENDENT SECTOR

David Joulfaian, Ph.D.
Senior Economist,
U.S. Treasury Department

Ann E. Kaplan
Director, Voluntary Support of Education,
Council for Aid to Education

John M. Kennedy, Ph.D.
Director, Indiana University Center for
Survey Research, Indiana University

Judith Kroll
Director of Research, Council on
Foundations

Linda M. Lampkin, M.S.
Program Director, National Center for
Charitable Statistics, The Urban Institute

Eileen W. Lindner, Ph.D.
Editor, *Yearbook of American and
Canadian Churches*, National Council
Churches of Christ, USA

Robert B. McClelland, Ph.D.
Senior Research Economist,
U.S. Bureau of Labor Statistics

Charles H. Moore, Executive Director,
Committee to Encourage Corporate
Philanthropy

Sophia A. Muirhead, J.D.
Senior Research Associate,
The Conference Board

Loren Renz
Vice President for Research,
The Foundation Center

Kathy L. Renzetti
Director, Communications and
Membership, Association for
Healthcare Philanthropy

Lester M. Salamon, Ph.D.
Center for Civil Society Studies
The Johns Hopkins University

Robert F. Sharpe, Jr.
President, The Sharpe Group

Frank P. Stafford, Ph.D., Director,
Institute for Social Research,
University of Michigan

Richard S. Steinberg, Ph.D.
Professor of Economics, Indiana
University-Purdue University
Indianapolis

For the Giving USA Foundation™

Leo P. Arnoult, CFRE
President, Arnoult & Associates, Inc.

David Bergeson, Ph.D. (*ex officio*)
Executive Director,
Giving USA Foundation™

Henry (Hank) Goldstein, CFRE
President, The Oram Group, Inc.

Richard T. Jolly
Marts & Lundy Inc.

Nancy Raybin
Managing Partner, Raybin Associates

Paul G. Schervish, Ph.D.
Director, Center on Wealth
and Philanthropy, Boston College

For the Center on Philanthropy at Indiana University

Melissa S. Brown
Managing Editor, *Giving USA*

Kathryn S. Steinberg, Ph.D.
Assistant Director of Research

Eugene R. Tempel, Ed.D., CFRE Executive Director

Patrick M. Rooney, Ph.D.
Director of Research

Staff

Melissa S. Brown, Managing Editor, *Giving USA*
Adriene L. Davis, Communications Manager
Heidi K. Frederick, Research Development Specialist
Patrick M. Rooney, Ph.D., Director of Research
Lois M. Sherman, Publications Manager
Kathryn S. Steinberg, Ph.D., Assistant Director of Research
Eugene R. Tempel, Ed.D., CFRE, Executive Director
Assistants: Emery Chen, Shruti Dubey, David Fleischhacker, Andrea Reamer, Diane Strong

Chapter authors

(All authors are research department staff or doctoral students at the Center on Philanthropy at Indiana University)

The Numbers: Estimates of Giving	Melissa S. Brown, Heidi K. Frederick, Patrick M. Rooney, Ph.D., Kathryn S. Steinberg, Ph.D.
Overview of Disaster Giving	Emery C. Chen
Giving by Individuals	Yue (Jen) Shang
Giving by Foundations	Melissa S. Brown
Giving by Bequest	Melissa S. Brown
Giving by Corporations	Larry Smith and Rebecca Scheer
Giving to Religion	Heidi K. Frederick
Giving to Education	Angela R. Logan and Melissa S. Brown
Giving to Foundations	Melissa S. Brown
Giving to Health	Janice S. O'Rourke
Giving to Human Services	Rebecca A. Scheer
Giving to Arts	Takayuki Yoshioka
Giving to Public-Society Benefit	Alvin S. Lyons
Giving to Environment	Nancy D. Goldfarb
Giving to International	Melissa S. Brown
Legal-Legislative Overview	Shariq A. Siddiqui
$5 Million and Over List	David A. Fleischhacker
Brief Summary of Methods	Kathryn S. Steinberg, Ph.D.

Index

African-American giving, 70, 71

Alumni giving, 125, 126, 128, 158

American Red Cross, 58-61, 64, 144, 147, 189

Arts education funding, 158

Arts, culture and humanities, giving to, 47, 154-162

Bequests, 6, 11, 33, 78-86, 88

Bird flu, 184

Center on Philanthropy Panel Study (COPPS), v, 2-4, 70, 71, 115-119, 125, 139, 151, 158, 167, 177, 183, 185, 214, 215

Corporate foundation giving, 95

Corporate giving, 5, 11, 35, 94-106

Corporate giving as a percentage of income, 40

Corporate profits, ii, 1, 6, 26, 35, 40, 94, 95, 213

Corporate sponsorships , 105

Direct mail fundraising, 69, 74

Disaster relief giving, 1, 6, 7, 14, 18-26, 57-65, 87, 96, 97, 99, 108, 146, 163, 166, 183, 189

Donor fatigue, 147

Donor-advised funds, 168

Education giving for health research, 124

Education, giving to, 42, 82, 121-130

Endowment giving, 8, 9, 68, 156, 157, 168, 170, 192, 193, 200

Environment and animals, giving to, 48, 82, 173-179

Family foundations, 90

Foundation grantmaking, 11, 34, 87-92

Foundation operating expenses, 90

Foundations, giving to, 43, 131-134

Fundraising research, 72

Fundraising, trends in, 73

Gift annuities, 80, 86

Giving circles, 72

Health, giving to, 44, 135-143

Higher education, 8, 61, 68, 121, 123-127, 216, 219, 225, 228

Household donation amount, 2-4, 69, 114, 115, 117, 125, 139, 151, 158, 167, 171, 177, 185

Hudson Institute study, int'l expenditures, 182

Human services, giving to, 4, 7, 45, 82, 144-153

Income, individual/households, 1, 11, 32, 66-77

International expenditures, 182

International affairs, giving to, 49, 82, 180-186

Internet, online giving, 74-75

Islamic charities, 194

Katrina Emergency Tax Relief Act (KETRA), 5, 32, 40, 67, 124, 187, 188

Legal and legislative issues, 187-195

Methodologies, 214-228

Museums, 154, 156

Native Americans, 91

Panel on the Nonprofit Sector , 193

Performing arts, 157, 158

Postal rates, 191

Poverty, low-income, 7, 149

Public broadcasting, 158

Public-society benefit, giving to, 46, 82, 163-172

Regional differences in religious giving, 113, 115

Religion, giving to, 4, 41, 82, 107-120

Rural philanthropy, 72

Stock market, impact on giving, 2

Tax rates, impact on giving, 95, 102, 124, 215

Tax reform proposals, 69

Unallocated giving, definition, 13

United Jewish Communities, 163, 166, 168

United Way, 58, 163, 166-168

Wal-Mart , 96, 98, 175, 176

Women, giving by, 68, 82

Order Your Copy of *Giving USA 2006* Today!

Required for order confirmation

First Name_____ Last Name_____

Organization_____ Address1_____

Address2_____ Address3_____

City_____ State_____ Zip_____ Country_____

Phone _____ Fax _____ Email _____

Prepayment is required in U.S. Dollars payable to Giving USA Foundation.

Payment Type ❑ Check ❑ Visa ❑ MasterCard ❑ American Express

Credit Card No _____ Exp _____

Credit Card Billing Address (if different than above) _____

Signature _____

Code	Publication	Price	Qty	Total
5003-246	**Giving USA 2006 Subscription - BEST VALUE!** *Giving USA 2006* – The Annual Report on Philanthropy for the Year 2005 *Giving USA Quarterly* – 4 issues *Giving USA 2006 Presentation on CD*	$200.00		
5001-247	*Giving USA 2006* – The Annual Report on Philanthropy for the Year 2005 *Giving USA Quarterly* – 4 issues	$130.00		
3006-244	*Giving USA 2006 Presentation on Transparencies* 8 full-color transparencies (8.5 x 11) of key data with talking points	$105.00		
1005-245	*Giving USA 2006 Presentation on CD* Full-color, ready-made computer presentation charts with talking points	$130.00		
5002-243	*Giving USA 2006 Quarterly* – 4 Issues	$85.00		
2002-241	*Giving USA 2006* – The Annual Report on Philanthropy for the Year 2005	$70.00		
2006-243	*Giving USA Quarterly*, Issue 1 - Annual Survey of State Laws Regulating Charitable Solicitations as of January 1, 2006	$40.00		
	*In the U.S. add $9.95 for orders up to $100	**Subtotal**	$	
	$13.95 for orders up to $149	**Shipping**	$	
	$18.95 for orders of $150+ Outside of U.S. add $25.00 for airmail delivery	**If delivered in IL, 8.25% tax**	$	
		Total	$	

Order By Mail:
Giving USA Foundation
4700 W. Lake Ave
Glenview, IL 60025

Order By Phone:
Have your credit card ready
800/462-2372
847/375-4709

Order By Fax:
866/607-0913
Intl. – 732/578-6594

Order Online:
Visit our web store at
www.givingusa.org

In the event of a miscalculation, I authorize Giving USA Foundation to charge to the above-named credit card an amount reasonably deemed by Giving USA Foundation to be accurate and appropriate.

GUSAB06

Order Your Copy of *Giving USA 2006* Today!

Required for order confirmation

First Name_____ Last Name_____

Organization_____ Address1_____

Address2_____ Address3_____

City_____ State_____ Zip_____ Country_____

Phone _____ Fax _____ Email _____

Prepayment is required in U.S. Dollars payable to Giving USA Foundation.

Payment Type ❑ Check ❑ Visa ❑ MasterCard ❑ American Express

Credit Card No _____ Exp _____

Credit Card Billing Address (if different than above) _____

Signature _____

Code	Publication	Price	Qty	Total
5003-246	**Giving USA 2006 Subscription - BEST VALUE!** *Giving USA 2006* – The Annual Report on Philanthropy for the Year 2005 *Giving USA Quarterly* – 4 issues *Giving USA 2006 Presentation on CD*	$200.00		
5001-247	*Giving USA 2006* – The Annual Report on Philanthropy for the Year 2005 *Giving USA Quarterly* – 4 issues	$130.00		
3006-244	*Giving USA 2006 Presentation on Transparencies* 8 full-color transparencies (8.5 x 11) of key data with talking points	$105.00		
1005-245	*Giving USA 2006 Presentation on CD* Full-color, ready-made computer presentation charts with talking points	$130.00		
5002-243	*Giving USA 2006 Quarterly* – 4 Issues	$85.00		
2002-241	*Giving USA 2006* – The Annual Report on Philanthropy for the Year 2005	$70.00		
2006-243	*Giving USA Quarterly*, Issue 1 - Annual Survey of State Laws Regulating Charitable Solicitations as of January 1, 2006	$40.00		
	*In the U.S. add $9.95 for orders up to $100	**Subtotal**	$	
	$13.95 for orders up to $149	**Shipping**	$	
	$18.95 for orders of $150+ Outside of U.S. add $25.00 for airmail delivery	**If delivered in IL, 8.25% tax**	$	
		Total	$	

Order By Mail:
Giving USA Foundation
4700 W. Lake Ave
Glenview, IL 60025

Order By Phone:
Have your credit card ready
800/462-2372
847/375-4709

Order By Fax:
866/607-0913
Intl. – 732/578-6594

Order Online:
Visit our web store at
www.givingusa.org

In the event of a miscalculation, I authorize Giving USA Foundation to charge to the above-named credit card an amount reasonably deemed by Giving USA Foundation to be accurate and appropriate.

GUSAB06